Journal of Pentecostal Theology Supplement Series
7

Editors
John Christopher Thomas
Rickie D. Moore
Steven J. Land

Sheffield Academic Press
Sheffield

Led by the Spirit

Toward a Practical Theology
of Pentecostal Discernment
and Decision Making

Stephen E. Parker

 Sheffield Academic Press

Copyright © 1996 Sheffield Academic Press

Published by Sheffield Academic Press Ltd
Mansion House
19 Kingfield Road
Sheffield S11 9AS
England

Printed on acid-free paper in Great Britain
by Cromwell Press
Melksham, Wiltshire

British Library Cataloguing in Publication Data

A catalogue record for this book is available
from the British Library

ISBN 1-85075-746-1

CONTENTS

ACKNOWLEDGMENTS

I owe thanks to many people for their contribution to this work. The administration, faculty, staff and students of Tomlinson College have encouraged me for several years as I labored with this project. I am especially grateful for the love and assistance extended during the illness and death of my mother in the Spring of 1991. Without the support of colleagues and students, a trying and painful time would have been much harder to bear. Larry Duncan, Vice-President for Academic Affairs, helped arrange a sabbatical in the Spring of 1990 in which the initial writing was begun. Gayla Cassidy, Librarian, helped secure hard to find materials on several occasions. Elsie Johnson, Gary Riggins, Phil Smith and James Wallace read and made helpful comments on earlier drafts of various chapters.

Members of the Theology and Personality Department, Emory University have also been a source of encouragement. The favorable responses to earlier proposals and presentations led to stimulating critique and dialogue that sharpened my focus and approach to this subject. Dr Charles Gerkin provided valuable comments on an early draft of Chapter 5 that helped me expand and redirect that chapter and Dr Theodore Runyon offered helpful comments on Chapter 6. Dr James Fowler's comments on the entire manuscript helped sharpen the presentation of the material. Dr Rodney Hunter provided invaluable help and encouragement during the progress of this study. His careful reading through several drafts of each chapter significantly improved the scope and argument of this work; during my mother's illness he offered understanding and encouragement when work on the study moved slowly.

I wish to thank John Christopher Thomas and the editors of the *Journal of Pentecostal Theology* for their help in bringing this work to publication. Innovative, interdisciplinary works can be difficult to market; I deeply appreciate their desire to give this study exposure to a wider audience.

I owe a special thanks to the people of 'King's Avenue'. My debt of gratitude to the people who appear as case studies in this project can never be expressed adequately. Their willingness to share their background and spiritual experiences has immeasurably enriched my understanding of the Spirit's work in 'earthen vessels'. Though they may not always agree with my conclusions, I will always feel a deep appreciation for what they have taught me.

My parents, Daniel and LaBerta Parker, have been a source of support and encouragement throughout my academic pursuits. My wife, Regina, and my son, Sean, have shown patience and understanding long past the allotted time for this project. Regina's encouragement provided impetus to begin again on several occasions; Sean's willingness to live with my absences also contributed to my ability to finish this endeavour. To them I owe the greatest thanks.

Chapter 1

TOWARD A PRACTICAL THEOLOGY OF PENTECOSTAL
DISCERNMENT AND DECISION MAKING

Introduction

> It is probably fair—and important—to note that in general the
> Pentecostals' experience has preceded their hermeneutics (Fee 1976: 122).

At the heart of Penetcostal practice is an experience of the Spirit's
immediate presence, an experience that often involves claims to direct
guidance from the Spirit for decisions and actions by Pentecostal believers.
Understanding and evaluating such claims has been problematic for
Pentecostals and non-Pentecostals alike. This study aims at the creation
of a 'practical theology' of Pentecostal discernment and decision making
that is true to the experiential nature of Pentecostalism and yet meets the
criteria for a 'critical' theology that can evaluate claims to being led by
the Spirit.

Friend (Fee 1976) and foe (Bruner 1970) alike have noted the tendency of Pentecostals to be more oriented toward 'experience' than
'theology', especially when talking about the central focus of their belief
and practice: Holy Spirit baptism. The earliest Pentecostal writings on
Spirit baptism had what William MacDonald (1976) called 'the character
of a "witness" experience'. Such 'witness' theologies, rooted as they
were in the oral-aural nature of Pentecostalism, offered 'testimonies' to
an 'experience' rather than reasoned answers to theological inquiry.
Their testimony-based writings left Pentecostals open to charges that
they uncritically appropriated Scripture and thus had neither biblical nor
theological groundings for their most distinctive belief and practice
(Bruner 1970).

In the attempt to answer such charges with more sophisticated
theologies (i.e. to show that they were critical and had biblical and theological warrant for their practices and beliefs), a new generation of
Pentecostals produced exegetical and historical studies to support the

Pentecostal positions regarding the 'normativity' of Holy Spirit baptism
and other charisms. The work of Burgess (1976), Elbert (1985), Ervin
(1968, 1984), Fee (1984), Hunter (1983) and Williams and Waldvogel
(1975) illustrate this effort.

While not impugning the importance of such work, it has created two
problems in Pentecostal theological reflection. First, it has tended to
narrow the focus of 'Pentecostal theology' to exegesis or, in some cases,
historical studies; and secondly, it adopted a more traditional theological
starting point of reflection upon the Christian tradition, including
Scripture, which tended to neglect or even contradict the centrality of
'experience' in Pentecostal faith and life.

There is thus a need for Pentecostals to expand their theological
reflections in several directions. First, there is need to expand their theological reflection beyond exegetical and historical dialogues in ways that
retain an emphasis on the role and authority of experience. The exegetical and historical dialogues tend to engage a rather narrow theological
spectrum, primarily fundamentalist Evangelicals. While acknowledging
the need for certain critical principles in relation to exegesis, this wing of
the Christian tradition tends to hold positions at variance with the
Pentecostal emphasis on experience. For Pentecostals, theology arises
from reflection on experience, yet these historical and exegetical dialogues have tended to reverse, if not abandon altogether, this primary
emphasis. The cognitive approach of Fundamentalism makes 'Holy
Spirit baptism' a doctrine reducible to propositional truths rather than
the lively experience of Pentecostal faith and worship. Its focus on truth
as propositional absolutes to be grasped cognitively seems alien to the
Pentecostal emphasis on experiencing the Spirit.

Furthermore, Pentecostal theological reflection needs to be constructive. The exegetical and historical battles tend to be defensive,
seeking to offer substantiation for the legitimacy of Pentecostal beliefs
and practices. While such defenses are helpful, it is only as Pentecostal
theological reflection seeks to be constructive and not only defensive
that it can hope to articulate its unique emphases within a larger tradition
perceived to be common to all Christians. The Pentecostal emphasis on
experience may well find more support from liberal theologies that are
critical in method yet make a place for the authority of experience and
the intersubjectivity of the knower and the known.

Thirdly, Pentecostal theological reflection needs to expand the critical
principles that guide it to develop intellectually. Pentecostal dialogue with

fundamentalist Christianity has acknowledged the need for critical principles in biblical study, but there is also a need to acknowledge how conscious and unconscious psychological processes influence theological reflection, and to develop corresponding critical methodological principles. Such principles could do much to prevent the kinds of abuses and excesses that have on occasion accompanied the enthusiasm of Pentecostal experience. However, the inclusion of principles for a critique of Pentecostal practice does not preclude the possibility that Pentecostalism may already have latent critical principles of its own that have not been sufficiently articulated. Cecil Robeck (1980) has suggested that there also operates in Pentecostal discernment and decision making certain 'transrational elements'. Any attempt at articulating the critical principles that are to be operative in Pentecostal theology must give attention to this notion of transrational criteria. Can such criteria be identified and articulated, and do such criteria offer a unique or distinctive evaluative critique of Pentecostal practice? Articulation of the transrational elements in Pentecostal discernment and decision making would offer Pentecostals insight into the distinctive critical features of their theological reflection and offer some defense against charges that these practices are irrational.

But if Pentecostal theological reflection is not to be subsumed as a variety of either Fundamentalist or liberal theology, Pentecostals need to make their own voice heard by expanding their theological reflection in ways that are more attuned to the Pentecostal emphasis on the authority of experience. Acknowledgment of the focus on experience as endemic to Pentecostalism, together with a method that incorporates this focus while yet meeting the criteria for a critical theology, may open the way for articulating the unique emphases of Pentecostal theological reflection.

This study proposes that the best theological method for drawing normatively on Pentecostal experience is construction of a 'practical theology', understood not as the application of theory, but as critical reflection upon the practices of a community of faith (Browning 1983). This understanding of practical theology is defined more fully below and seems more consistent with the way Pentecostals approach theology and a necessary supplement to systematic and theoretical reflections made upon Pentecostal practices.

The most logical practices to reflect upon in this way would be those practices that lead directly to action within the Pentecostal faith community, more specifically those practices associated with what Pentecostals

call the 'leading of the Spirit' or what may even more specifically be
termed 'discernment and decision making'. These practices are the focus
of this study for several reasons. Pentecostals are a people for whom
the leading of the Spirit is important and given the centrality of the
Pentecostal focus on Holy Spirit baptism it is not unusual for
Pentecostals to claim that certain actions or decisions are the result of
the 'leading of the Spirit'. However, while such claims hold enormous
potential for empowering Pentecostals in their actions, there are also
enormous dangers inherent in claims of Spirit leading. As one might
guess, both Pentecostals (Ervin 1985, 1987) and non-Pentecostals
(Benson 1975) have cautioned against the uncritical acceptance of claims
made in the name of the Holy Spirit. A people for whom the leading of
the Spirit is so important must have means for discerning what is of the
Spirit's leading and what is not. Yet when one seeks Pentecostal literature on discernment and decision making one finds very little. There is
thus a further need to explore how Pentecostal discernment and decision
making actually takes place and to elaborate the meaning and significance of these practices both for Pentecostals and the wider Christian
community. Finally, the inherent potential for destructive behaviour
and consequences as a result of claims to Spirit leading requires the
formulation of normative guidelines for evaluating such claims.

The major task of this study is to construct a 'practical theology' of
Pentecostal discernment and decision making. Practical theology, as used
here, involves the critical reflection upon the practices of a community
of faith and is not simply recommending 'applications' of a theory or
theology about Spirit leading. This also means that the primary focus of
this study is not the construction of a 'systematic theology' of Spirit
leading; this study is primarily a contribution to theological method
rather than to a doctrine of the Spirit. The practices of Pentecostal
discernment and decision making have been selected as a means to the
primary end of practical theological construction.

Definitions

Practical theology as used in this study refers to *critical theological
reflection arising out of and giving guidance to the practices of a local
faith community*. This definition draws from contributions to the
emerging field of practical theology and stands in marked contrast to the
traditional definition of practical theology as the minister's ability to

'apply' theoretically oriented material of a divinity curriculum (Bible, history, dogmatics) to the work of ministry (Farley 1983). Practical theology as used in this project does not refer to some appendices added to the prior work of theoretical reflection. It refers to a method of theological reflection that recognizes a logical and temporal priority to the actions or practices of a faith community as the beginning point for theological reflection and construction (Fowler 1983). A brief overview of practical theology as an emerging field is given in Chapter 3.

Pentecostal here refers broadly to *groups that affirm that the phenomenon described in Acts 2 is repeatable in contemporary times.* 'And when the day of Pentecost was fully come...they were all filled with the Holy Ghost and began to speak with other tongues, as the Spirit gave utterance' (Acts 2.1, 4). More specifically, it refers to *a religious phenomenon that emerged in the United States of America about the turn of the century* and subsequently spread to all parts of the world (Hollenweger 1972), whose distinctive, common feature is a focus on manifestation of the 'charismata' of the Holy Spirit, particularly that of 'speaking in tongues' or 'glossolalia' as evidence of the 'baptism in/by the Holy Spirit'.[1] *Holy Spirit baptism in Pentecostal circles is an*

---

1.   Synan (1987) distinguishes five major streams of Pentecostals which are further subdivided along theological lines (see Appendix I). This theological diversity is also noted by two other recent contributors to Pentecostal studies. Lederle (1988) points to considerable diversity regarding 'interpretations of "spirit-baptism" in the charismatic renewal movement' (the subtitle of his book), noting that not all within the Pentecostal-charismatic movement would agree as to the meaning of significance or Holy Spirit baptism. Similarly Dayton (1987) has cautioned against too narrow a focus on Holy Spirit baptism and tongues as the only distinguishing characteristic of Pentecostalism. He argues that a fourfold pattern distinguishes Pentecostal theology: salvation (an emphasis on being 'born again'), divine healing, baptism of the Holy Spirit, belief in the second coming of Christ. Land (1993) points to a fifth distinctive for certain Pentecostal groups: that of sanctification as a second definite work of grace.

While one should be cautious in assuming that Holy Spirit baptism and speaking in tongues are wholly adequate means for describing Pentecostals, nevertheless they remain useful distinguishing characteristics. All the groups Synan mentions have as part of their beliefs and practices an emphasis on the Holy Spirit and charismatic manifestations of the Spirit, including some mention of the role of speaking in tongues in relationship to the baptism of the Spirit. Even those who reject speaking in tongues as the initial evidence of baptism of the Spirit or as unnecessary to the 'baptism' of the Spirit, still allow for and practice speaking in tongues as a gift or charism of the Spirit (*Dictionary of Pentecostal and Charismatic Movements* 1988).

emotional experience described as being immersed in or indwelt by the presence of the Holy Spirit. Because this experience is so often tied to speaking in tongues, 'usually, but not exclusively, the religious phenomenon of making sounds that constitute, or resemble, a language not known to the speaker' (Spittler 1988: 335), Pentecostalism is sometimes referred to as the 'tongues movement' (Anderson 1979).

Practices are one of the organizing concepts of this project. *Practices* as used here *has its common sense meaning of frequent or usual activities* of a community of faith including externally observable activities (such as charismatic manifestations) and 'internal' or subjective activities and states of mind, such as characteristic thought patterns attendant upon decision making.

Regarding particular practices, 'the *leading of the Spirit*' refers to *inclinations to act in one way or another that are believed to arise from the Holy Spirit.* These inclinations may arise as spontaneous thoughts and feelings within the person but may at times be generated by the suggestions of another Spirit-filled person. But because Pentecostals do not attribute all inclinations to the Holy Spirit, the processes for determining the source of 'leadings' are called 'discernment'.

Discernment refers to the practices by which Pentecostals evaluate their leadings. In Pentecostal belief, leadings may have their source in the Spirit, in one's own desires, or in diabolical influence. Discernment may involve external criteria such as charismatic manifestations or more internal impressions that the choice one is making 'feels right' or 'feels good'. In any case, discernment ideally takes place prior to a commitment to some kind of action, such commitment being a moment of decision making. Pentecostals have 'inclinations' or leadings to do many things. Whether one follows through with a particular inclination is believed to be directly related to what one determines the source of the inclination to be. Discernment is therefore an integral moment in Pentecostal decision making, and references will be made to 'Pentecostal discernment and decision making' to indicate their integral relationship.

'Experience' is a word with many meanings and subtle variations.

The Pentecostal-charismatic movement has had a significant impact upon the Christian tradition particularly through the 'charismatic movement' which has been going on within the mainline churches for over twenty years and continues to exert influence upon the shape of contemporary Christianity. Worldwide the Pentecostal-charismatic movement is currently judged to be the fastest growing segment of Christianity (Wagner 1988).

The New World Dictionary of the American Language gives the following semantic range:

> 1. the act of living through an event or events; personal involvement in or observations of events as they occur; 2. anything observed or lived through; 3. a) anything that has happened to one in one's life to date; b) everything done or undergone by a group; 4. individual reaction to events, feelings, etc.; 5. activity that includes training, observation of practice, and personal participation; the knowledge, skill, or practice resulting from this.

It is the definitions given in 2 and 4 that indicate best the use of the word in this study. As used here *experience refers to a complex conscious, affective, physiological phenomenon, involving both cognitive awareness of external events and internal physiological, affective, and conscious reactions to such events*. However, this should not be seen to imply that the cognitive, affective and physiological dimensions are discrete and separable elements other than for purposes of description. Here this study follows Poling and Miller (1985) in defining experience as a multi-layered phenomenon not reducible to 'subjectivity'.

> This means that experience cannot be reduced to some part of experience, such as sense perception, conscious experience, cognitive experience, intuition and feeling, religious feeling, or any other kind. Rather, there is a thickness and depth to experience which is more than our attempts to describe and clarify it (Poling and Miller 1985: 67).

It is both 'source and authority for all reflection'. The Whiteheads (1980) similarly refer to the 'thickness' of experience by describing it as including the 'rational' elements of reasoned reflection and the 'extra-rational' elements of feeling and imagination.

The relationship between 'practices' and 'experience' is reciprocal. At times practices are the external, physical embodiments of experience, as when speaking in tongues becomes an expression of the sense of being filled with the Spirit. At other times practices give rise to experience as when charismatic manifestations generate heightened awareness of one's sensibilities or induce reflection upon or openness to matters of the Spirit. Practices would function similarly to Grimes's (1982) description of rituals: not only embodying but also generating experience. Goodman (1986) has also argued this kind of connection between Pentecostal ritual and experience. While the reciprocal connection between practice and experience is more observable in those instances where practices are external actions, the reciprocity would also be present in characteristic mental activities involved in decision making where the mental activity gave rise to belief that the Spirit was directing the decision. Such mental activity may then become a formulaic means to experience Spirit direction (cf. the use of 'fleeces' as described in Chapter 4).

Concerns that Generated this Study

I have been a member of a Pentecostal community for over 25 years. During this time I have observed many changes both in myself and in the Pentecostal movement and this study is an attempt to understand better a movement that has had a profound impact upon my life. But the relevance of this study goes beyond its personal interest to me.

The need to expand Pentecostal theological reflection beyond exegetical and historical methods which have sought only to confirm the validity or normativity of Pentecostal experiences was another concern that generated this study. While there have been a few attempts to do Pentecostal theology in a systematic way, most notably Williams (1988, 1990) and Nichols (1984), no one has tried to develop a practical theology in the Pentecostal tradition; one explicitly drawing upon the authority of Pentecostal experience while satisfying the criteria for a critical theology. Although Land's (1993) work on Pentecostal spirituality, reviewed and discussed in Chapter 7, is the most significant contribution to date toward meeting this need, it by no means exhausts the possibilities of practical theology from the Pentecostal tradition.

The possibility of lifting up and articulating some principle or insight operative in Pentecostal practice that may be relevant to the wider church was another concern that generated this study. When Pentecostals pray for the Spirit to guide them, they expect something concrete to happen because of those prayers—they anticipate direction from the Spirit. No one has specifically focused on discernment and decision making among Pentecostals so as to articulate what is going on and how this is similar to or different from decision making in mainline churches. Articulation of the similarities and differences between Pentecostal discernment and decision making and similar practices in mainline churches may suggest ways to enhance decision making in both traditions. The centrality of experience for Pentecostal decision making suggests that there is value in giving greater attention to the less cognitive dimensions of decision making. The role of charismatic manifestations in Pentecostal discernment and decision making also raises the question of whether there might be some transrational dimensions of knowing at work in such practices.

A further aim of this study is to make a practical contribution to Pentecostal practice itself, by helping Pentecostals understand themselves and their practices more critically and of formulating better guidelines for evaluating these practices. The need for Pentecostals to appraise critically the impact, positively and negatively, of these practices so as to guide future action was another motivation for this study.

This study claims a kind of 'dual theological citizenship'. It is conceived as 'Pentecostal theology'; that is, it is theological reflection and construction from within and for the Pentecostal community. Yet it also seeks to test a methodology for practical theological construction and thus make a contribution to practical theology more generally. It tests a methodology that combines ethnographic description of Pentecostal discernment and decision making with the method of 'mutually critical correlation' drawn from the emerging field of practical theology as a means for articulating the unique contributions of a Pentecostal approach to theological construction. This revised method should enable Pentecostals to engage in critical dialogue about their practices with other traditions and previously neglected perspectives while allowing their practices to be studied from the perspective of the Pentecostal experience itself, rather than simply from an imposed point of view alien to this experience. In this study the perspectives which are critically correlated with the Pentecostal one include ego and object relations psychology, and the theology of Paul Tillich. The choice of these perspectives is discussed in Chapter 3.

Some Questions

There are several questions that arise out of the nature of this study. How will Pentecostals reconcile the more ecstatic forms of their experience with critical reflection? Are there latent critical dimensions already incorporated into Pentecostal discernment and decision making? What is the relationship between charismatic manifestations and discernment and decision making? Does Pentecostal discernment and decision making involve transrational dimensions of knowing? What resources of the human personality are being tapped in these practices, either consciously or unconsciously? Is there some principle or insight that may be drawn from Pentecostal discernment and decision making that will enhance decision making in a larger context?

What about the end results of these practices? On the positive side, from a Pentecostal perspective, do they denote a more active presence of the Spirit, a sense of spiritual strength and direction, and unity among believers? In more obviously psychological and theological terms, do they promote an openness in relationships, create new possibilities for transformation of self and society, open up new understanding of God and God's will, encourage reconciliation and community, enrich one's decision making to include more illusive factors of feeling, intuition and unconscious processes? Or on the negative side, do they confuse personal desires or emotional excitement with the leading of the Spirit, or promote confusion and disharmony among believers? From the psychological and theological perspectives, do they legitimate or promote arrested psychological development or feelings that Pentecostals are superior to other Christians, divert and subvert energy that would be used in social action into a privatized emotionalism, or function as an escape from the ambiguities and negatives of life?

The Plan of the Book

In offering answers to the above and related suggestions the study precedes along the following plan. Chapter 2 is an overview of the role of experience in Pentecostal theological construction as well as a review of Pentecostal reflection on discernment and decision making. It points to several deficiencies in Pentecostal theological reflection including the need for a theological method that would retain the Pentecostal focus on experience yet satisfy criteria for a critical theology and the need for a more comprehensive means for understanding and evaluating Pentecostal claims to divine guidance.

Chapter 3 describes a methodology designed to meet the needs identified in Chapter 2. It is a method of 'mutually critical correlation' (Tracy 1975, 1981) that provides a means for critically correlating Pentecostal, psychological and theological perspectives on claims to divine guidance. This chapter also justifies the selection of the various explanatory and evaluative perspectives. The remainder of the book is given to evaluating the phenomena of Spirit leading from these various viewpoints.

Chapter 4 gives the reader a sense of the richness and variety of Pentecostal experiences of Spirit leading by including 'first-hand' reports from interviews with and participant-observations of people claiming divine guidance in their decisions. This material becomes the basis for articulating a particularly Pentecostal understanding of these experiences, giving the reader an insider's perspective and evaluation of these practices.

In Chapter 5 ego and object relations psychology provide the basis for a psychological evaluation of Pentecostal claims to divine guidance. Biographical information of selected individuals illustrates the impact of developmental history on experiences of being led by the Spirit. While acknowledging and illustrating the pathological potential of claims to Spirit-led activities, this chapter also presents evidence that certain claims to the Spirit's leading provide occasion for 'creative, ego-enhancing regressions'.

In Chapter 6 the work of Paul Tillich provides criteria for a theological evaluation of Pentecostal claims to being led by the Spirit. In Tillich's language, these are potentially 'revelatory' experiences—occasions when one is grasped by ultimate concern and experiences a connectedness to the 'ground of being'. However, examples from the interviews and participant-observation also illustrate the potential for these experiences to promote emotionalism and escapism, confusion of personal desires as the Spirit's direction, and disintegration of the Pentecostal community.

The mutually critical correlation of perspectives is concluded in Chapter 7 as the Pentecostal, psychological and theological understandings of these practices and experiences are brought together to produce multi-faceted guidelines for evaluating claims to the Spirit's direction. This chapter also reflects on the implications of this study for both Pentecostals and the wider, ecumenical Christian church.

Chapter 2

THE ROLE OF EXPERIENCE IN PENTECOSTAL THEOLOGICAL CONSTRUCTION AND THE PROBLEM OF DISCERNMENT AND DECISION MAKING

This chapter examines the role of experience in Pentecostal theological construction. It looks at how the Pentecostal response to the charge that they are too 'experience' oriented tended to narrow Pentecostal theological reflection to historical and exegetical battles over the legitimacy of Pentecostal experiences in ways that appear at odds with the Pentecostal emphasis on experience. This chapter also reviews the literature in which aspects of Pentecostal discernment and decision making have been studied, showing that little has been done here although there is recognition of the need for discernment given the emphasis on charismatic manifestations among Pentecostals.[1]

1.   It is beyond the scope of this study to provide an exhaustive review of the literature on Pentecostals which has reached voluminous proportions. Charles Jones's (1983) two volume bibliography of the Pentecostal movement, which lists 9883 items, has been described as 'incomplete' by Dayton (1987). Pentecostals have been studied by historians (Bloch-Hoell 1964), anthropologists (Abell 1982), psychologists (Kildahl 1972), sociologists (Anderson 1979), theologians (Bruner 1970), linguists (Samarin 1968, 1969, 1973), and folklorists (Lawless 1983, 1988).
    Most scholarly studies of Pentecostals, both by Pentecostals and non-Pentecostals, tend to focus on the question of the 'legitimacy' or 'deficiency' of Pentecostal practices and beliefs. Early studies of Pentecostals especially tended to judge Pentecostals deficient in some way, either psychologically (Cutten 1927), sociologically (Niebuhr 1929), or theologically (Ironside 1912). This approach continues to guide many recent studies which focus on the dangers and abuses of the movement, pronouncing Pentecostals to be pathological (Dominion 1976), deprived (Anderson 1979), or heretical (Dollar 1963). The emergence of the 'charismatic movement' or neo-pentecostalism led to a series of more recent studies that were more favourable to the movement, finding in it sources for emotional strength (Maloney 1982), socialization (DeVol 1974), and revitalization for the church (Mayers 1973).
    A wider introduction to Pentecostals can be found in Hollenweger (1972).

Literature Bearing on the Role of Experience in Pentecostal Theological Reflection

The locus of most Spirit baptisms is an emotionally charged and free-flowing worship service and the 'experience' of receiving the baptism of the Holy Spirit is received amid much enthusiasm. Pentecostals give exuberant testimonies to their experience, citing them as evidence of the presence of the Holy Spirit. Pentecostalism therefore stands in a long line of religious traditions that emphasize 'heart-felt experience', including the holiness tradition, the Wesleys, certain Anabaptist groups and Montanists (Knox 1950). Early Pentecostal literature in particular focused on such experiences (MacDonald 1976). One might say that the category of 'experience' is a central one for the movement (Abell 1982).

The Central Charge against Pentecostal Theological Construction
This focus on experience has led to charges that Pentecostals go about the business of theological reflection 'backwards', that their 'experience has preceded their hermeneutics' (Fee 1976). Fee is not alone in making this assessment; he was merely echoing the sentiments of other Pentecostal (Menzies 1979) and non-Pentecostal (Bruner 1970) writers. Menzies has acknowledged that a 'common complaint' against Pentecostals is that they 'first experience something, then rush to the scripture after the fact to reach for a rationale for what has happened to them' (1985: 12). Early Pentecostal 'theology' did indeed have the quality of simply a testimony to an experience and left Pentecostals open to charges of being uncritical in their use of Scripture, more given to emotion than to reason, and without biblical or theological warrant for their central beliefs and practices (Bruner 1970). Such charges implied that there was not only an unreflective and uncritical quality to Pentecostal 'experience', but that the experience itself was an illegitimate place to begin theological reflection.

Anderson's (1979) review of American Pentecostalism is a good supplement and provides good bibliography for further studies. The *Dictionary of Pentecostal and Charismatic Movements* (1988) is an excellent resource. More focused studies include a volume by Maloney and Lovekin (1985) which reviews and critiques most of the behavioural science research on glossolalia, and a volume by Mills (1986) which brings together almost thirty articles that treat glossolalia from exegetical, historical, theological, psychological, and socio-cultural perspectives.

Pentecostal Responses

Pentecostals felt the sting of such charges as a response by William McDonald indicates:

> This conserving of the value of experience does not deny that Pentecostal theology is a theology of the Word. We do not begin with Schleiermacher's man of religious feelings...Does this holy experience result in an experience centred theology? Hardly. The better way to label it is this: Christ-centred, experience-certified theology (1976: 63-64).

Even those like Menzies, Fee and MacDonald who affirm the Pentecostal emphasis on experience point to the 'problems' of such an emphasis. As Gause, another Pentecostal, has succinctly said, 'Pentecostalism has not faced the dangers of an emotion- and experience-centred theology' (1976: 114).

The primary Pentecostal response to the criticisms of the role given experience has been one that tends to reverse the pattern of moving 'from experience to reflection'. Pentecostals have sought to establish the legitimacy of their belief and experience by starting their theological reflection with the 'tradition' (particularly Scripture) and working 'forward' to their experiences. The attempts to legitimate Pentecostal experience by this means is obvious in the many 'historical and exegetical' studies provided by Pentecostals.

The historical approach to proving the legitimacy of Pentecostal beliefs and practices argues that charismatic manifestations such as speaking in tongues are not new to Pentecostals but have been present throughout Christian history. The most noteworthy recent attempts to argue for charismatic manifestations throughout church history include the work of Stanley Burgess (1988) and Cecil Robeck (1988). In two essays on the doctrine of the Holy Spirit in the ancient and medieval church fathers Burgess deals with the presence of the charismata in their works while Robeck writes on the presence of the gift of prophecy throughout Christian history. Other works along this line include those of Williams and Waldvogel (1975), Hunter (1980) and Kydd (1984).[2]

---

2. It is worth noting that another way by which early Pentecostal writers sought to demonstrate the historical legitimacy of charismatic manifestations was to argue that charismatic manifestations such as speaking in tongues were being 'restored' to the 'last days church' after centuries of absence. While the restoration motif seems to have been widely used by early Pentecostal writers, it is not appealed to much by modern Pentecostal scholars although one, David Faupel (1989), has argued that the 'latter rain' (restorationist) motif is central to understanding Pentecostalism. However,

The second way that Pentecostal scholars have sought to defend the legitimacy of Pentecostal belief and practice, and by far most significant in terms of the literature it generated, was through a biblical-exegetical defense of Pentecostal beliefs and practices. The works of Brumback (1947) and Riggs (1949) were early attempts to show the biblical warrants for such Pentecostal doctrines as 'tongues as initial evidence' and the doctrine of 'subsequence' (i.e., that there is a second [or third] blessing after regeneration). Over time these early responses have been supplemented, modified and replaced with responses from a new generation of Pentecostal scholars including work by Ervin (1968, 1987) Hunter (1983), Menzies (1991), Shelton (1991) and Williams (1990).

Howard Ervin's 1968 work, *These Are not Drunken as ye Suppose* (updated as *Spirit Baptism* [1987]) is a polemic 'directed primarily to an Evangelical and Pentecostal audience—a refutation of the harsher criticisms of the former, a defense of the Pentecostal hermeneutics for the latter' (Ervin 1987: viii). Ervin's work was one of the first thorough attempts to take into account the criticisms against Pentecostalism and thus shows a departure from the earliest works, such as those of Riggs (1949) or Brumback (1947), which still relied somewhat on 'testimonial' defenses. It offers a solid 'grammatico-historical' exegesis of Pentecostal teachings from within the framework of the emerging charismatic movement.

The Hunter book (1983) is a response to a double broadside suffered by Pentecostals in the exegetical battles over the legitimacy of their beliefs and practices. Two books, *A Theology of the Holy Spirit* by F.D. Bruner, and *Baptism in the Holy Spirit* by J.D.G. Dunn, both published in 1970, leveled serious charges against Pentecostals. Bruner's volume devotes much space to an exegesis of the so-called Pentecostal passages in Acts (1.1-2.47; 8.4-40; 10.44-48; 11.13-18; 19.1-7) and Corinthians (1 Cor. 12–14; 2 Cor. 10–13). It is critical of the Pentecostal interpretations of these Scriptures and remains a significant assessment of Pentecostal doctrine.

James Dunn also devotes much space to an exegesis of the passages on 'baptism in the Holy Spirit'. While concluding that water baptism and the baptism with the Holy Spirit are distinct works, Dunn similarly

Dayton is correct in arguing that Faupel probably overstates the case (1987). While at least one early Pentecostal writer took the approach expounded in the text (Lawrence 1916), it was clearly a minority position among early Pentecostal writers (Dayton 1987). It is now the preferred argument among Pentecostal scholars.

concludes that there is no exegetical basis for the central belief and practice of Pentecostals.

Although it took Pentecostals several years to respond, Harold Hunter's 1979 doctoral dissertation (revised 1983) takes the Bruner and Dunn books as his point of departure and offers an alternative exegesis using the same grammatical-historical method of exegesis employed by Bruner and Dunn. In a second major response to Dunn, Howard Ervin (1984) also used the grammatical-historical method of exegesis to challenge the legitimacy of Dunn's exegesis in a point by point refutation.

More recent interactions and challenges to the Bruner and Dunn works include the second volume of Rodman Williams's systematic theology (1990), which carries on some dialogue with the 'errors and inadequacies' of the Bruner and Dunn volumes in his chapters on the Holy Spirit and Spirit baptism and the works of James Shelton (1991, 1994) and Robert Menzies (1991, 1994b) whose redactional critical studies of the role of the Holy Spirit and the charismata in Luke–Acts not only engage Dunn's work but significantly expand the ways in which Pentecostals engage the exegetical debate.

It is of interest to note at this point that two related issues have emerged from the exegetical battles over Pentecostal beliefs and practices. One is the question of hermeneutics. In the early exegetical responses, a grammatical-historical hermeneutic was used. While this is a standard hermeneutical form in Evangelical circles, Pentecostals are divided over its usefulness for them. This division is observable in the varying answers to the question of whether there is a uniquely 'Pentecostal hermeneutic'.

On the one hand, Pentecostals scholars like Ervin (1985) argue that there is no uniquely Pentecostal hermeneutic. He argues that Pentecostals simply add to an Evangelical hermeneutic emphasis on the role of the Spirit in Scripture interpretation. It is the Spirit's presence, understood in terms of a personal experience of the Spirit's presence, that enables a correct understanding (and response) to the Scripture.

A related but different response to the question of a unique Pentecostal hermeneutic can be seen in the on-going dialogue over the priority of narrative for establishing the normativity of Pentecostal practices. While not arguing for abandonment of Evangelical hermeneutics, Menzies (1985) and Williams (1990), argue that the uniqueness of Pentecostal hermeneutics is the priority given to narrative Scripture for establishing normative doctrine and practice. As used in Evangelical circles, grammatical-historical exegesis generally carries the hidden assumption that hortatory or didactic material (such as the epistles) takes precedence over narrative material (such as the book of Acts) for establishing and judging doctrine and practice. The argument that narrative material might take precedence over didactic material is seen as the uniqueness of the Pentecostal appropriation of a grammatical-historical hermeneutics.

This proposal for the priority of narrative is really a variation of the problem of whether any hermeneutical perspective establishes a 'canon within the canon' from which it works and has sparked a lively, sometimes heated, debate among Pentecostals. Indeed, Dayton (1987) has noted that *the* issue in Pentecostal hermeneutics is the validity of using narrative rather than didactic Scriptures for establishment of behavior. The most recent articulations of this debate have been the series of exchanges between Stronstad (1988, 1993a, 1993b) and Fee (1976, 1991, 1993). Fee is much closer to the standard Evangelical position when he argues that narrative can be 'paradigmatic' only, without establishing 'normative precedent', while Stronstad's position challenges the hidden assumptions regarding didactic material and seeks to expand the influence of narrative material by outlining procedures for establishing normative practice by discerning 'authorial intent' of the narrative passages.

A third response to the question of a unique Pentecostal hermeneutic is seen in the work of Mark McLean (1984). McLean argues for a uniquely Pentecostal hermeneutic based on a unified understanding of God's presence in the world; that is, a view that God does not act differently now than earlier in history. While liberalism tends to exclude God from time-space reality and Fundamentalism tends to relegate God to a different realm than time-space reality, McLean argues that a Pentecostal hermeneutic, affirming that God acts now in the same ways God acted in biblical times, provides both an internal and an external witness of the Spirit for this age as well as the biblical age. McLean's argument for a 'pneumatic hermeneutic' tries to connect Pentecostal hermeneutics to its roots in experiential religion without capitulating to either a liberal or Fundamentalist theology.

A fourth response to the question of whether there is a uniquely Pentecostal hermeneutic emerges from a series of articles in a recent issue of *Pneuma: The Journal of the Society for Pentecostal Studies* (1993: 15 [2]). These studies place the question within the larger debate over the nature of hermeneutics as a multi-layered human interpretive activity and offer new paradigms for Pentecostal hermeneutics. Cargal (1993), for instance, argues that Pentecostals (as well as Evangelicals) need to move beyond the confines of a 'positivist historicism' to more post-modern understandings of the interaction between text and interpreter. Israel, Albrecht and McNally (1993) make a similar point in their proposal that 'texts' include not only written materials but 'rituals' and the 'communities' that live and practice their interpretations. Thus, Pentecostal practice and belief, including the understanding of Scripture, is seen as part of larger questions regarding both the nature of epistemology and hermeneutics. What is new in these studies is the argument that Pentecostal hermeneutics cannot be divorced from the lived Pentecostal tradition and that what is needed is a methodology that is aware of the various layers of interplay between the knower and the known.[3]

The second issue that the exegetical battles have generated is whether there is a *theology* that may be identified as uniquely Pentecostal. Just as some Pentecostal scholars argue against a uniquely Pentecostal hermeneutics, several Pentecostal scholars are also ready to concede that there is no uniquely Pentecostal theology: Pentecostal theology is again Evangelical theology with the proper emphasis on the Holy Spirit.

> Is there a Pentecostal theology? In one sense, the answer is a resounding 'no' ... the role of the Pentecostal may be seen as a calling of the larger church world to a *fuller* understanding of the theology of the Spirit, not an essentially *different* understanding' (Menzies 1985: 1, his emphasis).

---

3.   While it is not the intent or place of this study to resolve the hermeneutical debate among Pentecostals, certain questions that arise from this subdiscussion are pertinent to the methodology that is adopted. The case for the methodology is argued more fully in Chapter 3. Those interested in the most recent contributions to the discussion over the uniquely Pentecostal hermeneutic will find the articles by Dempster (1993), Cargal (1993) and Israel, *et al.* (1993) helpful. Dempster offers an excellent summary and analysis of the articles in the issue of *Pneuma* mentioned in the text. The Cargal and Israel, *et al.* articles from the same issue plow new and fertile ground in their engagement of postmodern hermeneutical theory. In a subsequent issue of Pneuma, Arrington (1994), Harrington and Patten (1994), Menzies (1994a), and Sheppard offer helpful critique and interaction with the Cargal and Israel, et al. articles. In addition to the articles by Fee (1976, 1991, 1993) and Stronstad (1988, 1993a, 1993b) mentioned in the text, other recent helpful framings of the problem of Pentecostal hermeneutics can be found in Anderson (1992), Arrington (1988), Johns and Johns (1992), Newman (1991), and Thomas (1994).

Menzies argues that while there is uniqueness to Pentecostal theology (the emphasis on the role of the Holy Spirit in theology that is missing from most theological efforts), there is no uniquely Pentecostal theology. Rodman Williams's (1988, 1990, 1992) new work, subtitled *Systematic Theology from a Charismatic Perspective*, is really an embodiment of Menzie's claim. Indeed, William's chief theologian of reference is John Calvin (more citations than any other name) and Calvin is mostly called upon to show that Pentecostal theology accords well with Reformed theology. He even sees Calvin as supporting certain Pentecostal distinctives such as the doctrine that the baptism of the Spirit is subsequent to regeneration. The only modern theologian with which Williams engages in any significant dialogue is Karl Barth (21 references, all positive). Significantly, the people with whom Williams most interacts in the second volume (on the Holy Spirit) are biblical scholars rather than theologians (cf. Cross 1993). Williams's later work tends to be further evidence of narrowing Pentecostal theological reflection to exegetical battles. 'My concern in this matter [writing the chapters on the gifts and manifestations of the Holy Spirit] is to give a thorough *biblical* presentation' (1990: 11, my emphasis).

The work of those who have argued that there is a uniquely Pentecostal theology has been sporadic and uneven. One of the earliest attempts at articulating a uniquely Pentecostal theology was by William McDonald. In the first of two seminal essays, McDonald (1976) argues that Pentecostal theology was to be found in its 'oral traditions' rather than its writings and that this oral tradition gave witness to and was rooted in 'experience', though he struggles with how to articulate the role of this experience ('does this holy experience result in an experienced centred theology'?). He suggested that one way Pentecostals could do theology was to commit the oral traditions to writing for the purpose of 'sifting' and comparing with other Christian traditions, remembering that for the Pentecostal, 'right theology is believed to culminate always in worship' (1976: 67). In a second essay, McDonald (1979) again took up the theme of worship and proposed that a unique Pentecostal theology might be termed 'temple theology'; that is, it would be rooted in the worshipful encounter with God. McDonald called upon his colleagues in the Society for Pentecostal Studies (SPS) to write this theology.

However, four years later the then president of SPS, Russell Spittler (1983), listed the writing of a distinctive Pentecostal theology first on his list of areas in which Pentecostals needed to do research. Spittler noted that a 'charismatic theology' had been produced by Gelpi (1978) but that no Pentecostal theology from the classical Pentecostal tradition had been produced. What Gelpi tries to articulate is an epistemology based on human experience. He argues that process theology and American pragmatism (particularly the work of Charles Pierce) provide the best bases for the kind of experiential theology that Pentecostal Charismatics want to articulate. By contrast Spittler notes that what classical Pentecostals have produced is more like outlines of theology, 'excerpted' from and heavily indebted to the standard reformed theologies of nineteenth-century theologians such as Hodge and Shedd. In 1988 the president of SPS, Ronald Kydd, reported on the progress since the Spittler challenge: two articles had appeared by members of the society and one book-length study was forthcoming.

The book-length study was the above mentioned work by Williams (1990) and the two articles cited by Kydd (1988) include McLean's (1984; noted above) and an article by Nichols (1984), neither of which were subsequently followed up.

Nichols (1984) engages in dialogue with the theology of Karl Barth in search of a 'Pentecostal structure in systematic theology'. Nichols identifies a 'spiritual ontology' (as distinguished from the dualistic onto-logies of Plato and Aristotle) as being at the heart of Pentecostal theology. This spiritual ontology overcomes the dichotomy between good spirit and evil matter and allows humans to recognize that though they still live in 'existence' (time-space continuum) they also live through the new being in Christ and participate in 'essence' (God and God's realm). Such Pentecostal theology purports to avoid the pitfalls of irrationalism (characterized by liberal nineteenth-century theology's pre-occupation with experience) and exclusive rationalism (the neoscholastic biblicism of Fundamentalism) and allows for the 'integration of the rational and nonrational (not irrational) aspects of the human experience of God' (1984: 74). Nichols's work is an attempt to move beyond an either/or split between liberal and Fundamentalist theology to find a unique approach or emphasis for Pentecostal theology.

Since the Spittler challenge the most significant work on Pentecostal theology to appear is Steven Land's (1993) monograph on Pentecostal spirituality. Land's work is a systematic exploration of Pentecostal 'affections' that plumbs the early roots of Pentecostal practice to offer a critique and revision of Pentecostal spirituality that illustrates the theological depth and significance of Pentecostal worship. Land's work clearly is an expansion of the way in which Pentecostal theological reflection and construction is done. It lies close to the aim of this project of constructing a practical theology through reflection on Pentecostal practice and is discussed in more depth in Chapter 7.

Consequences of the Pentecostal Response
However necessary work such as that of the historical and exegetical defenses may be for Pentecostals, its effect has not been entirely positive. It has no doubt been helpful in making the beliefs of Pentecostal more acceptable to Fundamentalists and Evangelicals (Ervin 1987). It has also made a credible claim that Pentecostal beliefs and liturgical practices have as much biblical warrant as some key doctrines and practices in the mainline churches (see Arrington [1988] on Stronstad [1984], Hollenweger [1972], Menzies [1991] and Shelton [1991]).

However, these defenses by Pentecostal scholars have also had a negative impact on Pentecostal theology. First, they have tended to narrow the realm within which theological reflection and construction is done as well as the means by which it is done. By focusing on historical and exegetical defenses Pentecostals tend to have fundamentalist Evangelical Christianity as their only dialogue partner. The chief critical principle in Evangelical hermeneutics is the use of the 'grammatical-historical' approach to exegesis. The grammatical-historical method recognizes that Scripture is not to be interpreted apart from its historical context, that common sense rules of grammatical construction are to be followed, and that interpreters bring certain presuppositions to their work. Nevertheless, it tends to regard Scripture as an objective form that stands apart from or over against the subjectivity of the interpreter. The truth of the Scripture is reducible to propositional statements supposedly uninfluenced by the conscious and unconscious motive of the interpreter. While critical biblical scholarship is necessary for theological reflection, grammatical-historical exegesis needs to be supplemented by hermeneutical models that are also attentive to the interrelationship between text and interpreter (Gadamer 1975) and between interpreter and social structure (Habermas 1971).

But even more importantly for Pentecostals, the crucial role of experience is diminished or lost in the battle over historical validity and proper exegesis. The attempt to define the role of the Holy Spirit in theological reflection may be seen as the dilemma of Pentecostal theological reflection. If theological reflection proceeds along Fundamentalist lines, the liveliness of experience that Pentecostals associate with the Holy Spirit is in danger of being lost and must be consciously reintroduced. Referring to the more narrow ways of doing theology embodied in Evangelical hermeneutics, Robert Johnston has observed that 'such a philosophical approach is but one of many options, one that would seem perhaps least appealing to an experientially centred movement' (1984: 57).

Furthermore, this general pattern of de-emphasis (even devaluing) of experience elaborated above has contributed to a concomitant lack of attention to focusing on Pentecostal practices as a locus for Pentecostal theological reflection and construction. What Pentecostals need at this juncture in their theological reflection is to expand beyond the confines of these early defenses. Pentecostals need to expand their theological dialogue to include partners other than Evangelicals and to expand their theological methods in ways that are more open to the Pentecostal emphasis on experience, that are more attentive to actual Pentecostal practices, and yet meet the criteria for critical theology. There are several signs that Pentecostals have been moving in both of these directions.

The work of Menzies (1991, 1994) and Shelton (1991, 1994) show a willingness by Pentecostal scholars to expand their approach to exegesis in ways that embrace the historical-critical methodologies of redaction criticism. This indicates expansion beyond simply grammatical-historical methods.

Also of significance are the articles by Cargal(1993) and Israel, Albrecht and McNally (1993) in the issue of *Pneuma* noted above. Both articles engage a wider dialogue in hermeneutical theory that raise questions as to what is considered a text, what is the impact of the interpreter's pre-understandings on interpretation, and what is the relationship between a text and interpreter (Dempster 1993). All of these are new questions with which Pentecostals are interacting. This series of articles point toward methodologies that are much more open to the ways in which Pentecostals do theological reflection, arguing that since anyone's experience always influences the way interpretation is done, what are ways to approach this problem without becoming lost in non-rational subjectivity.

Another particularly encouraging sign that Pentecostals are expanding their theological reflection beyond narrowly defined exegetical and historical approaches is the appearance of a new journal, the *Journal of Pentecostal Theology*. Edited by three teachers at the Church of God School of Theology, the journal began publication in 1992. The journal and its supplemental series of monographs show great promise as a forum for a new generation of Pentecostal scholars desiring to redress some of the inadequacies of Pentecostal theological reflection identified in this review.

This study also is an attempt to expand Pentecostal theological reflection and construction both in terms of its dialogue partners and its methodology. Its chief contribution is a methodology for Pentecostal theological reflection and construction that is congruent with the Pentecostal emphasis on experience but that also meets criteria for critical theology. The methodology of this study addresses some of the questions regarding the nature of 'texts', the interplay between interpreter and texts and the nature of the role of the interpreter's pre-understandings in theological reflection that have arisen in the recent debates over hermeneutical theory. It joins the debate on the side of those who argue that 'human life itself is *textual* in nature' and agrees with them that all Pentecostal practices participate in 'disclos[ing] the meaning of human life' (Dempster 1993). This study offers new insights into the meaning and significance of Pentecostal behavior and practice in the context of an expanded theological method that attends to the unique focuses and practices of the Pentecostal tradition.

Before offering a detailed description and justification of this methodology some review of the literature on the actual practices chosen for the focus of this study is needed. As important as the leading of the Spirit is for Pentecostals, the literature shows little work that consciously makes the practices associated with discernment and decision making a focal point for Pentecostal theological reflection and construction.

Literature Bearing on the Problem of Pentecostal
Discernment and Decision Making

While there are no major systematic studies that deal with discernment and decision making among Pentecostals, a few studies touch on the topic.

Pentecostals make decisions in many ways, though the leading of the Spirit is often connected to the various charismatic manifestations

that are part of Pentecostal belief and practice.[4] An early sociological/
anthropological study of Pentecostals observed that

4.   Charismatic manifestations among Pentecostals include the following:
(1) *Speaking in Tongues.* This has been much described and discussed in the
literature. (For introduction, see the works by Mills [1986], and Maloney and Lovekin
[1985]). The literature on this charismatic manifestation will confirm that all
definitions are problematical. Spittler has recently offered the following definition:

> Usually, but not exclusively, the religious phenomenon of making sounds that consti-
> tute, or resemble, a language not known to the speaker. It is often accompanied by an
> excited religious psychological state, and in the Pentecostal and charismatic movements
> it is widely and distinctively (but not universally) viewed as the certifying conse-
> quence of the baptism in the Holy Spirit (1988: 335).

(2) *Interpretation of Tongues.* In this charismatic manifestation speaking in
tongues is usually called a 'message' (in tongues) and the 'interpretation' gives the
sense or meaning of the message in a language known to the listener. The interpretation is considered to have a divine source. Spittler again has offered the following
definition:

> The spiritual gift (charisma) by which one so endowed makes cleare to the congrega-
> tion the unintelligible utterance of one who has spoken in tongues (1988: 469).

Such interpretations are seen as signifying the presence and intervention of the Holy
Spirit in the affairs of the person or group. In tongues the Spirit speaks in a way
unintelligible to the listener. While the speaker may be edified, neither he or she nor
the listeners understand what the Spirit speaks without an interpretation. The interpretation then is considered to be the Spirit speaking in a way that becomes understand-
able for the hearers (cf. 1 Cor. 14). While speaking in tongues may occur in group
worship or private devotion, messages and interpretations may be intended for
individuals. That such phenomena are sometimes responsible for certain decisions
among Pentecostals has already been noted.
    Prophecies. Prophecies are generally understood to be a more direct speaking
from the Spirit in the language of the hearers. Rodman Williams offers the following
definition:

> Prophecy...is an immediate communication from God in the common language. It is a
> 'speaking for' God by which a person's tongue is completely at the disposal of the
> Holy Spirit. The concepts and words do not derive from the speaker but from a divine
> source. So God communicates in a given situation a special message to His people
> (1990: 382).

In this sense prophecies are much like interpretations but without someone speaking
in tongues as a preceding event. While Williams's definition expresses a common
understanding of this manifestation in Pentecostal circles (McGuire 1982), other
definitions recognize less frequent understandings of prophecy as prediction
(Hollenweger 1972) or preaching (Robeck 1988).

> The life of a 'Spirit-filled' Christian may involve recurrent or sporadic experience of any or all of these [charismatic] gifts, but far more importantly it is characterized by a sense of the immanent presence of and guidance by the third Person of the Christian Godhead (Gerlach and Hine 1970: 16).

Another similar study noted that

> A second important assumption among Holiness-Pentecostals [the first is that emotional experience is a primary goal of worship] is that outward action (saying 'amen', clapping hands, stomping feet, running the aisles, dancing in the spirit, shouting, jerking, speaking in tongues) is a manifestation of God's presence in a person's life (Abell 1982: 125).

The Holy Spirit is understood and experienced by Pentecostals as an ever present reality in their lives. Several writers have noted that Pentecostals have made various kinds of decisions on the basis of diverse charismatic manifestations understood as manifestations of the Holy Spirit. Gause notes with concern that

> Experience (often a charismatic manifestation) is used to affirm a doctrine or a decision, approve or vindicate a man, sanctify a communion, or canonize a mode of worship (1976: 114).

Walter Hollenweger (1972), a long-time observer of the Pentecostal movement, has noted similar incidents.

> We have known marriages arranged, church business conducted, personal fellowship dissolved, family matters dealt with, money matters handled, by such methods [the charismatic manifestation of prophecy] (1972: 345, source unclear).

These same authors along with others also point out that decisions made on the basis of charismatic manifestations have not always led to positive

Other External Manifestations. In addition to the foregoing external manifestations, the Holy Spirit is believed to be present in and the originator of other external manifestations such as 'shouting', 'dancing', and other forms of 'getting happy' or 'blessed'. Shouting sometimes involves intelligible praise words, such as 'glory (to God)', 'hallelujah', 'praise the Lord', but may involve emotive exclamations— 'shewwww', 'whoooo'—and other such sounds harder to reproduce phonetically. Shouting is often accompanied by bodily movements best characterized as 'jerks' or 'shakings'. A more pronounced bodily movement is 'dancing in the Spirit'. This involves rhythmic movements of the feet (often to the beat of music being played). This dancing, however, is not understood to be something the person initiates, but something one simply yields to. Charismatic manifestations sometimes accompany the sense of things feeling right or good (cf. Land [1993]).

ends. McLean notes that one reason Pentecostal scholars have tried to show a close association between Pentecostal hermeneutics and traditional Evangelical hermeneutics is the 'recurring tendency of charismatic groups to abandon the canon for "fresh and authoritative revelations" of the Holy Spirit' (1984: 35). He cites a moving case of people close to his family who were caught up in new revelations of 'soul marriage' (defined as taking sexual urges to be the leadings of the Holy Spirit). These revelations led to multiple divorces among the participants, including eventually the divorce by the partners of the newly formed soul marriage. Conn (1955), an early Pentecostal historian, has documented the divisiveness and destructiveness of early charismatic 'excesses' among Pentecostals. Schwartz (1970) also noted some tendencies among the Pentecostals he studied to legitimate their own desires as the leading of the Spirit. These articles have many parallels. They also point to the need of 'discernment' as an important part of decisions made on the basis of the 'leading of the Spirit'.

In spite of the above citations showing the relationship between charismatic manifestations and Pentecostal decision making, it would be erroneous to assume that Pentecostals have been unequivocal in their endorsement of charismatic manifestations as the means for discerning the leading of the Spirit. The relationship of charismatic manifestations to discernment and decision making is more subtle than a one-to-one identification of charismatic manifestations as the leading of the Spirit. Charismatic manifestations might better be conceived as not only a means for discernment in some circumstances, but also as the very thing that needs to be discerned in other circumstances. Charismatic manifestations may be evidence of the Spirit's presence, yet they are not sufficient in and of themselves for discerning the Spirit's leading (cf. Land 1993 and Macchia 1992). For Pentecostals these manifestations may have any one of three origins: the Holy Spirit, oneself, or diabolical influence (Spittler 1988). If charismatic manifestations in and of themselves are not to be trusted as the Spirit's leading, what does one trust? Surely a people for whom the leading of the Spirit is so important have means by which to determine what is of the Spirit. Why are there not more incidents like those McLean (1984) describes? What are the means by which Pentecostals keep such excesses in check?

The literature shows that one means by which Pentecostals have sought to discern the leading of the Spirit is reliance on the Christian tradition, particularly as this is contained in the Scriptures. From this tradition some Pentecostals have sought to develop theological criteria for discernment of the Spirit. Hiebert (1985) and Robeck (1980) are illustrative. Hiebert, an anthropologist and missiologist, notes that allowance for a spiritual dimension in human affairs means that one also opens up to the possibility of manifestations of the powers of darkness. He offers a combination of several theological and more softly focused phenomenological criteria for discerning the work of God. Hiebert rejects more obvious phenomenological criteria such as tongues, healings or miracles as sufficient within themselves for discerning whether a given manifestation is from God or the powers of darkness, and suggests the following theological criteria: Does the particular manifestation bring glory to God, honor the lordship of Christ, and agree with the Scriptures? (Each of these criteria can create its own problematic, which again shows that most Pentecostal dialogue tends to be carried on with the more conservative, Evangelical wing of Christianity.) In addition to these, Hiebert suggests the following more softly focused phenomenological criteria: Does the person by whom the manifestation comes exhibit the fruit of the Spirit? Does he or she demonstrate maturity in the faith and a balance in presenting the whole of the gospel? Does the particular manifestation promote unity in the body of Christ and an understanding of the world that rejects the false dichotomy of spirit and matter?

In an article on discerning whether prophecies were genuinely from the Lord, Cecil Robeck (1980) developed criteria for judging prophecy. He proposed that there are both 'rational' and 'transrational' criteria for judging prophecies. The rational criteria include: (1) The character of the person giving the prophecy (is the person a mature and fruitful Christian?). (2) The method by which the prophecy occurs. Regarding method, two criteria are operative: (a) genuine prophecies are given for a specific group or individual at a specific time and place and thus should not be written down for distribution to larger audiences, and (b) genuine prophecies are for edification, not prediction. (3) The message itself (does it accord with Scripture?). Robeck does not elaborate on the transrational criteria other than to say that

> it may appear almost as an existential, intuitive sense that all is not as it may otherwise appear. It is a divinely given sense which enables the detection of the source from which the prophetic word arises (1980: 38).

He then footnotes the Catholic H. Martin's article 'Discernment of Spirits and Spiritual Direction' (1970) without further comment. Pentecostals Basham (1971) and Horton (1972) both have written small, popular pamphlets offering similar criteria to those of Hiebert and Robeck.

Another way by which Pentecostals judge the leading of the Spirit is through a reliance on hierarchical structures of authority within the congregation. This is manifested in several ways. McGuire (1982) was able to show how prophecy was carefully controlled in Catholic Pentecostal prayer meetings by restricting its use to 'core' members. What could be potentially disruptive is 'routinized, managed, and ultimately used for the validation of the leader's authority in the group' (1982: 93). McGuire records that the leaders of the prayer meetings also met in 'discernment' sessions. These sessions allowed the leaders to invalidate any prophecies they did not feel were from the Lord and made the discerners in actuality the most powerful members of the group. While Willems (1967) found that charismatic manifestations were one means for validating a leader's authority in the egalitarian ethos fostered by Pentecostal worship, McGuire's observations show that the ability to regulate charismatic manifestations is actually a more powerful leadership role.

McGuire's (1982) observation about 'core' members points to another way the hierarchical authority structure is evident: a stratification of members. Melvin Williams's (1974) study of black Pentecostals documents such stratification in the congregation he observed. Members who are more advanced or mature are allowed to participate more fully in Spirit leading activities. Similarly Kroll-Smith (1980) has shown that the form of one's 'testimony' gives evidence of one's status in the organization. The implication is that people who can give a certain kind of testimony are respected as being in closer union with God. This concurs with observations by Wilson and Clow (1981), according to whom the process of discerning when a person is truly Spirit possessed does not occur simply by means of observing objective behavior. It involves a more subjective judgment by 'good' members, which implies a hierarchy in which these good members function as discerners.

Another way by which Pentecostals judge the leading of the Spirit is through attention to the social context in which Spirit leading experiences occur. Spirit leading experiences occur in other contexts (cf. Chapter 4), but the most common context is the worship service. Within the worship service there are 'cues' that regulate Spirit leading activities. Paris (1982) is able to demonstrate in his study of black Pentecostals that what might appear as 'chaos' to an outside observer of Pentecostal worship is actually a kind of creative structure not unlike jazz composition. He further likens Pentecostal worship to a drama in which each participant knows the 'script' (or 'score') being played. The participants in the 'chaos' of Pentecostal worship thus know of and adhere to a kind of order and structure in their worship. This shared knowledge of the 'score being played' helps Pentecostals to know when the Spirit is leading. Abell (1982) has observed similarly that behavior such as speaking in tongues and shouting rarely occurred without certain verbal cues from the leader and more subtly perceived cues from the music used in the service.[5] Thus the literature shows Pentecostals discerning and making decisions in a variety of 'rational' ways.

However, such means for discerning the leading of the Spirit are only part of the story. As noted, Robeck (1980) and others have pointed to a 'transrational' dimension to discernment. Hollenweger (1972) speaks of a 'trans-rational mode of communication' in Pentecostalism and McGuire (1982) mentions the belief of Catholic Pentecostals in the effectiveness of 'nonrational ways of knowing (for example, discernment)'. Although several point to this dimension of Pentecostal belief and practice, no one has explored this transrational dimension in Pentecostal discernment and decision making in any depth or detail.

Conclusions

This review of the literature has demonstrated several needs in Pentecostal theological reflection, including the need to move beyond the narrow historical and exegetical battles that characterize much of Pentecostal scholarship. Such work has tended to reverse, and at times repudiate, the focus on experience that has traditionally characterized Pentecostal theology. Such a retreat was thought necessary if Pentecostals were to be able to justify critically their beliefs and avoid the excesses often associated with their practices. The consequences of this were that Pentecostal theological reflection tended to have only Fundamentalists as their dialogue partner and a central feature of the Pentecostal way of doing theology, the focus on experience, was lost.

Pentecostals would benefit from a theological method that would allow retention of the focus on experience while satisfying the criteria for a critical theology. This could also expand the possibilities of theological dialogue beyond the Fundamentalists and offer opportunity for any uniquely Pentecostal contributions to the wider theological landscape.

5.   Land's (1993) work provides the most helpful and creative guide to the theological content and meaning of the Pentecostal worship 'script'.

This kind of expansion also might help resolve the issue of whether there is a uniquely Pentecostal theology.

The review of literature also indicated the need for further study of the transrational dimensions of Pentecostal discernment and decision making. While such dimensions have been noted in the literature, there is need to clarify what is going on in such practices and whether such dimensions are suggestive for enhancing the discernment and decision making of non-Pentecostal groups.

Chapter 3

A REVISED METHODOLOGY FOR PRACTICAL
THEOLOGICAL CONSTRUCTION

Introduction

The purpose of this chapter is to describe a methodology for theological reflection that will meet the needs identified in Chapter 2. The methodology for this project seeks to combine data from ethnographic field methods, including 'thick description', participant-observation, and interviews with analyses of the data from psychological and theological perspectives in a 'mutually critical correlation' (Tracy 1975, 1981), as a means of constructing a practical theology of Pentecostal discernment and decision making. A practical theology so conceived will enable Pentecostal theological reflection to move beyond exegesis and historical illustrations in ways that are congruent with the Pentecostal emphasis on experience while meeting the criteria for critical theology.

Sources of the Methodology

The central feature of this methodology is a procedure which Tracy (1975) has termed 'mutually critical correlation', a concept which has become an almost standard part of the recently revived discussion of methodology in practical theology. To understand better what mutually critical correlation entails one needs to explore the larger context from which it comes.

The Emerging Field of Practical Theology
At least since Schleiermacher, 'practical theology' has designated the minister's ability to 'apply' the theoretically oriented material of a divinity curriculum (Bible, history, dogmatics) to ministry (Farley 1983). This understanding of practical theology, which sees practice as growing out of theory, has set the pattern for theological education into the present

time. Conceived in this way practical theology has been perceived as less important than the more theoretical theological disciplines in the divinity curriculum (Farley 1983). A recent renaissance of interest in practical theology questions the adequacy of this understanding and attempts to rethink the relationship of theory to practice.[1]

The relationship of theory to practice is certainly at the heart of the discussion over the nature of practical theology. Matthew Lamb (1982) has proposed a fivefold typology that summarizes the various ways in which theory and practice may be related and how these relationships impact the nature of practical theology. Lamb prefers the term 'praxis' rather than 'practice' to avoid confusion as to the type of action envisioned. Practice in modern usage often indicates simply technical ability or proficiency. Understood this way practice fails to capture the moral and social dimension of action that praxis is designed to imply. Praxis is not technique but socially transformative action. Lamb would agree with Tracy's definition of praxis as

> the action of moral agents guided by some goal of the good and virtuous life and directed to the development of a character possessing *phronesis* or practical wisdom (1983: 75).

The five ways theory and praxis have been related according to Lamb (1982) are:

1. Theory is accorded primacy over praxis. Classical scholastic theology best represents the practical theology that arises from this position. Scholasticism replaced 'the questioning attitude of the medieval *summae* with a dogmatic thesis theology dedicated to certainty and various forms of logical deductivism' (1982: 65). According to this view, theory embodies the eternal and necessary structures of reality that are not intrinsically changed by human actions.

2. Praxis is accorded primacy over theory. In this type theory is reduced to extrinsic reflection on praxis; it no longer embodies necessary or eternal truth. Theology, as theory, is understood as ever revisable approximations of the events of history and is no longer determinative of praxis. In this position, there is a basic commitment to the cognitive claims and ethical values of contemporary secular culture which may be

---

1.　Seminal contributions to the field include Browning (1983, 1991), Farley (1983), Mudge and Poling (1987), Poling and Miller (1985), and Whitehead and Whitehead (1980). Mudge and Poling give a helpful overview of many of the contributions.

expressed in several ways: a liberal Christianity that sees the eternal in the emotive-intuitive experience of believers, or a socio-political reform which understands revelation to communicate ideals by which people live rather than truths to be believed, or a revolutionary Marxist praxis whose purpose is to criticize the structures of domination in church and society.

3. The 'primacy of faith-love'. This position is represented by the neo-orthodoxy of Karl Barth. For Barth, Christian faith-love is not to be identified with human theory-praxis, either in the classical primacy of theory way or the modern primacy of praxis approach. Christian faith-love is wholly different (non-identical and paradoxical) from human thought and practice. God is not the object of theology but its subject who encounters humanity in Jesus Christ. Lamb notes that such a perspective has affinities with Pentecostalism.

> Likewise, the question of normativity is approached within this non-identical, paradoxical perspective: only God is normative in his revelation. The pentacostalist experience of the Spirit, or the mystic's dark night, or unconditional obedience to the Word—these are the touchstones of truth and life (1982: 75).

4. The critical theoretical approach. The last two approaches to the relationship of theory and praxis Lamb calls 'post-modern, critical' approaches which seek to develop a 'both/and stance of critical correlation' (1982: 65). This fourth approach accepts the nonidentity of Christian faith and theory-praxis but is critical of the supernaturalist, paradoxical mediation of revelation characteristic of type three. This perspective seeks to correlate the values of the Christian tradition with the values of modern culture, but in ways that allow neither to absolutize its claims to truth. It seeks 'to articulate a union of identity and nonidentity between Christianity and the categories of theory-praxis' (1982: 76) but without the reductionism of the first two approaches or the fideism of the third. David Tracy's work is seen as exemplary of this approach.

5. The critical praxis correlation. This is Lamb's own approach.

> This type of theological reflection on the relationship of theory and praxis, as the previous type, seeks a critical union of identity and nonidentity between the categories of theory-praxis and Christianity. It differs from the previous type, however, inasmuch as the critical correlation is placed in praxis rather than in theory (1982: 82)

Unlike the fourth approach which insists that the goal of theory must be praxis, this approach sees praxis (understood as action) as both the goal and foundation of theory. And unlike the primacy of praxis of the second approach, this one points to the 'impossibility of finding a practical reason that is pure or innocent' (Lamb 1982: 83) and aims for an ongoing transformation of academic, ecclesial and social structures via praxis as action.

The understanding of practical theology that emerges from the critical correlational models contrasts sharply with the 'application' of theoretical knowledge or acquisition of 'ministerial skills' model. In the former, theory is understood to derive from critical reflection upon practice; there is a 'temporal and logical priority of practice over theory' (Browning 1983: 13). But there is also a recognition of the reciprocal relationship between theory and practice (theory is reflection upon action or practice and all practice is theory-laden), and of the need for theological reflection to be done in dialogue (critical correlation) with other meaning systems. Such a method, Lamb argues, is the best way to do practical theology in a modern context; practical theology can no longer be conceived along non-critical or 'application' models.

Tracy's Method of Mutually Critical Correlation

The method adopted in this study is a modified form of Tracy's methodology and thus has a close affinity to Lamb's fourth type. Tracy defines theology as

> the discipline that articulates mutually critical correlations between the meaning and truth of an interpretation of the Christian fact and the meaning and truth of an interpretation of the contemporary situation (1983: 62).[2]

2.   David Tracy has offered a typology regarding three 'sub-disciplines' of theology (1981: 56-58). Depending upon its purpose theology may be fundamental, systematic or practical. These three sub-disciplines are distinguished by their primary reference groups (their 'publics'), their modes of argument, their particular ethical emphases, the particular stance taken toward the self-understanding of the theologian's own beliefs, and the criteria for what counts as truth.

For instance, fundamental theology has as its primary reference group the 'academy'. It uses argument designed to appeal to all 'reasonable' people. The ethics it engenders tends to be one of 'honest, critical inquiry' appropriate to the academy. The faith commitment of the fundamental theologian is usually not relevant to the claims he or she makes. Fundamental theology is concerned to show the adequacy or inadequacy of the truth claims of the theologian and his or her dialogue partners in the academy. There is generally some assumed agreement that truth claims can be established through 'objective argument'.

By contrast systematic theology has the 'church' as its primary reference group. It

'Christian fact' is Tracy's term for the broad Christian tradition that begins with the record of the Christ-event in the Scriptures and continues through the full 'range of classic texts, symbols, events, persons, rituals and practices' (Tracy 1981: 64).

By 'critical' Tracy first of all means 'reasonable'; that is, claims to meaning and truth are arguable on 'grounds public to all, that is, available in principle to all intelligent, rational and responsible persons' (1983: 64) whether or not they embrace one's own aims, methods or claims. But reason here is a 'more comprehensive' activity than either classical deductive logic or modern positivist instrumental rationality. Critical also implies an effort to

> unmask the systematic distortions in the person [sic], social, cultural, historical, and religious models of human transformation...[and] the systematic distortions in the critical theories...themselves (Tracy 1983: 78).

This is because 'neither Christianity nor the contemporary situation is present to us in immediate or static forms as objects-over-against-our-subjectivity. Both come to us in mediated and often unconscious forms, especially through verbal language and symbol' (1983: 63).

'Critical' thus means a methodology that is aware of one's method and presuppositions, attempts to become aware (inasmuch as this is possible) of unconscious motives and interests operating through it, and that is reflective and 'public'.

is concerned primarily with the re-presentation of the truth of agreed upon sources of truth from a particular religious tradition. The ethics it engenders are those of loyalty to the tradition it interprets. Here the theologian assumes some personal stance in his or her own faith commitment. What counts as truth is generally agreed upon *a priori* and the task of systematic theology is to illuminate new applications for the present.

Practical theology is different still. Its primary reference group tends to be some particular segment of the 'public of society'.

> More exactly, to the concerns of some particular social, political, cultural or pastoral movement or problematic which is argued or assumed to possess major religious import (1981: 57).

Thus the groups it addresses may or may not be in the church but they are concerned with causes that are considered to have religious import. Practical theology calls for transformation of society. Action, not theory is the arena for testing truth claims. Without transformative action the truthfulness of one's reflections remain only conjectural. Truth is discovered through involvement. The commitment of the theologian is again a personal one, either to the church or to the movement that bears religious significance.

The notion of public dialogue is also present in Tracy's use of 'mutually critical correlation'. When Tracy speaks of mutual correlation he has in mind a kind of public dialogue concerning issues of 'common human experience', more specifically, a conversation in which 'reasonable' partners who hold various perspectives on the issues of human broken-ness engage in dialogue about the transformation of this brokenness in ways that have the potential for changing either or both perspectives.

Tracy's use of correlation is different from that of Paul Tillich. When Tillich spoke of correlation he meant bringing together 'questions' from human experience with 'answers' from revelation, as when questions arising from the anxiety of human finitude are answered by the assur-ance of a power of 'being' sustaining one against the forces of finitude or non-being (Tillich 1951: 59-66). Tracy modifies Tillich's method to let answers emerge from common human experience as well as from what Tillich called revelation, and to let questions, not just answers, arise from revelation.[3] By 'mutually critical correlation' he means that one is open to the various cultural ways of explicating this experience, and brings these various explanations into dialogue with the Christian explanations in ways that have the potential for changing both. Thus disciplines such as psychology and sociology can raise questions about human experi-ences of brokenness, and are also free to provide answers for the trans-formation of this brokenness alongside answers from the Christian tradition. There is thus also in Tracy's method of correlation a respect for the various 'non-revelational' perspectives not present in Tillich's methodology of correlation. Tracy's methodology is designed to bring a 'public' quality to the dialogue and is particularly appropriate in contexts where there is a plurality of competing meaning systems. The claims of the theologian are seen as one among many. While such claims are important, they have no special status among the other competing systems of meaning. They may criticize and challenge but must also submit to critique and challenge in a manner acceptable to public dialogue. Mutually critical correlation refers to a methodology of letting

---

3.   Tracy's doctrine of revelation, if one might speak of such, is basically the understanding that all humans experience 'limit-situations' (e.g. finitude, contingency). Because they disclose the limits of human existence and the sense that 'the final dimension or horizon of our situation is neither one of our own making or under our control' such experiences may be said to have a 'religious dimension' (1975: 105-107). Revelation for Tracy is primarily a self-awareness of the limit-dimensions of *human* experience.

various languages of interpretation interact with each other in a way that places all at risk.

Tracy's methodology yields a model for practical theology as a collaborative enterprise with four steps. First is the development of various theological and cultural models of human transformation. Second is the analysis and evaluation of the public claims to human transformation provided by different concrete ideals for the future. These ideals are themselves judged by criteria of coherence (i.e., they are cognitively consistent), adequacy (they are inclusive of all human experience), and disclosure (they make known some essential aspect of human existence such as finitude). The third step is to unmask distortions in the above claims, and the fourth is that of making ethical decisions for action.

The practical theology developed in this study brings together Pentecostal, psychological and theological perspectives in a theoretical mutually critical correlation (Lamb's fourth type). The dialogue is conceived as a three-way exchange with each perspective interacting with the other two on equal footing. Use of this methodology is especially appropriate to this investigation for several reasons. First, it brings a needed reflective and critical dimension to claims derived from Pentecostal experience, thus addressing charges that Pentecostal theology is unreflective and uncritical.

Secondly, Pentecostalism's own explanation of its practices will be allowed to contribute to the dialogue and be critiqued by other perspectives, with the possibility that new understandings may emerge in a Gadamerian (1975) 'fusion of horizons' (cf. Gerkin 1984, 1986).

Thirdly, Tracy's inclusion of common human experience as a source for theological reflection can deepen and enrich the Pentecostal emphasis on experience. While the meaning of experience for Pentecostals includes a more immediate, personal dimension than Tracy's definition indicates, there also is some common ground in the two understandings. For both Tracy and Pentecostals, experience can refer to feelings, moods, commitments and attitudes as well as information received through the senses, all of which are subject to reflection and interpretation within a community context. But the importance of experience as theological source is enriched by Tracy's understanding of experience to include a 'non-sensuous experience of the self' as a self that is prior to and more fundamental than the interpretation of sensory experience. In the most important instances, appeals to experience are not appeals to verification by means of the senses but

> to what we may validate as meaningful to the experience of the self as an
> authentic self... When we state that an appeal to experience is meaningful,
> we often mean no more and no less than the fact that the appeal
> 'resonates' to our own immediate experience as a self (1975: 66).

However, such experience ordinarily is subjected to critical historical,
scientific, philosophical, or theological analysis within the context of a
community of authority and value.

> In the most important questions of our life, we turn not merely to the
> report of our five senses or even to controlled experiments. Rather we turn
> to that community of interpretation where the value of the self as a self is
> reverenced and where modes of raising that experience to conscious
> awareness are developed (1975: 66).

This understanding of experience as a source of authority rooted in the
sense of a self can enrich Pentecostal explanations concerning the self-
validating nature of Holy Spirit baptism (in addition to claims that such
experiences are validated by linking them to similar experiences in the
New Testament).

Although Tracy's work is used to help define the concept of mutually
critical correlation, several emphases in Tracy's method need modifica-
tion. For instance, his focus on the transformation of society as the goal
to which reasonable human beings work tends to reduce practical
theology to development of a public ethics. The church is conceived as a
subsystem in the larger society which is valued as the preserver of
certain traditions and as a source of scholars committed to bringing that
tradition to the public arena to compete with other traditions in the
creation of a public ethic. This focus on society as the locus of practical
theology tends to neglect the importance of the local faith community
for theology. As Poling and Miller observe,

> theology, as a discipline, as an academic exercise, does not spring directly
> out of the Christian tradition... Rather, theology is deeply dependent on a
> concrete community of believers... Theology... arises out of the need of
> Christian communities to define their identity in ways that make sense in
> the world (1985: 48-49).

Tracy's method is modified in this study insofar as the church is
considered the primary locus for practical theology.

Another way that this project modifies Tracy's method is in the
understanding of experience as the starting place for theological
reflection. The understanding of experience used in this project is closer

to the Whiteheads' (1980) understanding of this term than to Tracy's understanding.

The Whiteheads modify Tracy's concept of 'common human experience' by identifying two kinds of experience: common cultural experience (more what Tracy has in mind) and a more immediate personal experience (which may have individual or corporate dimensions; i.e. the experience of *this* congregation as distinct from the experience of the culture or Christian tradition in general). Culture is the information that arises from the 'symbols, mores, and sciences' of a people. It includes the meaning systems of the natural and social sciences, and philosophical and historical as well as contemporary interpretations of personhood and community. Personal experience means that experience which is unique to the individual. 'Christian tradition' refers not only to the revelations found in the Old and New Testaments but also to two millennia of ecclesial decisions that have shaped the interpretation of those revelations. While this tradition is understood to be pluriform and dynamic, certain interpretations (e.g. the Councils) are understood to carry more theological weight. Common cultural experience and particular experience overlap at times but it is misleading to equate them. In a similar criticism Roberta Chopp (1987) has noted that Tracy's common human experience is not always as 'common' as presumed, but is apt to be common 'white, male, dominant' experience. Awareness of differences between common cultural experience and an individual or group's particular experience aids the group or individual in becoming aware of how their specific experience both reflects and departs from that of their wider culture (Whitehead and Whitehead 1980). The same is true regarding the Christian tradition and personal experience. One's personal experiences of and interpretation of traditional symbols are not necessarily coextensive with the 'Christian tradition' though they are part of it.

The Whiteheads' distinction is helpful in clarifying the nature of experience and in valuing the experience of a non-dominant cultural group such as Pentecostals. Their form of mutual critical correlation brings together information from (1) the Christian tradition, (2) personal experience, and (3) culture. While aware that many would propose that one start theological reflection at the 'beginning' (i.e., with the Christian tradition especially as embodied in Scripture) and work forward to present experience, the Whiteheads make the point that present experience is the more logical place to begin 'practical reflections' (reflections that call for answers in the moment of a lived faith).

These modifications to Tracy's thought bring the definition of practical theology closer to that of James Fowler, who defines practical theology as 'theological construction and reflection arising out of and giving guidance to a community of faith in the praxis of its mission' (1983: 149). While Fowler's methodology retains the emphasis on public criteria and critical reflection present in Tracy, several features in this definition need to be highlighted in relation to the purposes of this study. First, as already noted, the notion that practical theology arises out of (and gives guidance to) communities of faith makes the locus of practical theology the church rather than society. Secondly, implied in this definition is that practical theology involves 'local' communities of faith; that is, one does not study abstractions like 'the church' in general, one studies particular communities of faith. Mudge and Poling have noted the implications of this understanding of the church.

> We begin to see that the church, or even the particular congregation, func-
> tions very much like a culture in its own right and must be studied as such
> without assuming from the start that the reality categories that apply to one
> instance also apply to another (1987: xxiii).

Thirdly, one studies the faith community in the midst of its attempts to live its mission. In the present project, this means focusing on the practices of Pentecostals (their experiences of Spirit leading) as the starting point for theological reflection and construction. Fourthly, practical theology goes beyond critical reflection to include theological 'construction'. Each of these points is relevant to this investigation.

At the level of methodology, this investigation is therefore a test to see if indeed the methodology of mutually critical correlation can produce a practical theology of Pentecostal discernment and decision making. It is thus a contribution to methodology more than to a doctrine of Spirit leading as such. It might further be conceived as a test of this methodology as an appropriate method for interdisciplinary theological studies involving the social sciences.

Selecting the Participants and Perspectives

The Congregation

As noted previously, in Fowler's (1983) understanding, practical theology is done in a specific faith community. His method might be considered a case study approach at the congregational level (Hopewell 1987).

The congregation selected for this study is from the International

Holiness Pentecostal Church, one of the classical Pentecostal denominations.[4] All of the five later streams of Pentecostalism share a historical relatedness to this classical stream; thus it may be anticipated that the data produced from this congregation will have some relevance to the other streams.

Secondly, this congregation was chosen because it is one to which I had easy access.[5] It is a congregation that I have frequently attended for the last several years and in which I have established some rapport with the members. Of course a danger of studying a familiar group is that one might overlook things that a stranger would observe (Heilman 1973). However, there also are advantages to such a long association with this congregation: it allows a 'thicker' description regarding the meaning and significance of certain observations which would probably not be available in shorter periods of association and the rapport that I have with the people made them less suspicious and more willing to talk about their experiences. I concluded that the advantages of familiar, unobtrusive access outweighed the disadvantages of studying a congregation in which I would have been a stranger.

4.   The name of the denomination is a pseudonym.

5.   The congregation selected is a fairly large congregation by International Holiness Pentecostal Church (IHPC) standards. The average congregation in the IHPC has less than 40 members. The congregation selected is one of only a few congregations having an average attendance over 200. A significant factor in the size of this congregation is its location in the town that is the denomination's international headquarters. It is one of two congregations where most of the international office workers and officials are members. Because of its location near the headquarters of the denomination it also attracts any retired ministers.

This raises the question of how representative the congregation may be for the denomination and for Pentecostals in general. While one certainly could not argue that it is a typical congregation in the IHPC in terms of its size, there are other qualities to suggest that it may be more representative of the kinds of people in the denomination than a smaller congregation would be. Given its location in the town where the denomination is headquartered, it draws a wider variety of people from within the denomination than would be true of smaller IHPC congregations. And while this is not a study of the denomination, but of one local congregation, this particular congregation offers a better chance that the people observed and interviewed represent the denomination more generally than other congregations would and thus probably tap a wider range of the kinds of people found in all Pentecostal churches. Those interviewed were sufficiently varied to include representatives from the different sub-groupings within this congregation.

The Perspectives
This study brings together the discernment and decision-making experiences of Pentecostals in a mutually critical correlation with perspectives on these experiences drawn from the Christian tradition and contemporary culture.

Pentecostal experience. The Pentecostal experiences of being led by the Spirit will be given voice through a modified ethnographic study that includes 'thick description', participant-observation and interviews. Because published accounts by Pentecostals regarding discernment and decision-making practices are deficient (as noted in Chapter 2), a modified ethnographic study of a local Pentecostal community appears to be the best way to provide the information needed for a Pentecostal analysis of its discernment and decision making.

'Thick description'. Ethnography, as developed by anthropologists, involves observation and description of a group's rituals, beliefs and events so as to understand them in their own terms with minimum imposition of theoretical concepts alien to the people studied. The method of observation and description envisioned here draws from the work of Clifford Geertz (1973) who defines ethnography as 'thick description'.

> In anthropology, or anyway social anthropology, what the practitioners do is ethnography... From one point of view, that of the textbook, doing ethnography is establishing rapport, selecting informants, transcribing texts, taking genealogies, mapping fields, keeping a diary, and so on. But it is not these things, techniques and received procedures, that define the enterprise. What defines it is the kind of intellectual effort it is: an elaborate venture in, to borrow a notion from Gilbert Ryle, 'thick description' (1973: 5-6).

Thick description seeks to record what Geertz calls the 'semiotic' function of behavior and beliefs, that is, to illumine the symbolic function or meaning of a behavior or belief in an attempt to construct as clearly as possible the meaning world of the people studied. By thickly describing groups in terms of the constructions they might use of themselves, Geertz hopes to gain 'access to the conceptual world in which our subjects live so we can...converse with them' (1973: 24). Thick description is thus distinguished from a 'what the camera saw' kind of phenomenological description; it allows one to distinguish between a 'twitch' of the eye and a 'wink', that is, between similar physical behaviors having different meanings. Although Geertz realizes that no observation by an outsider can be free of interpretive bias, his method is an attempt to 'see things from the actor's viewpoint'.

Participant-observation. One of the means for gaining access to the meaning system of a group so as to make observations of a thick descriptive kind is 'participant-observation', a method in which the researcher is both a participant as well as observer in the ongoing life of those studied. While such participation is rarely *full* participation—the researcher remains an observer—participant-observation is not simply observation; it involves genuine participation and thus certain risks.

> The difference between pure 'observation' and 'participant-observation' is that the latter requires encountering the group on its own terms and (in anthropological terms) the risk of 'going native' (McGuire 1982: 21).

This study began with an unannounced period of participant-observation in the congregation. For eight months (September–April) I participated in and observed a variety of services and activities conducted by the congregation, including 26 Sunday morning services, 24 Sunday evening services, 25 Sunday School class sessions, 11 Wednesday evening services or activities, five of six revival services, two fellowship breakfasts, one work day to paint Sunday School rooms, one district service and two meetings the pastor conducted with members concerned with the future of the congregation's ministry. I also participated in and observed three special occasion services: a baptismal service, a service in which young people formally joined the membership of this congregation, and a service in which the Lord's Supper and the Washing of Feet were practiced.

During this period of participant-observation I made notes on the activities of the services or meetings. Brief notes were generally made during the service or meeting when it could be done unobtrusively and supplemented after the meetings. Notes on matters such as the order or arrangement of the service or meeting, the songs sung, the comments made by those directing the meetings, who 'testified' and something as to the content of the testimony, were made. Some notation regarding the time that various activities took, the general theme and content of the preacher's sermons (which are all audio taped by the congregation), the content of 'prayer requests' and the prayers prayed were also made. I noted those who made an active contribution to the services and was particularly careful to observe and record services in which there was some 'move' of the Spirit that would set up a context for discernment and decision making.

Interviews. The participant-observation phase of the study was augmented by audio-taped interviews with selected members of the congregation. The interviews sought information regarding experiences of discernment and decision making as well as information about the person's perceptions of and relationship with God. An interview guide (Appendix II) contained questions on experiences of discernment and decision making designed to illuminate these questions further, while questions on perceptions of and relationship with God explored the possible links between Pentecostal experience and ego psychology and object relational understandings of early childhood experiences. The questions were drawn from and informed by similar surveys from studies using these theoretical frameworks (cf. McDargh 1984 and Rizzuto 1979). There were questions regarding one's earliest memories of God, one's current image of God, one's sense of obligation to God and how this impacts one's attitudes about oneself.

The interview began by having people share, in a general way, how they received the baptism of the Holy Spirit and its significance for them and then moved to more specific questions about Spirit leading and discernment and decision making. This seemed to help people feel more comfortable and the interview took on something of the air of a conversation about things that were important to Pentecostals and about which they had often talked with others. One person remarked that it was like sharing her 'testimony', something not unusual for a Pentecostal. The interview then moved to the questions about one's general understanding of and relation to God.

The questions, formulated with the use of Pentecostal terminology, were open ended in an effort to encourage those interviewed to tell the information their way. Because of this people often answered more than one question on the interview guide at a time. When this happened, I made adjustments to the order of questions. Since the purpose of the interviews was to give Pentecostals an opportunity to voice their own explanations of their practices, allowing the interview to flow like a conversation was deemed better than a rigid form. The interview guide gave a basic structure to insure that common ground was covered in all interviews.

Most of those interviewed indicated that they were glad to help and many expressed their appreciation at being able to share their thoughts and experiences. Some looked hesitant when asked to be taped but no one refused. Taping was explained as a way to help me remember and also to keep me from reporting that people said what I wanted them to say, if they had not said it that way.

Interviewees were selected from among the membership on the basis of their commitment to Pentecostal faith and practice. All interviewees were active members who professed Holy Spirit baptism. For the Pentecostal, Holy Spirit baptism is a prerequisite to experiences of Spirit leading and Spirit leading would be an important, if not essential, aspect of decision making for such people. A second consideration in the choice of interviewees was to approximate the social make up of the congregation (see Appendix IV).

Twenty-two interviews that lasted from a half to two and a half hours each were conducted. The initial three interviews were conducted with members of the congregation with whom I work. These interviews were used to help refine questions on the guide used in the other 19 interviews. These interviews were conducted several months later after the period of participant-observation had been concluded and included the two ministers then on staff.

The interviews were conducted in a variety of locations: four were done in my office, two in my home, six at the interviewee's place of work or office, and eight in the interviewees' homes. The interviews began with a word of thanks for the person's willingness to participate. This was followed by comments about the general nature of the study as an exploration of the ways people discern the leading of the Spirit, that not much had been done in this area, and that the author wished to talk with people about experiences of this kind they have had. When queried as to what the study hoped to find I offered to share the results when the study was finished. Five participants, selected to represent the range of Spirit leading experiences reported in the first interviews, were interviewed a second time to obtain further information regarding family and childhood background (Appendix III).

There are of course limitations to ethnographic methods. Chief among these are the lack of quantitative results and comparative data. Quantitative data is primarily a means of guarding against chance occurrence in one's findings and of indicating the breadth of distribution of the behaviors or events studied. Comparative data seeks to insure that one's findings are not idiosyncratic or contaminated by extraneous variables. While the addition of these types of data ideally give more reliability to one's findings, their absence does not mean their purposes are wholly unsatisfied by qualitative types of data. Carefully argued case studies can provide information for judging both the idiosyncrasies and generalizability of the findings, while presenting information that could not easily be quantified. Human behavior is a complex phenomenon and despite the bias toward quantifiable data, reducing complex human behavior to such categories often results in a narrowing of the applicability of the findings. The rich detail of a case presentation can offset the lack of comparative and quantitative data. Illuminating the practices of a particular congregation, with its strengths and weaknesses, should be instructive to those who observe and participate in other congregations.

A second weakness to ethnography is related to the method of participant-observation and the extent to which participation in a group influences the findings relative to the group.

> Although the participant observation offers the best possibility for understanding a group's meanings and assumptions, we can never be quite sure how the observer has changed the world she is observing (Ammerman 1987: 12).

The role and extent of observer neutrality is a debated issue among social scientists. There is a recognition by certain philosophers of science that observer neutrality is unachievable in the social sciences (Myrdal 1969) and perhaps in the natural sciences (Kuhn 1962). While it is beyond the scope of this study to resolve this issue, the presupposition than an investigator is not to influence unduly the results he or she achieves is a valid goal for research.[6] What is important in participant-observation is that one recognize to the extent possible where and in what ways he or she is influencing the results. In the present study my presence as a long time member of the congregation meant that no

---

6.   The problem raises larger issues which cannot be resolved here. While the notion of the researcher as unobtrusive observer is still held to be the ideal model for science, Thomas Kuhn (1962) has shown how pre-commitments to certain methods preclude the scientist's ability to deal sufficiently with anomalies in his or her research. Myrdal (1969) and Rosenthal (1976) have demonstrated similar effects in the social sciences and have also shown that the researcher's methodological commitments directly influence the findings. In a different context, Gilkey (1990) following Tillich (1951), argues that certain pre-commitments (e.g. to 'truth') are necessary to keep 'science' from degenerating to struggles for money and power (cf. the periodic reports of researchers changing evidence for the sake of funds).

intrusive formal announcement had to be made that I was observing the congregation. Thus the observations could be made without concern that the people would feel self-conscious about being observed. And while a few people observed me writing in a notebook on occasions, no one visibly altered his or her behavior because of this activity, though the possibility of more subtle forms of influence cannot be ruled out on that account alone.

Despite the obvious limitations of ethnography such methods have several advantages. Chief among them is the richness of detail and the depth in understanding ethnography can achieve.

> The foremost reason for choosing field research methods, such as participant-observation and intensive interviewing, is that these methodological approaches are best suited to trying to grasp the meanings of a situation for the participants themselves. Furthermore, they yield firsthand insights into the ongoing life of the group studied (McGuire 1982: 10).

The observations and interviews of this study sought 'Pentecostal answers' to such questions as the contexts in which one can expect the Spirit to lead, the ways in which the Spirit is apt to lead, how Pentecostals distinguish the leading of the Spirit from other leadings, the kinds of discernment and decision making experiences Pentecostals actually have, the kinds of changes they actually make as a result of these experiences, whether Spirit leading encounters open up or close off possibilities for people, and how Pentecostals handle the ambiguous and negative elements in these practices. Chapter 4 reports the answers to these questions.

Secondly, the ethnographic approach helps assure that what one says is being studied is indeed what is being studied. Paris (1982) has noted a tendency among 'functionalist' approaches to religion to 'explain away' the phenomena being studied. Because the ethnographic approach gives more immediate access, via thick descriptions, to the data on which analyses are made, it is less reductionistic; 'it is meant to reaffirm realities rather than dissect them' (Schrieter 1985: 58).

Thirdly, this approach allows the 'common' person to be heard. Those who write tend to be the intellectuals, whether internal or external to the movement, who may not always express how things are actually perceived by those about whom they write. Ethnographic descriptions of Pentecostal practices should be such that Pentecostals themselves could recognize the descriptions as true to their experience.

Psychological perspectives

One might well ask why choose psychology to represent what Tracy (1983) has called 'common human experience' or what Whitehead and Whitehead (1980) have called the 'cultural experience' pole of the correlation? Philip Reiff (1966) has written of the explanatory power of psychology for the modern world. The therapeutic language of psychology 'makes sense' to many modern people and has become a powerful language of explanation for the common experiences of this culture. A psychological perspective as correlation partner for this study becomes suggestive in two ways. One, it will offer explanations that 'make sense' of these processes for many people, especially those who look for more interpretive explanations than the narrative-descriptive explanations of these practices produced by the modified ethnographic study. But secondly, and this is important for the mutual correlation, such a powerful language stands in need of its own critique by the other partners in the dialogue, lest it be assumed that the psychological explanation is the only way to make sense of these phenomena.

But which psychology? The function of psychology in this study is primarily as a cultural 'language of explanation' which contributes to the mutually critical correlational dialogue essential to the construction of a practical theology of discernment and decision making. In this dialogue the language of psychology will bring to the analysis of Pentecostal discernment and decision making a methodology of 'suspicion and retrieval' (Ricouer in Reagan and Stewart 1978) that asks if there are ways to understand what is going on in these practices different from the indigenous Pentecostal explanation. As a 'hermeneutics of suspicion', it will look for pathology not obvious in the Pentecostal explanation. As a 'hermeneutics of retrieval' it will look for constructive ways to illuminate the basis and nature of certain discernment and decision practices, particularly the reliance on things 'feeling right'; are there positive psychological factors that lie at the root of discernment and decision making? Because of their focus on early developmental and unconscious processes, the psychoanalytic or dynamic psychologies seem best suited to an inquiry into the helpfulness and harmfulness of these practices.[7]

---

7. Two other psychologies, decision-making theory and attribution theory, suggest themselves at this point. Attribution theory appears to have particular relevance because the basic premise of this theory is that the fundamental human motivation is to make sense or meaning out of the world or experience. People make

The psychoanalytic psychologies chosen for this study are ego psychology and object relations theory. The understandings of developmental and unconscious processes offered in these psychologies will provide rich theoretical resources for understanding what is going on in Pentecostal discernment and decision making.

The use of psychology as a language of explanation for practical theological construction extends the ways in which these psychologies have been used in religious studies both in terms of subject matter and methodology. The expansion of the methodological use of these psychologies is their use for practical theological construction. The expansion of subject matter use is in the exploration of Pentecostal discernment and decision making. Those studies which have sought to apply ego psychological perspectives to Pentecostal behavior have focused exclusively on the phenomenon of speaking in tongues, arriving at variant conclusions (Maloney and Lovekin 1985). For instance, Alland (1962) suggests that a positive regression of the ego occurs in this behavior while Lapsley and Simpson (1964a, 1964b) argue that the regression in the service of the ego that occurs in tongue speaking is basically a defensive move on the part of the ego to save itself from destruction. However, no one has sought to apply ego psychological perspectives to Pentecostal practices beyond this context. Such application may help answer the question of whether Pentecostal practices, including but not limited to speaking in

'attributions' or inference about the sources or causes of events as ways to explain their world (Spilka, Hood and Gorsuch 1986). Thus this theory explores many of the same concerns of the ethnographic-descriptive approach. One of the key tasks of the ethnographic approach is to articulate the symbol (meaning) system of the group studied. Because Pentecostals attribute many decisions to the Holy Spirit the indigenous explanation developed in this study is in some ways an attributional explanation although it is articulated more directly in this study as ethnographic description.

Decision-making theory, however, is not suited to this particular study. Decision-making theory is primarily associated with the work of Irving Janis (1977) and focuses largely on descriptions of how people make decisions. Janis understands decision making as information processing and has developed complex models that included 'balance sheets' and generation and weighing of alternative gains and losses. While the name of his theory is suggestive, his theoretical and practical models are not as suited to this study as might appear from the name. The highly cognitive orientation of an information processing model of decision making is far removed from the exploration of the non-cognitive and affective dimensions of Pentecostal decision making. There is also evidence that people do not use the methods of decision making Janis proposes without specific training (Hillstrom 1985) which also suggests that Pentecostal decision making would not be of the kind Janis investigates.

tongues, are part of a more general openness by Pentecostals to the intuitive, affective, and unconscious dimensions of life.

Only a few studies in religion have employed an object relations perspective and only one has explored the implications of such psychologies for Pentecostal behavior. Two studies, those of McDargh (1983) and Rizzuto (1979), focused on the God representation or the object images one constructs of God. A third study (Jones 1991) explores the relationship between the formation of early childhood relationships and the experience of transcendence while a fourth, that of William Meissner (1984), has explored a wide range of religious thought and practice from the perspective of object relations theory, expanding the understanding of religious behavior as 'transitional phenomena'. The only study to explore Pentecostal behavior from an object relations perspective is a paper by Castelein (1984) dealing with narcissism and ecstatic experience. In addition to interacting with these previous studies, this investigation will explore other concepts in object relations theory, such as affective knowing, which have not been utilized in previous studies and may be helpful for understanding Pentecostal discernment and decision making.

Theological Perspectives

Theology, as used here, refers to the wider Christian tradition, a tradition which begins with the New Testament church and includes the historical reflections of the church upon the Scriptures and its mission. Tracy (1981) has called this pole of a mutually critical correlation the 'Christian fact'. Since Pentecostalism locates itself within the Christian tradition, any attempt to formulate guidelines or norms for evaluation of Pentecostal practices must involve critical dialogue with that tradition because it provides a language for evaluating reality and truth claims.

However, as with psychology, there are many variations in the Christian tradition. To which articulation of the faith does one appeal? As noted in Chapter 2, Pentecostals have sought a dialogue primarily with Evangelical exegetical theology. While some have questioned the appropriateness of such restrictions (Johnston 1984), there have been few attempts on the part of Pentecostals to engage in dialogue with modern, critical expressions of Christian tradition (neo-orthodoxy, liberalism, liberation theologies, existentialism) (see Chapter 2). This study proposes that the theology of Paul Tillich (1951, 1957, 1963) can be a fruitful dialogue partner for expanding Pentecostal theological reflection. Tillich's theology can enrich the construction of a practical theology of Pentecostal discernment and decision making by offering a language of explanation for Pentecostal practices consistent with the wider Christian tradition and by helping to formulate norms for evaluation of such practices.

But how compatible is Tillich with a Pentecostal approach to theology? At least one charismatic theologian (Gelpi 1978) thinks he is not at all compatible, and the dialogue between Tillich and Pentecostals is admittedly small. Evangelical scholar David Wells (1978) has criticized Tillich's theology, asserting that it 'fits with everything' and thus has abandoned true Christianity. To demonstrate affinities between Tillich and Pentecostal theology would be detrimental to the project of Pentecostal scholars who try to show that Pentecostalism is a variation of Fundamentalism; it would confirm Fundamentalists' suspicions that Pentecostals are not of their camp.

Charismatic theologian Donald Gelpi (1978) rejects Tillich's compatibility with a Pentecostal-experiential approach to theology. In an attempt to develop an epistemological undergirding for the experiential nature of Pentecostal theology, Gelpi gives Tillich's theology serious consideration but rejects it in favor of American process theology. Gelpi faults Tillich's methodology as well as his substance. According to Gelpi, Tillich insists that philosophy has no place in theology because it is detached and objective, whereas theology is existential, focusing on human experience. Gelpi sees this as an 'illegitimate' attempt to endow Tillich's own philosophical categories with an 'aura of holiness that put[s] them beyond the patient critique of other philosophical systems' (1978: 40), thus employing existential philosophy dogmatically rather than critically. Gelpi also finds Tillich's critique of philosophy as detached and objective untrue to his own experience of American philosophers such as Whitehead who were 'personally, even passionately involved in the search for religious meaning' (1978: 40). In addition, Gelpi argues that if one follows Tillich one must substitute the Tillichian category 'being' for the very different American category, 'experience'. Gelpi concludes that Tillich's language requires one to deny God as person or self and to deny that Jesus can be both divine and human.

How is one to respond to Gelpi's criticisms? Gelpi is correct to criticize Tillich for proposing a philosophical theology that tries to put itself above philosophical critique, but such critique can surely be supplied by others who would use his theology. The mutually critical

correlation requires just such a critique, which would appear therefore to
meet Gelpi's methodological objection.

Gelpi's other criticism, that one must substitute 'being' for 'experience'
in order to use Tillich's theology, is rooted in a concern that Tillich's
ontological language causes a loss of certain important expressions of
experience. The relationship of 'language' to 'reality' is not a simple
issue. Lindbeck (1984) argues that what often lies behind theologies such
as Tillich's (which Lindbeck calls experiential-expressive) is the assumption of a common reality or experience that can be expressed in different
languages. Against this position, Lindbeck argues that languages often
embody or refer to different realities and that they actively shape the
experience of their users; he thus cautions against assuming that meanings
of one language are translatable to another. Gelpi's last criticism rides
largely on this issue which, however, the method of mutually critical
correlation directly addresses. Tillich's theology is part of a multiple
dialogue that seeks to share meanings between and across languages of
explanation but in ways that do not reduce one language to another.
Thus, even granting Gelpi's reservations, it is possible to use Tillich's
theology in an exploration of Pentecostal discernment and decision
making within the practical theological methodology of this study.

Rodman Williams (1971), another charismatic theologian who has
sought dialogue with Tillich, finds more to affirm than criticize regarding
Tillich's relevance to Pentecostals. Williams is not without reservations.
He holds, for instance, that Tillich's notion of the 'mutual immanence'
of human and divine spirit does not sufficiently recognize the differences
between regenerate and unregenerate humanity and he dislikes Tillich's
concept of 'ecstasy', which he believes connotes emotionalism. Nevertheless, Williams finds Tillich's existential theology a possible framework
for developing the kind of 'experienced based' theology that characterizes
Pentecostalism.

> Thus Tillich is clearly an ally of all of us who are seeking to bear witness
> to the dynamic movement of the Spirit presently occurring (1971: 96).

> I would hold that no other theologian of our time has sought more
> seriously to explore the dynamics of the relationship between the divine
> Spirit and human spirit, and Tillich will continue to offer invaluable guid-
> ance in a day when people are increasingly concerned to find a faith that
> involves their whole existence (1971: 99).

Tillich is chosen basically because he takes 'spirit movements' (in
which Pentecostalism would certainly fall) seriously. Since this is the

system of thought from which the theological concepts and norms for evaluation will be derived, a theology compatible with the basic thrust of Pentecostalism should be helpful in the constructive task of this project. Tillich states at one point that the whole of Part IV of his system ('Life and the Spirit') is intended to defend 'the ecstatic manifestations of the Spiritual Presence' against its psychological and ecclesiastical critics (1963: 118). But while Tillich is quick to discuss safeguards necessary for spirit movements, he nevertheless affirms them and takes a stand against those who would forbid their emergence or reduce the ecstatic dimension to psychological dynamics. Though Tillich may not fit with all Evangelical presuppositions about Pentecostalism, dialogue with Tillich appears to provide Pentecostals one promising way to move beyond the narrowness of their previous theological reflections.

Chapter 4

A PENTECOSTAL UNDERSTANDING OF DISCERNMENT AND DECISION MAKING: AN ETHNOGRAPHIC STUDY OF A LOCAL CONGREGATION

Introduction

This chapter sets forth a Pentecostal understanding of practices that Pentecostals call 'the leading of the Spirit' or, alternately, discernment and decision making, developed from ethnographic data collected from a local Pentecostal congregation. It draws upon information from participant-observation in the life of the congregation and interviews with members about their experiences of Spirit leading to describe times and places where discernment and decision making have occurred, patterns of discernment and decision making, criteria by which discernment is made, and the kinds of subsequent activities that reportedly result from these practices. It also includes a 'thick' description of a Pentecostal worship service as a locus of certain Spirit leading experiences. The theory and methods employed in this ethnographic study are described in Chapter 3.

The data from these observations and interviews will provide answers to the following questions: what kinds of decisions are attributed to the leading of the Spirit, by what criteria do Pentecostals discern that it is the 'Spirit' that directed them, and what impact do these decisions have on the person? Related questions include: What aspects of these decisions are uniquely Pentecostal? How are the discernment criteria used? and What is the relationship between discernment and decision making and charismatic manifestations?

Background and Description of the Congregation Selected

Location

The King's Avenue congregation is located in Antioch, a town of about 30,000 in Northwestern North Carolina in the heart of the Smoky

Mountain Range of the Appalachian Mountains.[1] Antioch, like the surrounding region, shares a deeply rooted tradition in southern, Fundamentalist religion. Dayton, Tennessee, home of the famous 'Scopes monkey trial', is less than two hours from Antioch.

The growth of Antioch has been closely associated with the growth of Pentecostalism. One of the oldest classical Pentecostal denominations moved its administrative operations to Antioch in 1907 (population 5000) and by 1913 had built a publishing plant that was producing and distributing church literature to several states and the Carribbean Islands. Locating the central headquarters for the denomination in Antioch also meant that several of the more charismatic and qualified leaders of the organization made Antioch their home over the years.

The Pentecostal influence in Antioch can be seen in several ways. One is in the number of buildings belonging to Pentecostal organizations. No fewer than four Pentecostal organizations call Antioch their headquarters. Besides the numerous church buildings that dot the town, the two larger Pentecostal organizations have publishing facilities, church sponsored colleges, and multi-storied general office buildings in the town. One of the most imposing structures in Antioch, located on the main north–south road through town is a 10,000 seat auditorium with 30 acres of paved parking lot owned by one of the Pentecostal denominations. This auditorium is the sight for the 'general assembly' of this organization, an annual event that brings about 20,000 additional people to Antioch for a week. The colleges and publishing houses, together with various denominational bureaucracies, also generate significant revenue for the town.

Pentecostal influence is also evident in the significant number of Pentecostals active in or employed by civic groups, government, the public educational system, and private business and industry in the area.

Denomination

The King's Avenue congregation belongs to the International Holiness Pentecostal Church (IHPC), a classical Pentecostal denomination, the second largest of the Pentecostal groups headquartered in Antioch, and owner of the 10,000 seat auditorium. Some history of the King's Avenue denomination will help to understand better the meaning and significance of Spirit leading for this congregation.

The IHPC traces its roots to an 'outpouring of the Holy Spirit' among

---

1.   The names of the congregation and its location are pseudonyms as is the subsequent identification of the denomination and its founding leaders.

some holiness people in the mountains of North Carolina around the turn of the century. In 1903 a charismatic leader named John Thomas Anderson joined the group and was soon selected as its pastor. By 1904 he had moved from the mountains of North Carolina to the small town of Antioch and was pastor to three of four affiliated congregations in the three states of North Carolina, Tennessee and Georgia. In 1907 the group made Antioch the center of its administrative operations and by 1911 had grown in size to the point where 'overseers' had to be appointed to supervise almost 2,000 members in several southern states. The group built cohesiveness among its members by holding annual 'general assemblies' beginning in 1906. In the 1914 General Assembly, following several 'messages [in tongues] and interpretations', Anderson was selected as 'General Overseer for life'. When sharp disagreements between Anderson and other church leaders led to his separation from the denomination in the early 1920s, he formed another organization with about 3000 members from the larger denomination. It is this later group that became the IHPC; it continued to view Anderson's selection as 'General Overseer for life' as the Spirit's direction to the group.

It is fair to characterize the IHPC as a denomination in which the leading of the Spirit is considered a central aspect of its denominational identity. The minutes of its general assemblies often carry parenthetical notations that there was a 'move' of the Spirit following a sermon or song. Particularly important were times the Spirit was felt to direct the general assembly in deciding doctrinal or policy matters. Such leadings of the Spirit were often accompanied by various charismatic manifestations, particularly messages in tongues and interpretations. The IHPC also prides itself that its business decisions in the general assembly are passed by 'unanimous agreement'. It is felt that such harmonious agreement could not be reached without the Spirit's direct intervention. While such unanimous decisions are actually a form of majority rule (those not in agreement are asked to 'submit' so that in the final passage 'unanimous' means no one stood publicly in opposition to the measure), much is made of the Spirit's ability to help the group come to agreement.

Another significant example that the IHPC points to as the leading of the Spirit was the selection of the General Overseer to succeed Anderson when he died. The group, gathered to select a successor, experienced a 'move of the Spirit' in which there was an 'interpretation' of a message in tongues that was understood to point to Anderson's younger son, Philip, as the one to be the new General Overseer. When Philip

Anderson retired after serving over forty years the denomination underwent the selection of a new General Overseer. When Anderson's successor, a man whose selection by the 'presbytery' (all State and National Overseers) had included dissension, was presented as the permanent General Overseer at the general assembly there were several messages and interpretations which were understood as the Spirit's selection and confirmation of the new leader.[2]

Formation of King's Avenue[3]
As an IHPC congregation, King's Avenue shares this tradition regarding the importance of the leading of the Spirit. First formed in the late 1950s following a revival by an itinerant IHPC evangelist, initial membership of the congregation consisted of six people converted to Christ in the revival and about twenty people who transferred their membership from other IHPC congregations. Growth was slow and erratic until the late 1960s when the congregation experienced a significant period of growth which evenuated in a move from an older, historic part of town to its present structure which is located on a well-traveled street.

There were at least two factors that aided the growth of this congregation. New housing was expanding in this part of town which made it closer to the homes of several members of other IHPC congregations which transferred to King's Avenue. The relocation of the church college to Antioch during this period also provided a significant student body that might attend a more conveniently located congregation.

King's Avenue has had a succession of pastors since its formation with three years being the average length of stay. The period of growth and re-location described above occurred during an atypical pastorate that lasted for six years. After this pastor, growth has been moderate and no further building has taken place under subsequent pastors, who

2.   General Assembly decisions would seem appropriate for further investigation given their attribution to the Spirit's leading. However, Spirit led assembly decisions tend to be associated with charismatic manifestations and thus do not offer the breadth of discernment and decision making characteristic of Pentecostalism. Focus on a local congregation's discernment and decision making provides contact with a wider range of these practices and also offers more immediate access to the participants.

3.   Some identifying information about the formation of the congregation has been changed to help obscure the identity of the members who appear in the case studies. While this results in some loss regarding the unique history of the formation of this congregation, minimal changes that aid preservation of member's anonymity outweighed inclusion of details that would readily identify the congregation.

served three years, four years, three years and four years respectively. This study was done during the fourth year of this last pastor. In the year following the study, another pastor began his tenure. All pastoral changes were made by the State Overseer of North Carolina who is responsible to appoint pastors to all IHPC congregations in his charge.[4]

Membership Composition

In the IHPC formal membership is considered a serious matter, one in which the Spirit's direction should be sought, and thus members are generally expected to live by a stricter set of rules regarding acceptable conduct than non-members. Children accordingly are not encouraged to join at early ages. This serious approach to formal membership gives rise to a curious phenomenon among IHPC congregations: the regular attendees in a given congregation rarely coincide with the membership list. Thus the official membership list at King's Avenue includes many members who no longer live in the Antioch area and do not attend the congregation, while the list of regular attendees includes many 'friends' of the church and children who are not official members. Conversations with the pastor showed that King's Avenue has 332 members, only 280 of whom reside in or near Antioch. Of them, the pastor estimates that about 225 attend services at least once a month. In addition, however, there are approximately 125 'friends' and children who attend at least once a month. Friends of the church are generally restricted in terms of their participation, being rarely allowed to serve in any kind of leadership capacity, however small. There is an assumption that the Spirit works primarily among 'members', particularly those that claim the

---

4.   The polity of the IHPC uses an appointment system for selection of its leaders. At the close of each general assembly the General Overseer appoints about 35 denominational leaders for such areas as evangelism, missions, youth, Sunday school, literature translation, television and radio ministry, pastoral care, education, etc. In addition he also appoints State and National Overseers to administrate the work in the respective states or countries. In turn the State and National Overseers appoint state and national leaders for the ecclesiastical concerns mentioned and also appoint pastors for the congregations under their charge. Pastors of the local congregations in turn appoint their local congregational leaders and committees. The denomination teaches that appointments duly made are to be understood and accepted as the 'will of God'. The IHPC refers to their understanding of the appointment system as 'theocracy'. The appointment system is an interesting variation in the way the members of the IHPC experience the leading of the Spirit and sometimes generates tension for them when contrasted with the freedom the Spirit is believed to exercise.

baptism of the Holy Spirit. The pastor reports that 245 of the 332 claim this experience. All of those interviewed in this study were chosen from the membership list of those currently residing in or near Antioch who claim the baptism of the Holy Spirit.

The membership records of those currently residing in Antioch, show that the 280 come from 146 households with 36 of these being children still living in their parent's home. There are 131 male and 149 female members, 47 of whom work at the international headquarters, publishing house or church sponsored college. Twelve are denominational officials and five are instructors at the church sponsored college. The congregation includes ten Hispanic members from three families, and 13 black members from four families, including two families that are West Indian blacks.

Because so many of the King's Avenue members work for or are retired from the denomination, 36 ministers are members of the congregation. This may seem a large number but it is only a little above the denominational norm: in the United States the IHPC averages one minister to every twelve members, a ratio that would predict 28 ministers in a congregation the size of King's Avenue. Nineteen of the 36 ministers at King's Avenue are retired.

The lower middle class status of the congregation is noticeable in the type of work the members do, the clothes they wear, and cars they drive. More than 30 women members work in clerical positions, while the men tend to be small business managers (or owners in a few cases), skilled craftsmen (printers, photographers, carpenters), or lower level professionals such as teachers and accountants. A few members are unskilled laborers. On Sunday mornings, most men wear suits or coats and ties purchased from local department stores; women wear ready made dresses or dress suits. On Sunday and Wednesday evenings, men often forego the coat and tie. Few families drive anything other than family style cars; luxury and sports class cars are rarely seen in the parking lot.

Building and Seating Patterns
The physical structure of King's Avenue church consists of two main buildings joined by a well designed foyer. Seating up to 350, the main building, erected in 1973 to accommodate the growing congregation, is rectangular in shape and houses a large open beam sanctuary with a choir loft, two offices, a baptistery, nursery and two classrooms. With

few exceptions the people voluntarily seat themselves by age groupings. The families of the ministerial staff and musicians occupy the front left pews. Behind them sit retired members and a few denominational officials. Retired members tend to occupy the center left aisle seats for several rows. Pews in the back half are occupied by mostly middle-aged members. In the center section the first two or three pews remain empty. Retired ministers and denominational officials sit in the next few rows with more middle-aged members filling the middle rows. The last third of this section is occupied by retired members, primarily ministers and their companions. The young people of the congregation sit on the first and last rows of the right hand section with the middle rows filled by younger middle-aged members. Most members sit in the same general area each time. The ministerial staff sits on a raised area at the front of the sanctuary that holds the piano, organ, a bass guitar, drums and a special area for the choir. The pianist also sits near the piano even when not playing. The choir occupies the choir area only when singing; members of the choir sit in the pews after the choir has sung.

The second building is squarish in design and serves as the educational wing and fellowship hall. In addition it contains a kitchen area, restrooms and offices. Rooms for Sunday School classes are made by drawing flexible dividers across the normally open spaces that form the fellowship hall. This space is occasionally used for church dinners.

Pastoral Staff[5]

During the time of this study the congregation had three paid ministers, all male: Bill Smith, the senior pastor who is appointed by the State Overseer of North Carolina; Ed Rollins, the minister of music, and John Avery, the minister of youth and Christian education; both of whom are selected by the congregation and serve on annual renewable contracts. The senior pastor holds a critical position in IHPC congregations; he (or she) is usually the only paid minister in most congregations and usually wields a good deal of power and influence. The senior pastor tends to

---

5.   Names of the pastoral staff and members are pseudonyms and certain identifying information has been altered to preserve anonymity. A note on the nature of the quotations is also in order. Spoken language is very different from written language and therefore a judgment on how to punctuate is sometimes difficult. I have retained the words actually spoken even when not grammatically correct and have tried to punctuate to make the quotations as readable as possible. Longer quotations come from sustained comments by the person; gaps are identified by ellipses.

set the pace for what will or will not be done by a congregation. Pastor Smith moved to King's Avenue four years ago following twenty years of successful pastorates in the West. He tends to be a serious individual although he has a humorous side that occasionally comes out during his sermons. He is very sensitive to the congregation's thoughts and moods and will often interject comments or lively mannerisms to let the congregation know he has sensed their boredom, confusion, or uncertainty about agreement with his last point. He has two years of college and is the father of a fifteen-year-old son. His wife is visible but not particularly active; this congregation does not demand heavy involvement by the pastor's wife. She works part-time in the church office.

The minister of music also holds a key position in the congregation, especially in directing corporate worship. A good minister of music (or song leader in smaller congregations) sets the tone or mood of the service by the choice of songs and the way they are led, either creating a smooth flow or sense of disjuncture.[6] The music leader is the key figure for getting the congregation to participate in the service through clapping, vigorous singing or making songs the basis for prayer. It is believed a good music leader will be enthusiastic and sensitive to the congregation's energy level, which will help determine whether a verse or refrain to a song needs to be repeated. The song leader is also key to the smoothness of transitions from one song to the next or from a song to the next part of the service.

Ed Rollins was hired as the minister of music at King's Avenue the summer before this study was done. Prior to his coming the music was done by a part-time choir director/song leader. Ed is white, in his early thirties, the father of two children. He has a college degree in music and prior to coming to this congregation had been minister of music at another IHPC congregation in a neighboring state. He is also actively

---

6.   Music is a central part of Pentecostal worship; its presence or absence helps control the mood of the service. The pianist is the lead musician; he or she sets the pace which the others seem to follow. The drums and guitar punctuate the rhythms of the already lively songs, creating an atmosphere in which physical gestures, such as clapping, seem appropriate. Accordingly, playing of the drums and guitar is often omitted when the music chosen creates a quieter, softer mood. The organ is rarely played alone at King's Avenue, probably because this congregation is part of a movement in which few people could play one (or congregations afford one); thus people are not accustomed to this. Organ music alone also tends to be associated in the Pentecostal mind with more 'formal' churches (cf. Abell 1982).

involved in the denomination's radio and television ministries. Somewhat self-effacing but lively and passionate when leading the congregation or choir in song, Ed is energetic but generally serious in temperament. He supports the senior pastor's decisions and defers to him when there is a question regarding how the service should be directed. His wife sings in the choir, but is not particularly active otherwise.

John Avery is from Canada, having come to King's Avenue two years ago. He is in his mid-30s, married with two teen-agers, one girl and one boy. His wife is more active in the congregation than the other two minister's wives, functioning as an unpaid 'assistant youth minister'. Energetic and affable, John saw himself an advocate for the youth. During his time at King's Avenue he had several conflicts with Pastor Smith over the youth ministry and ended up leaving the congregation at Christmas. His departure caused some confusion among members because he said at one point that he 'felt led of the Lord' to make this move. He was not replaced for over a year.

The employment of a multipastoral staff has been a gradual develop-ment for the congregation. Ten years ago the congregation added its first full-time paid youth minister. When this person left he was not replaced for about a year, during which time there was also a change in senior pastors. The youth minister hired as a replacement did not have his contract renewed after only one year due to disagreements with the senior pastor over his duties. The position again remained unfilled for about two years until John Avery was hired. The lapses in filling vacant positions seems to have been the result of ambivalence by the senior pastors about having assistants rather than economic factors. About six years ago the congregation also began to pay a part-time minister of music. This continued until the summer before this study began when a full time paid minister of music, Ed Rollins, was hired. Renewal of this position in the budget for the following year signaled the congregation's ongoing commitment to (and the senior pastor's acceptance of) a multiple staff of full-time paid ministers.

Activities

The people of King's Avenue gather for a variety of regularly scheduled meetings and activities, most of which seem geared to building relation-ships among the members. Once a year the church holds a stewardship banquet where the general financial resources and needs of the congre-gation are laid out to the congregation and support for the upcoming year is solicited. (A large portion of the King's Avenue budget is met through 'tithes' paid by members; tithing is a 'prominent' teaching of the IHPC.) Once a quarter the congregation observes the Lord's Supper and Feet Washing in a special Sunday evening service. A quarterly 'business conference' is also held to discuss matters of finance and general church concerns but tends to be poorly attended, averaging around ten who are primarily the members of the finance committee which meets as needed but usually once a quarter just prior to the business meeting. Each member of the congregation is encouraged to attend small group home prayer meetings conducted by local lay leaders once a month, although attendance at these also is small and some lay leaders do not conduct their meetings each month. Poor attendance at these functions is partly attributable to the perception that 'not much Spirit' is present in the meetings, and partly to the attitude that these are necessary to satisfy denominational requirements rather than to meet felt needs of the congregation. A 'men's fellowship breakfast' held the first Saturday of each month averages around 30, mostly older men.

Each week 17 different age related Sunday school classes meet prior to the Sunday morning services with an average attendance of about 200. On Thursday evenings six to twelve people visit new people in the community as part of an evangelism program. On Wednesday evenings a variety of activities that attract about 100 people is scheduled. Adults usually meet in the sanctuary for a traditional service while the young people meet in the educational wing for their own service. Once during the course of this study this pattern was abandoned for about ten weeks to try a series of 'classes'. In the sanctuary, classes on 'the church in the last days' were conducted by a retired minister, while in the fellowship hall, other adults attended classes on marriage and child rearing consisting of video tapes for the marriage sessions and presentations by a psychology instructor from the church college for the child rearing sessions. During this time the young people also held services in the educational wing. After about ten weeks the former patterns were resumed; the congregation preferred the more traditional services.

The adult choir meets regularly twice a week for practice and attracts about 40 people. A high level of participation is aided by the perception of music as an activity that facilitates the moving of the Spirit. During the eight months of intensive observation, two 'revival' campaigns lasting from Sunday to Wednesday were also conducted. Revivals are considered special times in which a move of the Spirit can be experienced.

Worship Services

At the heart of all King's Avenue gatherings are the Sunday morning and evening services for corporate worship, occasions that consistently draw the largest participation. On Sunday mornings Sunday School classes are conducted from 9:45 until 10:35. Service in the main auditorium begins at 10:45 while children's' church (4-12 years of age) begins at the same time in the educational wing. Sunday morning services generally end shortly after 12 noon. Sunday evening services include all age groups and begin at 6 pm and variously last until 7:30 or 8:00 and longer.

With few variations Sunday morning services follow an identifiable pattern: musicians play what will be the first 'chorus' sung as the people emerge from the Sunday school classes. It is usually a chorus and not a full song or hymn, and is led by the song leader or minister of music. Generally the music is familiar and the people know the words. Singing is almost always done with the congregation standing. Following each song there is usually a time for prayer or praise (praise includes utterances such as 'thank you, Jesus', 'bless the Lord', 'praise God', etc.). Prayers are 'congregational prayers,' meaning that the entire congregation prays at the same time. After the singing, which tends to be lively, the congregation is seated and an offering is received followed by a dedicatory prayer by a member of the congregation. The choir then sings and the senior pastor comes forward. Until this point the song leader or minister of music has directed the service. When the pastor comes he has the congregation stand and join hands in a prayer for their families, both within and beyond the congregation. Following this is the sermon, usually an energetic presentation with the pastor coming down into the congregation several times. The sermons always begin with a biblical text but focus on encouragement and lessons for practical Christian living rather than expositions of biblical history or context (Various titles include 'Why it Is Better to Have Faith', 'How to Have Joy', 'Transformed by God', 'Be Excited about your Religion'). After the sermon the congregation is dismissed by a prayer that the pastor leads.

The Sunday evening services vary this pattern in the following ways: the choir does not sing, there is time given for 'prayer requests' or 'testimonies' or sometimes both, and there is usually an 'altar call' near the end of the service. Testimonies are opportunities for people to stand and share their perceptions of how the Spirit is at work in their lives.

Prayer requests are times for people to vocalize something for which they would like the congregation to pray. The more routine requests are of two types: requests for someone who is sick, or for someone to be converted. A third type, occurring less frequently, is one that requests prayer for some personal problem or need. Altar calls are invitations for people to come forward around the front of the sanctuary to kneel and pray. If the altar praying is rather lively there may be times of 'rejoicing' and charismatic manifestations. More singing usually accompanies and follows such altar services. It should also be noted that the Sunday services are one place where the leading of the Spirit is experienced.

Conversations about Spirit Leading

This section reports conversations with members of King's Avenue regarding experiences of Spirit leading. Interviews chosen illustrate the variety of Spirit led decisions reported. The method employed in these interviews is discussed in Chapter 3.

Allison
Allison is 27, married and mother of two girls, two and four, and a son, six; she does not currently work outside the home. She grew up in a small town in the mountains of North Carolina, the oldest of three girls and a son born to her parents, both of whom worked while she was growing up. Allison reports being cared for by a babysitter, a member of the local IHPC congregation, after school and during summers up to age nine when she began to stay home with her first sister. By age ten Allison was taking care of both sisters and her brother and assisting with household chores including preparing the evening meal. From age five until after she left home, her family lived in the same house.

The most significant memories of Allison's childhood involve a two to three year period when she was about twelve to fourteen and her parents were on 'nerve' pills. She describes this as a very, 'chaotic, wild, violent' time in which she reports being 'slapped around a lot'. She remembers vividly a time when her mother 'went crazy and started knocking me all over the hall' for not folding the towels correctly, and reports that to this day, she (Allison) refolds the towels anytime her husband folds them. Allison reported feeling estranged from her mother for many years—'Mom was too busy to show affection'—and has only tried to talk to her mother about these childhood memories within the last year.

Allison remembers her father as only moderately more available emotionally than her mother. Long hours at work often made him physically unavailable. Allison recalls an incident when she was eight of consciously deciding never again to kiss her dad after he did not look up from the television when she kissed him good night. Her father rarely showed affection physically or verbally; she can only remember him kissing her mother once or twice and she reports that he never told Allison he loved her until after she was married. However, during the 'wild' years she does remember being able to talk with her father about boyfriend problems or problems with her mother, 'but never about us'.

Allison's most positive memories of childhood center around monthly visits to her grandmother (her mother's mother) who is described as a soft-spoken, godly woman who lived about an hour and a half from Allison's family. Without material wealth, she is described as always having time to talk with Allison. This grandmother died during Allison's time at college.

After a year at college, a basically positive time that gave Allison the emotional distance from her family to allow some 'healing' to begin, she quit school and moved to Antioch to work at the IHPC headquarters as a secretary. She began attending King's Avenue where she met her husband, a member of the IHPC from a neighboring town who was attending a denominational function at King's Avenue. After dating for six months they were married and she and her husband decided to live in Antioch because he felt 'led of the Lord' that this was where they should live. When her first child was nine months old, Allison quit work and began to stay home at her husband's urging. Being home with her children generates mixed emotions for Allison; she loves working outside the home, yet because of memories associated with the unavailability of her own parents while she was growing up, she feels being home with her children is the 'best thing' for now.

Church life has always been important to Allison and her current involvement includes teaching Sunday School and singing in the choir. Since childhood she attended an IHPC congregation in which her parents were active lay leaders. She describes her earliest memories of God as those connected with church activities, Bible stories read by her mother, and singing gospel songs at family gatherings. She also was active in this congregation, holding positions as youth leader and Sunday School teacher.

Allison describes her baptism with the Holy Spirit at age six as a time of intense yearning and struggle praying for over an hour, before she spoke in tongues. She attributes the lengthy struggle to concerns that she might be overly influenced by her early exposure to Pentecostalism and wanting to know in her own mind that what she was experiencing was God and not herself.

Allison reports that the Holy Spirit has been a source of joy and strength, particularly helpful to her during the chaotic years. Prayer and church services provided a way to 'find peace, to find some sense, some reality' from the craziness at home. However, the juncture of church and home also created some confusion for Allison. She found it impossible to reconcile her mother's actions at home with the 'anointing of the Spirit' her mother experienced when testifying or leading worship service. Allison now attributes such behavior to God's graciousness; 'He knew her health, but He also understood her heart. Her heart was always in the right place, even though her actions may not have always been'.

An immediate sense of God's presence is very important to Allison; times of its absence are miserable. She describes experiencing God's presence as analogous to the relationship with her husband and children; it is 'my spirit with the Spirit of God...constantly saying hello to each other'; it is 'like when I take time to give the Lord a hug'. Yet times of greatest closeness are said to be experienced when she is alone, when 'I just stop and be with Him'. While growing up Allison reports she would often pray alone in her room after everyone had gone to bed, 'talking to God as my best friend, like I'm talking to you now'.

Allison describes a time in college when she lost the ability to sense God's presence. The 'crisis' was brought on by sexual behavior which Allison felt caused a great rift in her relationship to God. She felt herself to be very distant from God, unable to sense God's presence. Allison identifies this experience as a turning point from which she feels she learned not to take her relationship with God for granted. The time of being unable to sense God's presence came to an end after several especially intense weeks of struggle over the spiritual impasse she felt.

> I was driving to work and had been through this for weeks, crying and bawling, and I remember screaming in the car, 'God, I can't stand this,' and I remember instant peace, instant God, instant power and grace. At church I just get through thanking Him for His grace when everyone else is finished [praying]. I am so grateful He didn't keep His voice from me. I am grateful He had mercy on me, to forgive and love me. That is why I am the way I am. I think that [a period of being unable to feel God's presence] was to show me what I could have been [without God].

Allison has a tendency to overcommit herself, which has an analogue in her relationship to God. She reports that her sense of closeness to God is enhanced when she is 'doing what God expects me to do… living the way I am supposed to, being faithful in church, working in VBS'. However, her heavy commitment to church services and activities is also a source of frustration and drain on her family. And while she sees this pattern of overcommitting herself as a pattern rooted in childhood actions designed to win from her parents the same kind of favor they bestowed upon the middle sister, she confesses an inability to curb it sufficiently. (While in college Allison carried a load of 22 and 24 semester hours, worked two part-time jobs and traveled with a ball team.)

Allison experiences God as a gracious, loving provider for a variety of needs: financial, spiritual, emotional and physical well-being. Her experiences of Spirit leading are often directly connected with such needs, making her feel especially valued and protected by God. One kind of experience that Allison identified as an example of Spirit leading was a strong, instantaneous feeling that she should slow down while driving home one night. She did and a few hundred yards around a curve a man was crossing the road, a man she would have hit at her previous rate of speed. She reports that she knew the feeling was from God because it was a feeling she has learned to recognize over the years, a feeling likened to the uncomfortableness she sometimes feels when people are 'gossiping'; a feeling that this is not right and to be avoided. She 'knew God slowed me down to keep from killing that person'. Overwhelmed by this intervention in her behalf, she began speaking in tongues and continued to do so 'the rest of the way home'.

Allison also identified a decision about whether to buy certain property as resulting from the Spirit's direction.

> Even before we bought this house I saw [another] house that I really wanted but we didn't have enough money down. So I knelt in that house and told God, 'I want this house but not if You don't want us to have it'. I said, 'I am going to ask You for a sign, something that I will know is You. I am going to ask my mother for the extra [money] needed for the down payment and if she told me 'no', it would be God's will. I prayed that sincerely though I wanted that house bad. I called and she said 'no.' And as disappointed as I was I didn't question. And now I know why. Because this [their current house] is what God wanted us to have, and why He said, 'No'. He was waiting for something better for me to work its way out.

This particular incident illustrates the use of a 'fleece' for discerning the Spirit's leading. Use of fleeces to discern the leading of the Spirit finds its origin in the biblical story of Gideon (Judg. 6). When called by the Lord to go up against the Midianites, Gideon laid a sheep's hide (a fleece) upon the ground and asked the Lord to let it be wet with dew while the ground was dry if the Lord would indeed be with Gideon. The procedure was repeated in reverse (ground wet, fleece dry) before Gideon actually led his armies. From this story has come the practice by some of 'putting out a fleece' to determine the leading of the Spirit. With a fleece one sets up conditions and observes the outcome; 'if x happens, then I will know the Lord wants me to do y; if x doesn't happen, then it wasn't the Lord's will'. Fleeces provide Allison what she feels is unambiguous direction from the Spirit. They are a way to sort out her desires from the Spirit's. There is no second guessing; one has a settledness about the decision even when it is not what one had hoped for.[7]

A third way in which Allison experiences the Spirit's leading is persistent urgings that lead to charismatic manifestations in the context of worship. These kinds of decisions create intense anxiety for Allison because of concern over others' judgment of her worthiness to speak in God's behalf. The 'complete fear of what other people will think' can be almost paralyzing for her, but

> when something happens; when God speaks and people's hearts are changed or when the service is freed and you know that everything followed the way God wanted it to be that is wonderful. There is a peace in that; in knowing that God used you for what He wanted to do.

When asked how she discerns the Spirit's leading to interpret messages in tongues she continued

> Well it is something that (short pause), it is so strong, it is not like, 'Hey, this is the message' for me. Every time—and I will have to say there have been times I felt it and did quench it—I allowed my thought and what others would think of me, I did quench it. This feeling was here, where the Holy Ghost is so strong and it is like the Holy Ghost is, uh, possessing you; all consuming you and you are fighting it or saying, 'No, I know what they will think; they won't believe me', so that you don't yield. It is

---

7.   A retired minister who used fleeces in decisions regarding major career moves confirmed this advantage of fleeces, stating the greatest gain from their use was the peace of mind in not having to wonder whether one had followed the Spirit. He had suggested their use to many people over the years.

simply that. But as far as the message right there, no (short pause), it is more or less as you open your mouth it comes out. For me it is just like when the Holy Ghost starts speaking in other tongues and you don't know what syllables or words will come out of your mouth when you are speaking in tongues. It was that same type of thing for me. Every time it has been that way for me. It was not like the pastor was preaching on love and so this message [I feel from the Spirit] is going to be on love. It wasn't that way for me.

This quotation illustrates two criteria Allison uses for discernment in these kinds of decisions. One is the persistence of the urging she feels rather than a particular content about what should be said. While such urgings ultimately can be resisted, there is a 'consuming' quality to urgings that are Spirit directed. When such feelings are resisted there can be misgivings that one has missed the Spirit's direction. Allison mentioned an occasion when she consulted Pastor Smith after feeling 'disappointed' in herself for resisting an urge to sing a song in the service. He told her that 'generally if the feeling stays with you beyond the service, it should have been done. If you can let it go, leave the service and things are okay, then it probably wasn't [the Spirit's leading]'. This particular urge had stayed with her several days after the service.

A second criterion Allison uses for discernment is the impact of the manifestations on the congregation. In Spirit led manifestations there is a sense of release or freedom, a feeling that barriers to the work of the Spirit have been removed; people respond. On the other hand, 'if it is just kind of dead and lays there, then you know it was you [and not the Spirit]'.

Fernando

Fernando is a retired State Overseer (a denominational official responsible for the oversight of IHPC congregations in a given area), a native of Puerto Rico whose energy and initiative have helped him have a significant influence on the larger denomination for the last three decades. He is in his 60s, married, the father of five children with seven grandchildren. All his children are married; two live in Antioch, one lives about two hours away in a neighboring state, and two live in Texas. He has attended King's Avenue since moving to Antioch about five years ago following his retirement from denominational appointment. He currently serves as Sunday School teacher for adults.

Fernando grew up in one of the smaller villages on the southside of the island, the third of ten children and the first son born to his parents.

His father was a farmer who raised his own food and occasionally worked in one of the clothing mills in a neighboring town. Fernando recalls having plenty of food growing up but not much money for anything else. His father tended to save any extra money, even for things his mother might think necessary, lest his family be left destitute if he met with an accident at the mill. Fernando describes his father as a 'godly man', active in the local IHPC congregation in his village. Although his father could be 'severe in his rebuke; he could really put you in your place', Fernando's mother was the chief disciplinarian. While Fernando spent time during summers helping with the farming he did not feel especially close to his father.

Fernando remembers his mother as 'always there', a woman attentive to her children and their needs, often intervening with his father to persuade him that the children's needs required spending some of the money he was saving. He described his mother as a 'wise, perceptive, tender' woman who encouraged her children in pursuits that would lead to a 'better life' than the local village supported. Fernando remembers fondly his mother's frequent prayers for her children, although he reports she was more active in rearing the children than in church activities.

Fernando describes his early years at home as basically pleasant and without incident, his bout with tonsillitis being the only serious childhood illnesses or accidents experienced by any of the children. His fondest memory from childhood is the birth of his last sister at home. He recalls this as a tender occasion for his family and remembers being amused by the role reversals in the household, particularly seeing his father performing tasks such as cooking while his mother convalesced.

Fernando describes his selection at age 14 to become a teacher in training in the school system as the most significant event of his years at home. This work opened up further opportunities for employment and at age 17 Fernando left his village to work as a teacher in San Juan. By age 19 he was principal of a local school. An intelligent and ambitious young man, Fernando married at age 20, was appointed pastor of a small congregation and in two years had tripled its membership. During this time Fernando also attended night classes at college and was active in civic affairs.

Fernando was converted at an early age in an IHPC church in Puerto Rico and began preaching when he was 15. He received the baptism of the Holy Spirit in his early 20s. He moved from Puerto Rico to the United States in 1965 when he was appointed overseer for Spanish-speaking congregations in a Southwestern state. He reports being angered by his first encounters with American racism.

God is a persistent goad to Fernando, always judging his motives and prodding him to greater self denial and service. He attributes his not receiving the baptism with the Holy Spirit until his 20s to a struggle over trying to conquer all 'human' desires. One evening while praying he felt he had reached a point in which his 'supreme desire was to obey God' and he began to speak in tongues.

God is caring, in that he desires Fernando's growth but maintains an emotional distance lest Fernando become unable to handle such special attention.

> I think, at times, God keeps from me how He really feels about me...I don't think He lets me know; I don't think He can afford to let me know because it just may not be good for me. I think He knows that in my best interests His approval of me has to have severe limits. In other words, I don't think God would do anything to feed my pride, even my pride in good things. I am a weak person that way.

With a laugh Fernando described his experience as similar to Job's, one in which God made a 'wager with Satan' and left Fernando 'on [his] own to struggle through it'.

Certain leadings of the Spirit reflect this emotionally distant God for Fernando. For him the best way to know the Spirit's leading is retrospectively; one looks back and makes judgments as to whether it was the Spirit's leading by asking whether one grew from the experience. Fernando finds a certain contentment with this means of discernment.

> The leadings of the Lord have been through groping and searching for me. They have not been quite as specific as I hear some people testify. Mine is more confirmed in retrospect and in a sense of being occupied with what is pleasing to the Lord in a given time. I follow the principle, 'do with your might whatsoever your hand findeth to do'. That leads to the opportunities that God would have you in...Even [when he was an Overseer] some of the negative things I have struggled with for fifteen years I have felt that God was working to grow me in those circumstances. I try to look at all of life that way: that He is the leader, [that] this is committed to God, and that I have to grope to find Him. I don't find that insecure.

Retrospective judgments of the leading of the Spirit included such things as finding books that helped Fernando on his spiritual journey, a wife that has helped his ministry, and career moves. In such instances, the elements of time and outcome are indispensable tools for judging claims to Spirit direction.

A second type of decision described as a leading of the Spirit by Fernando was one to write an 'open letter of repentence' to be distributed from the IHPC to other Pentecostal denominations asking forgiveness for dividing the kingdom of God and seeking ways to bring Pentecostal denominations together. This inspiration came to him as he was praying, following the selection of the new General Overseer. During the years he was a State Overseer, Fernando felt a special mission of challenging the organization to transcend the white, southern, working class perspective evident in much of its general assembly debate and rulings and to be more inclusive of other cultures and their contributions to the denomination. Feeling that the denomination had turned a corner in leadership and direction, Fernando was praying about the direction his ministry should take.

> I thought, 'We are finally getting in the arena where changes are being made', and I thought 'If I can no longer preach reformation, if we are at the place to do the reformation', I thought, 'Where do we go from here? How do we begin'? In praying about this I asked the Lord to show me where we go from here and right there in my prayer a very strong presence, one of those spiritual hunches, came to me and it came in the form of a question: How about beginning with an act of humility? And next you think, 'What would that be'? I went home that night and the ideas around this concept began to flow and I began to write and I now have a draft of this which I am asking some of my friends to critique. I think that is one example of the kinds of leading that you can get that you need to follow. They are not so much definitive, as they begin as an impulse. But they evolve as you see the rightness of what you are trying to do. I will present it to the General Overseer for his study unofficially [i.e., privately] so he will not feel it is a mandate that he has to respond to, and will continue to refine it with my friends and their help. There doesn't seem to be any historical precedent for a group to do this although individuals have.

Here one can see the 'groping' element in discerning the leading of the Spirit as Fernando submits his 'impulses' to the assessment of friends. He also discerns this to be of the Spirit because repentance as an act of humility emerges as a 'right' thing to be doing upon reflection.

Finally, like Allison, another kind of decision Fernando attributed to the Spirit's direction was to give a message in tongues and interpretation. He related an incident that occurred at a national IHPC gathering he attended in Haiti. The congregation was engaged in a prayer of repentance when Fernando began to speak a 'message in tongues'.

But I tried to restrain myself because I was timid about trying to give an interpretation in French [a language he speaks less than fluently]. But I got such an overwhelming, repeated presence each time I would try to restrain it that it would come upon me so that I had to get up and literally walk to the pulpit. I couldn't help it. I mean I could help it ultimately but I would have felt like I had really disobeyed. Walking to the pulpit I am giving this message in this language [what sounded like a native dialect to him] and then I interpreted in French and they understood perfectly what I said. It was a confirmation from the Lord that He had seen their repentance.

Fernando continued his reflection on how he knows it is the Spirit by stating that he has a certain feeling, a 'spiritual hunch', that he decides to follow and then looks for confirmation from the congregation's reaction. Those 'messages' that are truly from the Spirit will be confirmed by others in the congregation; others will also feel that this was something the Spirit wished to say and may voice this during or after the service.

Spiritual hunches also have

a feel of rightness that grows out of our relationship with God. That is the best way I can put it: a sense of I must do this, an urging that comes in our spirits. That is really my best barometer for knowing how He leads and when He is leading: there is a sense of rightness.

Here Fernando discerns the leading of the Spirit through 'feelings'; feelings that are 'right' and persistent. This sense of rightness seems to be influenced by certain criteria that Fernando has appropriated from A.W. Tozer (1961), a writer of Christian devotional material: is this demeaning to the Scripture, does it exalt Christ, does it fit with the general demeanor of Christianity? Fernando reports that this 'feel of rightness' was instrumental in his decision to 'correct' an interpretation to a message given in a service at King's Avenue about three years ago.

I felt condemned because another person had given an incorrect interpretation and I knew it was incorrect and I was under a tremendous load of condemnation and what I did was write down the interpretation and read it subsequently rather than giving it at the moment. But I didn't forget it; it didn't leave me.

This action created some confusion but was received by the congregation as from the Spirit out of respect for Fernando's spirituality.

Sheila

Sheila is African-American, 40, single, and the director of a social service office serving the elderly. Eight years ago she adopted two girls, then aged eight and ten, when their mother died. She has been a faithful member of King's Avenue for over 15 years, having first attended when she moved to Antioch to work at the denominational publishing house. Although she states that she does not know where she really 'fits' in this congregation, Sheila and her children can be seen in most services and both she and her children are active in church activities. The congregation has occasionally given her financial assistance for the children.

Sheila is the second of four children; she has a sister one year older, a sister two years younger and a brother five years younger than she. Her father had been married before and had two sons by that marriage, aged twelve and nine when he married Sheila's mother. When Sheila's mother was pregnant with her first child, her father's youngest son was killed while trying to jump onto a freight train during a visit with relatives he had taken with Shelia's father. Family members have told Sheila her father was never the same after that incident, apparently blaming himself for the boy's death. She reports that from the time she was eight until she left home her family moved about 20 times, sometimes from one coast to the other, because of her father's search for work.

Sheila's childhood is filled with mixed images of her father, described as an overly protective man 'who would hardly let us out of his sight' yet physically abusive, more toward the mother than the children, especially under the influence of alcohol; 'he [was] like two personalities'. She remembers being 'scared to death' seeing her father hit her mother, but also remembers many good times with her father because 'he did a lot of payback kind of things' to make up for his abusive behavior. Sheila reports that she seems to have had significant influence with her father, being able to persuade him to change his mind about going places with the family or allowing the children privileges. As she got older and stronger she would 'talk back' to her father, telling him his abusive behavior was wrong.

Sheila describes her mother as a quiet person whom her father dominated. She did not work outside the home until Sheila was a teenager. As Sheila got older she adopted a protective stance toward her mother in relation to her father's abuse. She thinks this need to protect her mother was a factor in her not leaving home until she was in her 20s.

Sheila began attending the IHPC at age seven with her mother; her father did not attend and occasionally expressed resistance to Sheila and her mother's church involvement. Her baptism with the Holy Spirit, which occurred at age 17 during a church youth camp, included the experience of an altered state of consciousness. As she walked through a line formed by those praying for others to receive the baptism of the Holy Spirit

> I started speaking in tongues. It just sort of fell on me and I don't even remember beginning to speak in tongues. I wasn't like [lying on] the floor out, but I was somewhere else. I don't know what happened to me; I was like out in the Spirit and when I came to, woke up or something, I was way on the other side of the building. I don't know how I got there. I heard myself speaking in tongues and I thought 'I'm speaking in tongues', and it sort of just dawned on me. It was probably an hour later and I don't remember anything in between; it was kind of incredible.

Feelings are an important gauge of Sheila's relationship with God; God's presence is 'felt' and when she cannot feel it, she knows things are not right in the relationship. She recounts a time about five years ago when she 'couldn't feel God', feeling confused and angry with God because of a hysterectomy, foreclosing any possibility of having a child of her own, a long time desire. She felt God to be unfair in allowing this to happen to her; after all she 'had kept the rules': she 'didn't sneak off to movies or wear make-up' and even told on her sister who did. Her anger and confusion continued for about two years until one night in a service in which the congregation was praising God she remembered that as a child she had told God, 'I want your will in my life. Even if I don't like it, I want to do your will'. She felt the hysterectomy might be a testing of this desire. She began to praise God and as she did she began to feel some release from the anger. 'It was kind of like pouring oil on my insides; the feeling was really different.' Further release from the anger has come through talking with others and an awareness that she is not the only one ever to question God or resent what had happened to her. However, this issue continues to be a source of tension in her relationship with God.

Feelings also lie at the heart of much of Sheila's experience of Spirit leading. She recounted several decisions made on the basis of feelings which she attributed to the Spirit, including decisions concerned with the children's care and rearing, career opportunities, and speaking with others about concerns for them. Although Sheila reports this as an unusual experience for her, an incident in which she decided to buy groceries even though she had no money illustrates how certain feelings play a central role in her discernment of the Spirit's leading.

So one day I was coming home from work and it was as if someone really nice put their arm around my shoulder and said, 'It is going to be okay'. It was like I wanted to look around and see who it was. It was like they said, 'You just go ahead and go to the grocery store and get what you need; write a check for it and tomorrow when you need it you will have the money for it'. And I said, 'Yeh, God, you can get in trouble for doing things like that'. But it was like the most gentle calming (short pause), it was like when you are little and you fall down and your dad picks you up and says, 'Honey, it is going to be all right'. But it was almost like an audible voice. It was warm, gentle. I said, 'Okay, fine'. I went and got what I needed, wrote the check. The next day I was on my way home from work and I thought, 'I wonder where this money is going to come from; it is supposed to be today', and the same voice spoke to me and said, 'It is in the mailbox', and I thought, 'Wheww'! and the closer I got, for two blocks I could see my mailbox and it looked gigantic and it was like, 'It is there, it is there', and I got home and saw this envelope and I thought, 'It is here'! You know, we don't believe what we pray, at least I don't. I opened it and it was a check for $800. And there was no way I knew I would get that at that time and that amount. That was just a marvelous experience.

For Sheila the Spirit is discerned through intimate dialogue with a very special presence that conveys warmth, concern, and confidence; she feels especially cared for by a divine father/provider.

The hints at reception of special knowledge in this experience are more obvious in other examples of Spirit leading reported by Sheila. She receives what she described as a Spirit inspired insight into certain situations. These insights come mostly through very strong feelings about a person or situation (although some have come through dreams) and confirm Shelia's closeness to God; 'the Spirit of the Lord will tell you things if you are tuned in'. She described such insights regarding the youth pastor's resignation, a minister's relationship with a woman, and an attempted molestation of one of her daughters. In all instances the persistence of the feeling or insight, a sense that something was not right, and subsequent events that confirmed it were her indicators that these came from the Spirit. The incident with one of her girls is illustrative. She had taken a neighbor's child to ball practice, leaving the two girls at home with her brother and another man who were installing a television antenna.

About half way through the trip I felt I should go home immediately but I thought if I got some burgers now I wouldn't have to go back out so I ignored it and that is when the incident happened. The person went in and upstairs and my brother felt impressed to follow him but didn't. This

> person found one of the girls alone and attempted something. But I had
> talked to the girls and they knew what to do. I was devastated because God
> had warned me and I ignored it. Anytime I have had a super strong feeling
> it has proved out that way. It is like proof comes after the fact.

However, prior to confirmation of these insights by subsequent events,
Sheila is reluctant to attribute all such feelings to the Spirit and is content
to say that it is her concern that moves her. She tends to use this
approach when she feels the need to speak to the person about whom
she has had the insight (such as the minister). Such a posture not only
saves Sheila potential embarrassment, it also reflects certain difficulties
she experiences in sorting out her feelings.

> Sometimes I am not sure and think, 'That is just me', and sometimes I am
> sure and the only way I can specify it is the way I feel about it. There have
> been times I knew absolutely for sure God warned me about something
> and I knew it was God because the devil is not going to do anything good.

This quotation introduces a criterion for discernment rooted in a tradition about the nature of God: if it was a good thing to do, God was in it.

This means of discernment, along with a version of retrospective
judgment, lie behind Sheila's adoption of the children. In this case the
leading of the Spirit was discerned, not so much in feelings, but in
evolving circumstances that indicated adoption as a viable course of
action. Sheila did pray often about whether to adopt the children but felt
no special direction. Conviction that it was indeed the Spirit's direction
came as she looked back over the decision and the things that happened
prior to and after the decision. Sheila was to have been out of town on
the weekend the children's mother died but had delayed agreeing to a
speaking engagement. When the mother died Sheila stayed with the
children for a while and then took them under foster care, saying that at
first she never really thought it through, but just did it, citing the
Scripture, 'whatsoever your had finds to do' as her justification. But she
also continued her own plans which involved leaving for the mission
field within the year. When approached by the Department of Human
Services (DHS) about adopting the children if she got a medical subsidy,
she was unsure. Having felt what she thought to be God's direction
about the mission field she was confused about what to do. While
traveling back from a wedding the weekend before she was required to
give DHS an answer, she took a shortcut that had been told her and
passed a church marquis with the words 'Where God guides, He
provides'. She took this to be God's answer to adopt the children. 'It

was like the words on that sign jumped off and into the car with me. I said, "Okay, God you do it and I'll follow".' What followed this decision were several incidents of provision for Sheila and the children, including the one with the groceries.

> But I really felt like the Lord, looking back on the set of circumstances, that the Lord had control and was directing me even though I argued with Him for a while because I had looked forward to the mission thing for a long time and felt the Lord was dealing with me.

Gwen

Gwen is in her late 30s, married, mother of two, a daughter, 17, and son, 21. She and her husband have been members of King's Avenue for twelve years. She grew up in the IHPC in the Northeast and first moved to Antioch when her husband decided to attend the IHPC sponsored college. She is a secretary at a local community college.

Gwen is an only child. When she was eight her family moved from a farm where 'there was really no family and friends we were involved with' to a city of about 50,000 so her father could find work; her mother did not work outside the home while Gwen was growing up. Gwen continued to live in this town until moving to Antioch.

In the new town her family found many 'friends' in an IHPC congregation in which they became very active. Gwen's mother taught Sunday School, baked pies and was the women's missionary leader. Gwen's father, while active in the church, did not take the leadership role of her mother. She remembers that her parents would frequently invite visitors and evangelists to their home.

Gwen describes her father as a quiet man that did not communicate much with his family and with whom Gwen never felt able to communicate effectively. Described as a hard worker, 'his whole life was work', he might not say a word during the entire evening meal. She remembers her father's lack of communication as creating conflict between her parents which her father tried to ignore. Gwen thinks this also caused her mother to invest an 'unhealthy' amount of emotional energy in Gwen to make up for the loneliness her mother felt in relationship to Gwen's father.

Gwen's memories of involvement in the church while growing up are both positive and negative. She remembers the local church which her parents joined when she was eight as a 'good church' with 'good values'. 'It gave me a stability that some people don't have'. Yet because of the

Pentecostal antipathy to 'worldly' activities, such as 'skating, bowling, dances', Gwen often felt awkward during her junior high and high school years. Gwen thinks her desire to 'fit in' and be accepted contributed to her getting pregnant her last year in high school. Although she finished school she felt she had no option but also to get married. This has had a profound impact on Gwen who has told both of her children that while they would be responsible for the baby should anything like that happen to them, she would not want them getting married simply because of the pregnancy.

Gwen received the baptism of the Holy Spirit at 17 during a state level denominational gathering in which she 'recommitted' her life to Christ shortly after her marriage. Since then she describes a growth in her understanding of the Holy Spirit as 'little more than speaking in tongues to realiz[ing] the Holy Ghost affects your life in many ways', but primarily in bringing a consistency, a 'leveling out', to her Christian commitment. She reports that the Spirit has been especially helpful to her this past year as she struggled over what to do after becoming aware of her husband's marital infidelity.

This experience led to an introspective re-evaluation of her life and relationship with God. She describes a process in which she is becoming more aware of her own internal desires, and the need to give those attention, rather than being so driven by the wishes of others. She has had to rethink her understanding of the leading of the Spirit, expressing doubts as to whether she can rely on 'fleeces' anymore, a past means of discernment for decisions about whether to buy property or change jobs. Her relationship with the Lord has taken on an immediacy and inner directedness not experienced before.

> It seems I have been forced into a more moment by moment relationship with the Lord, saying 'Lord, I will do what I think is your will for this moment'. But as far as any long range things (short pause), for instance, there was a job opening in another state and I could not even pray, 'Lord if it is your will, blah, blah, blah', at least not at this point. I guess it has become a lot more personal walk and just knowing in my heart that this is what the Lord is doing in me at the present moment. I don't know if any longer I can go by circumstances and fleeces and those things... Maybe what I am saying is that I am deciding more what the Lord is doing in me instead of listening so much to what other people are saying. I know there is a danger there too, but I have not been able to cope in any other way. I have found that as I had to depend totally on God when everything else was knocked out from under me, I found that his presence, even when it

wasn't as we say 'felt,' there was a quiet knowing that He was there and as I had to live second by second, His word and grace came to me in abundance.

The growth in Gwen's inner directedness, brought on by her struggle over whether to leave her husband must be viewed in the light of official denominational doctrine which teaches that divorce is sinful and to be avoided because it leads to remarriage which is strictly prohibited by the IHPC. Gwen experienced the leading of the Spirit opening up possibilities and choices, including an option to leave her husband if she wished and to feel good about that decision, where previously she had felt trapped by the denominational teachings, feeling she had no choice but to stay in the marriage.

> I have definitely felt the Lord leading in relationship to my future. I really did consider leaving, but I was sincerely honest that I wanted to please the Lord. So I studied and searched [the scriptures and other literature], and in my own heart I feel justified that I could have. But I don't think that was God's best for me. I felt a definite leading of the Lord saying, 'You have this choice; you can do this if you want to, but this is not my best for you. It is not the best for you. It is not the best for your kids, and not the best in all circumstances.'

Gwen concluded that this leading to stay in the marriage was from the Spirit because of a 'very strong inner peace' that came following her turmoil over what to do. This sense of peace was rooted in both her new found freedom to choose and in the choice made.

> When I did begin to decide what I could do, what options I did have, it made me feel, 'I do have a little part in deciding', and it made it easier to hear what God was saying, and that in turn brought the peace...When you are walking in [the Lord's] will, it will bring a calm and peace that takes away the disharmony and brings a clarity of thinking. When you are walking in turmoil and finally there comes a point where you say, 'Lord, I want what you want', then a peace comes in. I had peace when I said, 'Lord, yes, I am going to take your best'. That didn't make it easier except for the sense of peace I felt about the situation.

The sense of peace in knowing that the Spirit has directed her brings strength and a courage to cope. Subsequently, Gwen has felt the Spirit's direction in the restoration of her marriage by helping her overcome negative feelings about her husband.

This sense of peace is also used to discern the Spirit's direction in other contexts, such as a decision to pray with Linus, a well loved denominational official diagnosed with cancer. Upon her arrival at the hospital, she found several other ministers telling Linus how the Lord would heal him and not let him die because of his value to the denomination which made her embarrassed to speak at first. Feeling a sense of peace that she had received something from the Spirit to comfort Linus in his suffering she was emboldened to share.

> When it is the Lord, there was a peace and a stillness in my spirit. I didn't feel uptight or nervous, but a peace and a boldness that I could give them something that was not from me but the Lord.

Finally, it should be noted that the 'danger' Gwen sensed in this new inner directedness was lessened through consultation with others. She mentioned several conversations with a married couple that helped her gain a sense of perspective on her feelings during this time.

Brad
Brad is Gwen's husband. He is in his early 40s and currently builds houses for a living. He resigned his positions with the congregation following disclosure of his marital infidelity and his ministerial credentials were suspended. After a period of about 18 months in which he was not active in the congregation other than to participate in worship, he is now assistant Sunday School teacher to an adult class. Brad's reincorporation into a position of leadership was aided by a move of the Spirit in a Sunday morning service described below.

Brad grew up in rural, southern Idaho, the last of six children (three daughters, three sons). When Brad was born his father was in his 50s and suffered from chronic emphysema so that his memories of his father are of a 'tired, old man' who was never able to work very much. His father had a heart attack and died when Brad was 17. He does not remember his father doing much with him and never felt particularly close to his father. Brad's earliest memories date from a time when his family were migrant farm workers, very poor people, living on a government check and moving often, sometimes twice in a year, though never leaving Idaho. His mother is described as a 'domineering woman' who could get really angry with her husband and children. Brad does not remember much affection, either verbally or physically, being shown between the parents or to the children and describes his memories of childhood as 'mostly negative'.

A significant image from this period that colored Brad's self-understanding was being called 'poor white trash' by other children.

Having to adjust to so many schools, and trying to make new friends caused Brad to become very introverted as a young man. He found such adjustments so hard that at the age of 15 he told his mother, who seems to have been the one behind the frequent moves, that he would quit school if they moved again, which he did the next time they moved. By this time his sister had married and moved to the Northeast, so he went to live with her and was persuaded to finish school. Brad feels that leaving Idaho was the best thing that ever happened to him, an act of 'God's grace and mercy'. It opened up 'a whole new world to me. I saw there were people who did something besides dig potatoes'. It was while in the Northeast that Brad met Gwen and began the line of work he is in today. After getting married he approached a local housing contractor, was hired, trained at his employer's expense and had become a journeyman carpenter when he decided to attend the church sponsored college to study for the ministry

Brad's family were always active in the IHPC; his earliest memories are of his father going early to fire up pot bellied stoves in country churches. He describes his father as a 'great prayer warrior'. His mother pastored a small congregation for a short while and held a state level denominational position for a time. Brad was also active in church activities, teaching himself to play guitar for worship services at age 12. (While he does not remember his mother showing much affection, he cites her helping him get this guitar as one of the ways he knew she loved him.) Brad received the baptism of the Holy Spirit in an emotion filled service at the age of 14, having sought the experience for two years. He reports that receiving the baptism of the Holy Spirit brought a 'personality change', from being shy, introverted and uncomfortable with people to being unafraid of others and thus able to share his faith more openly.

Brad reports that the deeper his relationship with God has grown the less emotional he has become.

> I used to run and shout with the best of them and if the Spirit moved me today, I would do that. But I used to shout when I was young and that felt good. But I wonder, 'What did I take home'? A good feeling. But I realize now that what I need is the Word. I wonder, was it the Lord or was it Brad?

He describes his relationship with God as a process in which he is learning to appreciate the 'father' qualities of God which include 'love, forgiveness, long-suffering' rather than an understanding of God as having 'a big stick out to get me'. Rethinking the qualities of God has been especially helpful to Brad in his attempts to rebuild his life and family following his infidelity. He reports that insight into the more loving, forgiving qualities of God emerged from reflections on his love for his children; he realized he loved them, 'even when they fail[ed]', and wanted them to 'try again'. He came to believe God shared similar feelings toward him and thinks this new understanding of God and the new relationship it fostered is probably the most valuable thing he has learned from this experience. This new understanding has given him a strength to remain at King's Avenue and 'prove myself again'.

Through this experience Brad has begun to rethink the nature of his relationship to God in terms of 'being' rather than 'doing', a change mirrored in his relationship with Gwen as well. Brad describes his and Gwen's relationship prior to these events as one in which he felt Gwen demanded 'perfection' from him as a husband and father. This led to much 'tension' and little communication. Brad now describes the emerging relationship with Gwen as one in which he feels 'accepted for who I am'. This change in focus also has had an impact on the way Brad views the leading of the Spirit. The Spirit is seen to lead in a more general way regarding what job to take.

> I used to worry, and still do to some extent, about what God wanted me to do, especially considering the [call to ministry] God gave to me. I was so concerned to do the right thing, to be at the right place and do the right job. I suppose there is some validity to that kind of thinking, but as I deepen my relationship with my Father, I am more concerned about being. As I become more like Jesus, an infinite process, my focus has changed. Rather than trying to find exact times and places, there have been times I felt that way, but right now I sense God saying, 'Do what you want but be a Christian'.

Brad's experience of God is one of a supportive and present 'father' who wishes him to succeed in rebuilding the relationship with Gwen, his children, and the congregation.

A second way Brad has experienced the leading of the Spirit is in worship services. From this context Brad offers an additional criterion to the persistence of feelings used by some. The Spirit's leading is judged by the persistence of the feeling and whether it fits with the order of what is happening.

> Telling whether it is the Lord or Brad is difficult. There have been times when I was sitting on the pew minding my own business when I would feel an unction, an impression to do something. Once I felt the desire to

lead a song and that was the key to that service. I don't do that often,
because of this idea that it might be me. [How did you decide?] There was
just such a terrible urge, and in the context of my personality, I am not one
who does that. There was a spirit of worship and you felt the Lord was
wanting to do something and there had to be a catalyst. And it wasn't out
of order. I guess that is one way you know: it is not out of order.

This remark reminds him of another incident that occurred at a retreat
where the leader felt impressed to have people stand and sing a certain
song as they felt led. People began standing up here and there and 'it
was like a wave of the Spirit hit that place'. But then a lady stood up
and decided she would sing a different song. 'It killed the spirit.' When
the leader asked her to be seated and began the other song again, 'the
Spirit renewed what He was doing. So there must be order.'

Brad also refers to the sense of release Allison mentioned when leadings are genuinely from the Spirit; things are unlocked so that the Spirit
can work. That is the meaning behind a 'key' to the service. The leading
of the Spirit brings a sense of power and purpose to Brad's participation
in worship; without such leadings he tends not to be very visible in the
service.

Example of Spirit Leading in a Service

This section supplements the conversations on Spirit leading with
observations of a worship service in which decisions attributed to the
Spirit's leading were made. The service described here is not typical in
the sense that these are activities that occur in most services (such
services are rare), but it is typical of those services in which a 'move of
the Spirit' leads to experiences of Spirit leading. A 'move of the Spirit'
can be defined as a time in which there is a heightened awareness of the
Spirit's presence and an openness and freedom is given for people to
express their feelings, praise and devotion, often through charismatic
manifestations. These are times, accompanied by high levels of emotion
and energy, when Pentecostals feel that the Spirit is almost visibly
present. An outside observer might conclude that the emotions bring on
the move of the Spirit; a Pentecostal would argue that if it is a true
move of the Spirit, the latter brings the emotion.

Description of the Service[8]

The congregation begins gathering in the sanctuary following the dismissal of the age related Sunday School classes. There is pleasant chatter as people greet each other with hand shakes and an occasional hug. The repeated nature of this behavior, for it is part of every service, serves several functions; it symbolizes the 'brother and sister in the Lord' relationship that the congregation understands itself to share (one is greeting members of an extended 'family'); it reinforces for members that this is a 'friendly' congregation; and one senses that it is also a time for genuine exchange of greetings among friends.

There is music in the background as the musicians, which include a pianist, an organist, a bass guitarist and a drummer, are already in their place up front. At 10:44 the choir enters from the back and walks single file along one of the side aisles to the choir area behind the pulpit where they seat themselves. They are led by Ed Rollins, minister of music, who goes to the pulpit area and invites everyone to stand and sing 'I Will Enter his Gates with Thanksgiving', a lively worship chorus based loosely on Psalm 100. The liveliness of the opening song serves to invite people to participate in the service. The opening song is chosen for its familiarity so that people are free to sing without the encumbrance of holding hymnals or having to learn new words. Many clap to the familiar rhythm. Such lively singing generates a positive energy among the congregation and brings a sense of harmony of purpose and expectation; God hears these songs of praise. The music sets the mood for the service. Here it is upbeat and communicates to the congregation that worship is a time for one's spirit to be uplifted. The congregation sings with enthusiasm and seems to enjoy singing through this chorus several times.

After this chorus Ed asks the congregation to lift their hands in 'praise' unto the Lord and he himself models this behavior. The 'praise' which he leads includes phrases like 'Thank you, Lord', 'Bless the Lord', 'Praise the Lord'. There is a unified cacophony as the people

---

8.   The service took place on a Sunday morning. This service does not contain all elements involved in Spirit leading but description of an actual service, supplemented by further observations and interviews, is preferable to constructing a service that would include all elements by conflating several services. This approach allows the reader insight into an actual rather than an artificially constructed service, even though some elements of Spirit leading will be missing from this particular service. The description is cast in the present tense to give the feel of being in the service.

extend hands and arms upward, vocalizing their praises.[9]

There is more congregational singing and times of praise between these songs. Ed contributes to the flow of the service by interspersing comments that indicate the relevance of the songs chosen to daily Christian life. Here 'Living by Faith', a slower testimony type song, and 'I Feel like Traveling On', an upbeat camp meeting song, are introduced with comments on the need to live by faith and encouragement to keep serving the Lord. This last song is again very familiar and many in the congregation clap and sing with much enthusiasm. The drums and bass guitar add to the sense of energy with their punctuated rhythms. At the end of this song, the people are told they can be seated but the energy level remains high as Ed asks for 'one testimony where the "Lord has been so good to me"' (a line from the last song). This call for testimonies on a Sunday morning is unusual and is probably prompted by the presence of a member who came in during the singing. Linus is about 55 years of age, a very popular denominational official known for his great faith and service to the denomination. He is a long time member of the congregation and is well liked and respected by the members. In addition to his denominational service he has made several profitable investments over the years and is one of the wealthier members of the congregation. He had come in during the singing and sat about midway down near a center aisle in the left section of pews. There were obvious looks and glances to acknowledge his presence and a few reached over to shake his hand in welcome because this is his first time to be in service after being diagnosed with cancer and learning that he does not have long to live. Most members are aware of this situation and his presence brings a certain intensity to the service. The minister of music's invitation builds an expectancy that he will be the one to testify. Most members are also aware of his decision not to undergo surgery or chemotherapy but to 'trust the Lord to heal me or take me on'. There is a mixed atmosphere that is both tense and expectant.

However, the first response to Ed's invitation comes from Patricia, a woman of about 30 whom the congregation knows to be undergoing chemotherapy for cancer. Patricia has held positions of prominence in the congregation (she was director of the Vacation Bible School before becoming ill with cancer) and remains active in the children's ministry of

9.   In the Pentecostal tradition all members are accustomed to pray at the same time. Such 'congregational prayers' may be jarring to those unaccustomed to such worship, but brings a feeling of familiarity and solidarity to Pentecostals.

the church, helping to direct Sunday morning services for the children despite her illness. She is seated in the center section near the front but stands and speaks enthusiastically.

> The Lord has been so good to me. Living by faith is so much better than living by sight. Living every day—day by day. God has been so good to me.

Her testimony reinforces the belief that despite unpleasant circumstances one can find something uplifting in serving or worshipping God. When she is seated Linus stands to speak. There is still an air of expectancy as he rises. He speaks slowly and with purpose.

> It is good to be in the house of the Lord and to know that in the midst of so much bad news that God is good. I thank God for the health that I do have this morning.

He emphasizes 'health I do have' in such a way as to acknowledge, by implication, that he would like to have better health. While there is restraint in his testimony, his presence, his condition, and the people's awareness of his condition, bring an intensity to his testimony. As he is speaking Ed becomes teary eyed and lifts his hands as in prayer or praise. It is obvious other members of the congregation also are moved by this man's testimony. Several audibly utter 'Bless him, Lord' and words of praise as he finishes. His testimony reaffirms publicly his faith in God even though he has not gotten the answers to his prayers that he would like. It is also a request, by implication, that the members continue to pray for 'better' health for him. There is a poignancy to Linus's testimony in light of the official denominational teaching on 'divine healing' which encourages dependence upon divine rather than medical assistance when sick. His testimony as given does not challenge this doctrine; rather, his actions have shown him to be one who is trying to practice this belief faithfully, and perhaps more faithfully than most.

The atmosphere is still filled with expectation, as though the congregation is waiting to see what God may do for Linus right now. At this point a woman in her 80s, the wife of a retired denominational official, stands and speaks. She is a rather quiet lady but shouts occasionally when there is a move of the Spirit. This time she does not speak long and is almost inaudible. When she is seated another middle-aged woman stands and thanks God for helping her daughter through an operation. This woman is not a prominent or influential member of the congregation although she attends regularly. Her testimony, while picking up the theme of God's help during an illness, seems to lessen the energy level which is restored through what could be described as 'murmurs of praise' ('thank you, Jesus', 'bless the Lord', 'praise the Lord', 'have your way, Lord') uttered softly by the congregation during these 'testimonies'. The murmurs seem to come from all over, although young people seem to do less praise murmuring than older people and it appears the more vocal murmurers were more apt to engage in charismatic manifestations. The praise murmurs seem to be evocations or invitations to the Spirit, acknowledging the Spirit's availability. But more, they heighten the awareness of the Spirit's presence and keep the energy level of the service high.

When the last woman is seated, Ed lifts his hands as in praise, again is teary eyed and after a moment says, 'I can't seem to go on'. This brings more murmurs of praise from the congregation. This remark signifies several things. It indicates Ed's uncertainty of what to do next because he is feeling that the Spirit is present and wanting to work and that what he has planned will interrupt the current mood of the service. He is further indicating to the congregation that there is now a freedom to seek and yield to the Spirit's direction.

At this point Ian, a retired denominational official and the husband of the lady who spoke too softly to be understood, stands and says:

> I have a Scripture. 'Delight yourself in the Lord and He will give you the desires of your heart.' Ask your neighbor, 'What do you need'? Think about that. It's rich! Tell your neighbor, 'You're too quiet!'

At this point he utters something like 'whoop, whoop' and begins to speak in tongues. During the active part of Ian's ministry he was very influential in the denominational power structure, delivering a keynote sermon at the general assembly for several years. Although his influence has diminished with his retirement, he is still respected among the congregation, partly for his years of service and partly for his age. The 'whoop, whoop' is a peculiar characteristic of Ian when he is 'rejoicing in the Lord' and everyone knows that some of this is just his way of being 'happy'. So characteristic is the 'whoop, whoop' that when imitated in conversation, most listeners know who is being talked about. His speaking in tongues leads to more praises and prayers from the congregation and signals that one person is already feeling blessed by the Spirit and opens up an opportunity for others to speak about what they are feeling.

At this point Fernando stands and reads a Scripture in which the Lord is invited to be in the midst of the congregation. It is read as though its invitation is being issued by this congregation now. Use of the Scripture in this way identifies this congregation as also the people of God as much as the people of the Bible; as the people of God, God's direction is anticipated this morning. Another man testifies that he is glad to feel the Spirit in his 'heart' and not just his 'head'. There are murmurs of praise during and following this testimony and two women can be heard speaking in tongues during this time. The Spirit is experienced as close at hand because the Spirit can be felt and heard as the Spirit gives forth praises in a 'heavenly language'. And yet there is still an uncertain expectancy in the air; no one is quite sure yet just what the Spirit may do.

As the congregation waits expectantly, Iva, a woman in her late 20s and the daughter of a finance committee member, stands. She and her husband, who had been pastoring in another state, moved to Antioch about a year ago because of her health. She and her husband have been active with the youth ministry of the congregation, particularly since John Avery, the youth minister, left in December. She is teary eyed and speaks haltingly.

> The devil has been fighting me over this. 'What will people think about you?' (a pause). I have a special need in my home and need the church to pray.

This confession indicates several things. To the woman it is an admission of weakness, an admission she is unsure will be received positively. It is made because there is a heightened awareness of the Spirit's presence and therefore this may be a time to receive a special answer to her request. To the congregation her confession is an opportunity to show concern and support through prayer in her behalf. It is also understood as one of those moments of heightened awareness of the Spirit's presence; times in which people may have needs met as they follow the direction of the Spirit. These are times of great expectation coupled with moments of uncertainty as one tries to discern what it is the Spirit wants to do in the service. Pentecostals sometimes speak of someone holding the 'key' to the service, meaning that by speaking up or doing something this person has followed the leading of the Spirit which brings a sense of openness to the service that makes others feel free to express their praise or testimony. The congregation believes that if people will obey the Spirit's leading in these times (and not 'quench the Spirit') then the Spirit can and will bless the people. To Ed, Iva's confession confirms that he did the correct thing to wait rather than proceed with his plans; he has given the Spirit liberty to lead. It also gives him a sense of direction now; he decides to invite Iva to the front to pray.

When she starts for the front another woman also starts toward the front. As they make their way forward, the minister of music says, 'Others of you may want to come if you have a need'. The other woman's going forward indicates her desire also to receive the blessings that may come in this time of the Spirit's special presence; she does not want to be passed by. It also draws some focus away from Iva. Splitting the congregation's concerns this way might be understood to have positive effects in that it diffuses the focus on a potentially embarrassing problem. However, given the positive response Iva had received from the congregation, this particular instance seems to draw attention away that might have been better focused on Iva and her need. Ed's invitation avoids any embarrassment to the second woman and gives a freedom for others to experience an answer to their needs. Five more, two men and three women, go forward. Ed invites those who 'feel moved by the Lord to pray for one of these' to come forward.

This invitation moves Ed and the congregation to more familiar ground and away from the ambiguity and intense energy connected with waiting for the Spirit to lead. The invitation refocuses this intense energy into a time of prayer for specific people and their needs. The invitation also affirms for Iva that her speaking up was in order. The prayer in behalf of those who had gone forward is an opportunity for the congregation to express their special concern. A visible sign of this concern is the 'laying on of hands' which is a touch to the back or shoulders of those prayed for. The time of prayer also confirms a repeated observance that there is a distinction between groups that might be designated 'those prayed for' and 'those who pray'. Some members almost never appear in the group that prays for others; still other members move back and forth between the two groups and 'membership' in the groups tends to be more fluid 'when the Spirit is moving'. Those who pray for others this morning include Linus, Fernando, Ian, several other ministers and lay people, both men and women. As the sound from the prayer dies down, those at the front begin to return to their seats.

The remainder of the service includes the offering, songs by the choir and choral group, remarks by Pastor Smith (but no sermon as such), and a second altar invitation for 'those who need help'. The pastor's remarks are chosen to fit with the earlier activities of the service, indicating his understanding that it was the Spirit that has been at work and Pastor Smith's willingness to adjust to the new time frame. His remarks show sensitivity to the ambiance created by the earlier activities and give coherence to the service.

> I knew I would not be able to share all I wrote down. I was going to preach on Jonah. Jonah tried to run from God but God found him. There is no escape from God. Sometimes we run from God because we don't want to think about what He wants, only what we want. That keeps us in our sins. We don't want to think about others, only ourselves. It's hard to admit who we are: people who need help. As I get to know you I realize I deal with a people who have a rich heritage in experiences with the Lord. God loves you enough He will not let you escape. God found you this morning to signal something is not right in your life.

Pastor Smith thanks Iva for sharing her need and then comments:

> I think we would have more healings if people had the intestinal fortitude to ask for help. I have a feeling more need help here this morning. Would anyone here this morning say 'I need help. I have sin in my life and I need help'!

This becomes the basis for an invitation to those who need help to stand. No one does. This is probably because of his last remark; in the 'holiness-Pentecostal' tradition from which this congregation comes, remarks about 'sin in my life' are understood to refer to 'sinners' not the 'saints' who make up the majority of the congregation. The invitation, as given, was probably heard to exclude most people there. Sensing that he may have chosen his words poorly, Pastor Smith says with obvious exasperation, 'Well, I need help' and asks again for others who need help to stand. The pastor's remark that he is included among those who need help is heard to widen the audience for whom the invitation was intended. This time a man in his early 30s stands and begins to go forward and as he does others begin standing at the pews. The pastor further invites those who are standing to come forward to the altar, about half of whom do while the others remain standing. The remainder of the congregation is invited to pray. Most remain quiet although there are some soft murmurs of praise.

During the second altar invitation, there is an outburst of speaking in tongues by two women. The first woman is a relative newcomer to the congregation, having moved to Antioch about a year ago so that she and her daughter might attend the church sponsored college. She tends to be emotional when she prays, but the congregation's response to her has been warm and accepting. The second woman often gives messages and interpretations in this congregation and so at this outburst, the congregation gets very quiet for a few moments to see if this is a 'message' in tongues and not just someone's individual praise in tongues. Ed, who has been playing music during the altar service, also pauses momentarily. Cessation of the music here is a way of focusing all attention on what the Spirit may wish to say. After a few moments with no interpretation Ed resumes playing softly. This again demonstrates the need of sensitivity on the part of musicians so that they enhance rather than disrupt the mood of the service.

Those praying at the altar begin to rise and linger near the front. Brad, who has been among those at the altar, goes to the piano where Ed is playing and leads the congregation in the chorus. For the congregation this activity becomes an act reincorporating Brad into a leadership role; he himself evidently understands it to be the Spirit's personal direction to him that this is what needs to be done at this time in the service and as a time for him to become more actively involved in the congregation once again. After the chorus is sung through twice, Pastor Smith comes forward and says,

> those who are saying 'yes' to the Lord stand and sing this chorus once again. The Lord is helping us. This is God's grace. I believe it. I feel it today.

Brad leads the chorus once again before the service is dismissed by an enthusiastic congregational prayer (everyone praying at the same time). After the prayer members exchange handshakes and comments about the service ('Wasn't that a good service?' 'The Lord was with us today'.) as they leave.

Examples of Spirit Leading in the Service
There are two points in the service in which discernment and decision making were evident. One was Ed's decision not to proceed with what he had planned because he discerned that he was feeling the presence and desire of the Spirit to work; the other was Brad's decision to lead a song because he felt the Spirit leading him to do that at this time.

Summary Observations

One should begin by noting that Pentecostals, like other groups, employ a wide variety of means for making decisions. The local congregation was observed making decisions in several customary ways: committees discussed and recommended or decided on several issues relative to the church's disbursal of funds, members concerned about specific issues often talked informally among themselves or with the church's leaders about what to do, and the pastor held meetings with concerned members regarding several issues. McGuire's observation that 'although members of such groups appreciate nonrational styles of cognition in certain aspects of life, they desire and utilize rational modes in other aspects' (1982: 212) could not have been more evident than in much of this congregation's decision making. Not only did members rely on functional rationality for the everyday kinds of things McGuire mentions (wanting airline pilots who were not in trances, employers who did not award jobs through divination, etc.), functional rationality was operative in many decisions Pentecostals might label 'spiritual' in nature. In one instance a meeting was called to discuss what to do about selection of a new youth pastor. Several members suggested that those who apply for the position be sorted through by the pastor who would then present to a committee of concerned parents a list of the top three to allow their input before a final decision was made. While such a suggestion may allow for the leading of the Spirit, for instance in terms of how the pastor eliminates candidates, the suggestion assumes a functional rationality for this decision.[10]

However, the interviews also reveal that there are many times, places,

10. The actual selection procedure used shows a combining of functional rationality with a reliance on 'things feeling right or good', a common criteria among Pentecostals. Procedures for choosing the new youth pastor involved selection by the pastor of a committee of parents who sat down with the pastor and talked over the qualities they desired in a youth minister and sorted through the nine vitas that had been sent to the pastor after the position was advertised in the denominational magazine. The committee selected three candidates that came closest to meeting their verbalized qualities and invited them for an interview. The interviews were conducted in a member's home by the committee of parents and selected members of the finance committee. After the interviews the group had prayer before sharing their feelings about each candidate. Although the prayer was serious in nature, (a couple of people were teary eyed as the prayer ended) there were no charismatic manifestations. After everyone had opportunity to speak their thoughts and feelings the group disbursed to meet in four days for its final selection. At this later meeting some reservations were expressed but all felt good about giving the person selected 'a try'. This attitude may be taken as an indication that what leading of the Spirit was experienced in the selection of this youth minister was not through extraordinary means.

and activities in which the leading of the Spirit is experienced as an extraordinary presence. It is these experiences that are the focus of this study.

Kinds of Spirit Led Decisions

These extraordinary leadings of the Spirit were experienced in a variety of everyday contexts: at home, riding in the car, while praying and conversing with friends. Others reported the leading of the Spirit in decisions concerning career moves, employment, choice of schools and buying property. Choice of marriage partner, avoidance of accidents and provisions for financial needs were also named as Spirit directed activities as were decisions to talk with someone, to work on the restoration of a marriage, and to adopt children whose mother had died.

Spirit leading was also experienced in the context of corporate worship. Here people felt led by the Spirit to speak, to sing, to invite someone to pray and to engage in various charismatic manifestations. Certain leadings of the Spirit, such as those to give a message in tongues or interpretation of tongues were restricted to worship services. The most commonly identified experience of Spirit leading in a worship context was to speak to someone (usually to invite them to pray). This is probably because many charismatic manifestations (shouting, speaking in tongues) are understood as general expressions of praise. The language of 'Spirit leading' was used to refer to such experiences only if there was something special about the manifestation (e.g. if it was a 'message' or 'interpretation'.)

When asked to name experiences of Spirit leading there was no obvious preference for worship over daily contexts; the Spirit was seen as active in all of life. However, experiences of Spirit leading were considered special; everything is not Spirit directed for the Pentecostal.

It is also of interest to note that Spirit led decisions fit a more privatized pattern of religion than a socially active one for Pentecostals. No one named occasions where the Spirit directed them into public social or political actions. Even when there are social consequences (such as the adoption of children or marriage), Spirit leading retains a private individualistic quality restricted to the family unit.

Discernment Criteria

While Spirit leading is very much a part of Pentecostal life, one should not assume that discerning when the Spirit is at work and when another

influence is at work is easy for Pentecostals. The need for criteria by
which to discern was apparent in Pentecostals who sometimes found it
not only hard to distinguish the Spirit's leading from their own desires,
but also hard to determine where the Spirit was leading. In the interviews, Brad noted this difficulty, as did Fernando and Sheila. Regarding
her call to the mission field Sheila remarked:

> I really felt the Lord in that, at least I thought I felt the Lord…Sometimes it
> is hard to know.

Fernando noted how he groped to discern. In one instance, he reported
that he volunteered to take a church for which the Overseer could not
find a pastor:

> And I don't know if this was a leading of the Lord or just my strong
> feelings [of concern for the Overseer].

Thus, discernment lies at the heart of Pentecostal decision making; it is
discernment that actually allows one to speak of 'Spirit' leading. Before
noting the various criteria Pentecostals use in discernment, one can see
the integral relationship between discernment and decision making by
distinguishing three phases that characterize this process:

1. Presentation. Something presents itself as from the Spirit. This
'something' may involve a stimulus external to the person, for instance,
a statement by someone else that 'so and so' is the Lord's will or leading; or a charismatic manifestation, which always carries an implicit
implication that this is the Spirit speaking; or a set of fortuitous circumstances that are perceived as an indication of the Spirit's direction.
However, internally, the 'something' is perceived as an impression, a
cognitive awareness of a desire that one ought to do 'such and such'.
Recognition that something has presented itself as from the Spirit leads
to the next phase:

2. Testing. This phase is the attempt to discern the source of the
presentation. Discernment is necessary before one actually takes action
because one does not wish to engage in activities or desires that are not
truly of the Spirit's leading. Once the person is assured that this
presentation is of the Spirit, the person then moves to the third phase:

3. Action. This third phase involves actually making a decision to do
something and following through. Such actions involve the types of
things mentioned above.

The interviews revealed that Pentecostals employ a variety of discernment criteria including retrospective judgment, reliance on tradition,

charismatic manifestations and reliance on internal feelings. The following paragraphs examine these criteria in the light of three issues: (1) whether the locus of the criterion is external or internal to the discerner, (2) the distance from the deciding moment at which the criterion can be used, and (3) whether the criterion is unique to Pentecostal discernment.

Retrospection. One criterion that Pentecostals used to discern the Spirit's leading was retrospective judgment; if things worked out for the good, then it was the Lord's leading, if they did not, it probably was not. Sheila used a form of this criterion in her decision to adopt the children, and Allison used it to judge charismatic manifestations in worship. Fernando used this in a variety of decisions and noted that this is the surest way to know whether the Spirit had directed any given course. The lapse of time gives one the advantage of being able to judge outcomes and subsequent behavior. However, its unavailability as a criterion at the moment one needs to decide limits its use. Because retrospection involves temporal distance, it is located furthest from the deciding moment of any criteria used and use of outcomes to judge the Spirit's leading makes the locus of this criterion external to the discerner. Needless to say, use of retrospective judgments as a discernment criterion is not uniquely Pentecostal.

Use of fleeces seems related to retrospection in that one judges outcomes. Furthermore, their use seems to respond to a desire for safe and sure discernment criteria that can be used closer to the deciding moment. The reason for their use indicated a desire for an unambiguous means of knowing the Spirit's direction. Fleeces are external in locus, but closer to the deciding moment (one decides once one sees the conditions have been satisfied). Their use is not unique to Pentecostals; asking God for 'signs' is a general characteristic of Fundamentalist religion. Fleeces differ from retrospection in that fleeces do not seem to require any further reflection upon one's decision, while retrospection can remain more reflectively open. For this reason fleeces have enormous potential for abuse.

Reliance on Tradition. This refers to a cluster of criteria that share a common source of authority: their faithfulness to tradition. Appeals to certain interpretations and use of Scripture, especially those that deal with charismatic manifestations, fit here along with other traditions drawn more broadly from Pentecostal practice. One tradition that influences discernment is the idea that the Spirit leads one to do good things. If some action is a good thing to be doing anyway, it is much more apt to be judged as the Spirit's direction. The Scripture 'Whatsoever your hand finds to do, do it with your might' (Eccl. 9.10), is used to justify this criterion. Fernando used this criterion in decisions about his ministerial career and Sheila mentioned this in connection with her initial taking on of the children.

A second, related tradition that influences discernment is the idea that the Spirit works in people of good character. Pastor Smith notes that 'sometimes you have to look at the credibility of the person who gave the interpretation'. Almost everyone interviewed voiced similar thoughts, particularly when charismatic manifestations were involved.

A third tradition that influences discernment is the understanding that the Spirit does not physically harm, confuse or embarrass anyone. Thus times when people become violent or disruptive are judged not of the Spirit. Allison judges charismatic manifestations by this criterion; 'I don't think there will be confusion; the Bible says that'. Similar ideas are voiced by two retired ministers.

> I have always believed in government and that the Holy Ghost doesn't do things that are out of order or that will embarrass anyone. It won't confuse people either.

> The Holy Ghost will not behave Himself unseemingly, the Lord's Spirit will not hurt anyone physically. Any demonstration [charismatic manifestation] is potentially injurious. If that happens, that is an automatic indication that that is out of line.[11]

Reliance on tradition, in its various forms, is external to the discerner in locus and is not unique in its use by Pentecostals although some elements of the tradition relied upon may be unique (those traditions about charismatic manifestations, for instance). Distance from the moment of decision can vary but generally tends to be close; a charismatic manifestation can be judged the moment it gets disruptive. Judgments of character or assessments of the goodness of an act may involve the passage of time but need not.

---

11. Gerlach and Hine (1970) report a similar tradition among the Pentecostals they studied.

> The Holy Spirit, a visitor or seeker is likely to be reminded, is a gentleman and is not likely to be rude, to disrupt a group meeting, or to offend the sensibilities (1970: 15).

Charismatic Manifestations. A uniquely Pentecostal criterion for discernment is the use of charismatic manifestations. The relationship between charismatic manifestations and discernment and decision making is not always a simple one; there is no one-to-one correspondence. As signs of God's presence and power, charismatic manifestations sometimes function as the criterion for discernment. Allison spoke of them in this manner:

> I take it seriously when the Holy Ghost speaks; seriously about reverencing the speaking in tongues, the interpretation, all of that... God just spoke to us.

Another informant told a story of his father, a Pentecostal pioneer, who was trying to decide where to begin work for a new congregation.

> After the prayer he said that I feel we need to do it this way. When we are driving down the streets of A___ and the Holy Ghost falls on all of us at the same time we will know that is the place to stop.

At other times charismatic manifestations function as powerful confirmations of other discernment criteria. Pastor Smith commented on the selection of the new General Overseer:

> I think something like that [a message and interpretation] would be more in order as confirmation than as the selection itself.

Still other times it is charismatic manifestations themselves that have to be discerned. Pentecostals exhibit an ambivalence about the sufficiency of charismatic manifestations by themselves for discerning the Spirit's leading. Sheila gives voice to this concern:

> I have seen people speak in tongues and whatever and I am sitting over there going, 'No, no'... Someone can get up and do their own version of an interpretation and what if we took that?

As already noted, such manifestations are sometimes judged through assessment of character and reliance on tradition. One way this works in practice is the congregation's deference to and reliance upon certain people as those through whom most messages and interpretations come.

As a discernment criterion, charismatic manifestations have little distance from the discerning moment and may be either external or internal depending on whether the discerner is the one having the charismatic experience.

Internal Feelings. A fourth criterion by which Pentecostals discern the leading of the Spirit is their own internal feeling; a deep sense that this 'feels right'. Sheila mentions this as one way she knows it is the Spirit leading.

> Sometimes I feel something and I say, 'God, I don't know about this'. A strong feeling that something is not right... There have been times when the Lord absolutely (pause) I knew (pause) it is a feeling I guess... Sometimes I am not sure and think that is just me and sometimes I am sure and the only way I can specify it is the way I feel about it.

Fernando also refers to a growing sense of 'rightness' as he discerns the Spirit's leading.

> So it is only in retrospect that we can be more definitive about God having been in a certain incident. However, there is a feel of rightness that grows out of my relationship with God. That is the best way I can put it; a sense of I must do this. An urging that comes in our spirits... That is really my best barometer for knowing how He leads and when He is leading. There is a sense of rightness.

Discernment on the basis of feelings should not be understood to say that Pentecostals believe 'if it feels good it must be the Spirit'; this is not a sanction for whatever feels good. Nor should it be confused with certain physiological states that are sometimes reported as accompanying charismatic manifestations. Sensations of 'pressure', 'tingling', 'swelling up' and the like are often reported by Pentecostals in personal charismatic experiences. While the language of discernment by feelings seems at times to refer to such physiological sensations, it also seems helpful to distinguish these from a more deeply rooted feeling state.

This is an important distinction. When Allison credited the leading of the Spirit, through an internal feeling, with causing her to drive more slowly one night, her feeling of impending tragedy seems more akin to the sensations associated with charismatic feelings than to the deeply felt sense of things being right (or not right as in this case). This interpretation seems confirmed by the disclosure that she spoke in tongues the rest of the way home. When the word 'feeling' is used to describe these kinds of physiological sensations, such feelings function the same way as charismatic manifestations in terms of discernment. Sometimes they are the means for discerning the Spirit, but at other times they themselves must be judged.

One way Pentecostals try to sort out such feelings is the quality of persistence. Those feelings judged to be from the Spirit have a persistent quality, especially when resisted. The persistence seems to point to something deeper than physiological sensations for the Pentecostal; if it can be resisted it is not the more deeply rooted feeling.

The feeling of rightness also has an aesthetic quality. Things feel harmonious and coherent; there is a sense that things are orderly and fit with what is transpiring. For instance, Ed Rollins reports that he sometimes feels led to sing various unplanned choruses during worship. He judges whether these impressions are from the Spirit by their appropriateness to the mood of the service.

> If a chorus came to mind that was totally out of character with what was happening [in the service], then I would shut it off [as not from the Spirit].

Brad mentioned a similar quality to his discernment that it was right to sing a song in service.

> There was a spirit of worship, and you felt the Lord was wanting to do something and there had to be a catalyst. And is wasn't out of order. I guess that is one way you know; it is not out of order.

The aesthetic quality is felt as a sense of completeness and fulfillment for all present. By the same token, feelings of confusion, disorder or incompletion are judged not to be of the Spirit. This is particularly true when judging charismatic manifestations. Gwen notes that when such manifestations are not of the Spirit

> there is a real feeling of disorder, disharmony and uncomfortableness for those not involved [in the observed activity].

Pastor Smith also points to the sense of direction and completeness that accompanies genuine moves of the Spirit.

> My overall experience of the Spirit is more of wooing and drawing than threats. God doesn't have to threaten. This lady would just go on and it would be obnoxiously loud; screeches and carrying on that created more of a disturbance than it did peace of mind. But when the real Holy Ghost move comes...there is always a direction. When it is right there is a culmination, and wild fire [disruptive manifestations] tends to go on and on with no satisfying conclusion.

Another informant reinforced this understanding of the criterion of things feeling right in his account of an occasional attendee at the church where he grew up.

> We would all sit down and he would keep speaking [in tongues]. This
> never felt right... There was never any interpretation of his tongues. I felt
> nothing. I did not feel the Spirit of God. I did not sense any reverence
> among the congregation.

These instances point to a relationship between the criterion of things
feeling right and certain Pentecostal traditions. Judging the Spirit-
directed quality of charismatic manifestations in worship on the basis of
internal feelings draws upon the tradition that the Spirit does not harm
or confuse. Here the distinction between external and internal locus is
less clearly drawn; tradition feeds a sense of what is harmonious.

In terms of distance from the deciding moment, discernment on the
basis of things feeling right tends to occur very close to the decision; in
terms of its use, it is not unique to Pentecostals.[12]

Relationships among the Criteria

Use of the various criteria seems to be more circular than hierarchical;
that is, any one of the four seems open for use in judging the other
three. Decisions made on the basis of things feeling right can be judged
in retrospect (Sheila's call to the mission field, Fernando's letter), by
tradition (was it a good thing anyway), or charismatic manifestation (as
confirmation); decisions made on the basis of tradition can be evaluated
in retrospect (Sheila's adoption of the children began as a good thing to
be doing but was validated by how things turned out), things feeling
right (Fernando's emerging sense of rightness about his letter), or
charismatic manifestations (as confirmation). Decisions made on the
basis of charismatic manifestations can be (and usually are) judged by
the other three criteria. Fernando judged such manifestations by things

---

12. Sometimes Pentecostals report conferring with recognized authority figures to
help them in their decision making. Since this simply shifts usage of the criteria
elaborated here to the authority figure, reliance on the pronouncement of an authority
figure is not treated as a separate discernment criterion. Authority may be either
formal (one holds an authoritative office) or informal (one is judged to be 'spiritual').
Use of this means to aid decision making can take various forms and was referred to
by several of those interviewed. Allison asked Pastor Smith to interpret her feelings
that she should have sung a song. Another woman told of feeling led to lead a
'march' around the church building but of consulting with the person moderating the
service before doing so. Gwen consulted a friend whose spirituality she valued to help
her sort through various leadings thought to be from the Spirit. Reliance on authority
is also evident in the repeated expressions of confidence in the pastoral appointment
system used in the IHPC.

feeling right; others judged them by tradition (reliance on character and orderliness) and in retrospect. In this way, charismatic manifestations might be considered hierarchically inferior to the others.

In some sense, retrospection might seem to be hierarchically above the others, but even retrospective judgments are not necessarily without further evaluation. Retrospection relies on outcomes but judgment of 'good' outcomes was sometimes tied to tradition (where charismatic manifestations were concerned, for instance: did it embarrass or confuse?). However, the practical need of having to decide closer to the discerning moment reduces the hierarchical superiority of retrospection in practice. Its superiority as a discernment criterion is achieved only by greater distance from the deciding moment.

Impact of Spirit Led Decisions

Spirit led decisions impact Pentecostals in several ways, both personally and corporately. Summarily the observations and interviews suggest the following: First, Pentecostal discernment and decision making empha- sizes, encourages, and legitimates an openness to affective, intuitive, and semi-conscious dimensions of knowing. Pentecostal worship in particular gives people a context in which reliance on intuitive, unconscious processes of knowing are given explicit meaning and value. Because of the belief in Holy Spirit baptism, Pentecostals often connect this affective dimension of knowing with charismatic manifestations, but charismatic manifestations are only one way that an openness to these dimensions is signified. More important apparently is the criterion of things 'feeling right'. Charismatic manifestations, though understood as presentations that the Spirit is present, are considered insufficient as discernment strategies ultimately; they are judged by the criterion of things 'feeling right', and openness to this criterion is fundamental to Pentecostal practice. Sheila judged on this basis:

> I didn't feel right in my spirit...One of the interpretations didn't feel right to me and there was another one that felt right to me.

Secondly, Pentecostals believe the Spirit to be at work in these trans- rational psychic processes, and thus Pentecostal practices, particularly worship, may be said to ritualize the opening of boundaries between God and humans, creating opportunities for the Pentecostal's under- standing of God, self and others to change. In the service, the woman who revealed a potentially embarrassing need seems to have undergone a small but important increase in self-esteem: she will risk admitting her

weakness to the congregation during this time of openness created by
the move of the Spirit. This time of openness was signaled by the
minister of music's decision to change the order of the service. Gwen
also indicated the potential for transformation of understandings of self
and others in her description of how the Spirit was leading her to rebuild
her marriage. At times, however, she prayed

> 'God I don't want to do this and in my flesh I refuse to do it', but yet this
> other part prays, 'God, I want you more than anything and to please you'.
> In the daily living I feel the Lord saying you need to do thus and thus
> toward him and so there has been that confidence that the Lord is working
> to restore; but it is an extremely painful process.

Thirdly, these practices create opportunity for community building.
The community building dimensions of discernment and decision
making can be seen in the service when people were enabled to share
potentially shaming or embarrassing concerns by their testimonies and
prayer requests. The move of the Spirit empowered them to speak,
opening up a time for confession and relationship building. These times
for confession almost always draw a sympathetic response from the
congregation ('Bless her, Lord', 'Yes'). Praying for one another's
needs, physically and ritually reinforced by the laying on of hands,
obviously builds congregational solidarity.

The building of congregational solidarity was most dramatically
evident when Brad lead the song at the end of the service. The Spirit's
leading made possible his reincorporation into a position of leadership,
overcoming what had been a serious negative event in the life of the
congregation. A similar incident was observed in a service following
John Avery's decision to resign his position. Because he was going to a
different denomination and because he had claimed that he felt led of the
Spirit to make this move even though it was a very abrupt decision,
Pastor Smith had decided that John would be immediately removed
from all responsibilities and forbade him to call any meetings to explain
his actions. The pastor and some members viewed John's decision
to move to another denomination as a betrayal of this denomination and
its traditions. Shortly after Pastor Smith made his decision there was
a service in which a move of the Spirit occurred, and he decided to
let John address the congregation 'from his heart'. The move of the
Spirit had created an openness in which Pastor Smith could change
his mind, and in which those who felt betrayed were willing to listen to
John speak. Again this gave the congregation opportunity to work

through some negative elements of its life together.

The community building function of Spirit leading also can be seen in the opportunity it creates for a wider involvement of members in the service. In more routine, less inspired parts of the service those persons most often called upon to pray for others are male ministers, but prayers that accompany moves of the Spirit draw in a wider spectrum of the congregation, including women and non-ministers.

The interviews confirm this judgment. Members themselves indicate that feeling led to sing or speak to someone in worship is a means by which members can express their concern for others as well as a way for the Spirit to speak to the congregation. Allison recalled a service in which

> The Holy Ghost was moving on the service so strong and I just felt strongly that a certain song should be sung... It was two days before Darrell's father died and I told them at the funeral home that God was trying to warn them or comfort them in that service and I felt so bad that I didn't just go ahead and stand up and sing that song for whoever it was for.

Brad recalled a similar experience.

> Once I felt the desire to lead a song and that became the key to that service... There was a spirit of worship, and you felt the Lord was wanting to do something and there had to be a catalyst.

In his interview Ed Rollins discussed the service described in this chapter in the following way:

> I don't know if you were here when Iva stood up and said she just had to have a need met that morning and she came forward and about six or seven more came forward. That was a case, that was a confirmation too, I changed hymns... We sang that song and we were supposed to go on with something else and I couldn't go on. It was like a roadblock and you can't go on and then out of the clear blue she stood up and said, 'I have a need' and it just went from there. That was an instance in which the Lord confirmed to me that the hymn was right; I should have changed and that I should have stopped. It feels good when that happens. I was glad I did that.

Finally the community building aspect of discernment and decision making is seen in the patterns of order and restraint operative in Pentecostal worship; all is not chaos (cf. Paris 1982). There is an orderliness, apparent to the long time observer, that underlies and prevails over the spontaneity in the worship and that contributes to the building of community.

Patterns of order are evident in the use of music to guide congregational response, for instance. One senses that the music played during altar
services has different functions; there seems to be 'go on praying' music,
'pray vigorously' music, and 'stop praying' music (cf. Abell 1982).
Cessation of the music in the service was a way to honor the leading of
the Spirit. Music is usually played all during the service up until the time
of the sermon. Here the momentary absences of music during the Spirit
leading activities was a way to acknowledge that the Spirit was at work.

Order is also discernible in the way charismatic manifestations occur.
Certain charismatic manifestations themselves contribute to the management of this activity. For instance, 'messages and interpretations'
often bring a sense of closure to the highly charged atmosphere just
prior to such manifestations. At other times messages and interpretations
clearly bring a sense of reassurance to the congregation. If no
'interpretation' is forthcoming (a potentially disruptive event) the congregation, usually at the leader's direction and modeling, will begin to
murmur praises again. In this way the murmurs, sounding much like
invocations of some sort ('Yes, Lord', 'Help us, Lord', 'Lord, have
your way'), are a way to manage the flow of charismatic manifestations.

A distinction between 'tongues' that are for praise and 'tongues' that
are a 'message', that is, a prelude to an 'interpretation', is another
pattern to the way charismatic manifestations occur. While the auditory
distinction is hard to describe, tongues that are a message appear to be
spoken louder than tongues that are praise. One voice rises above the
sound of the various tongues and murmurs of praise. With the louder,
more persistent tones of such tongues, the congregation becomes quiet
to see if an interpretation is forthcoming. The ability to distinguish
between these two types of tongues indicates that Pentecostals know the
worship 'script' (Paris 1982). The distinction between tongues for praise
and for messages is also aided by the fact that most messages and interpretations tend to be done by a small core of members. Hearing certain
voices quiets the congregation in anticipation. The murmurs of praise
that await interpretations after a message might be understood as
encouragement to those who usually interpret. To extend Paris's (1982)
metaphor, knowing the script also means knowing the main 'players'. It
also is of interest to note that in this congregation the pastor is not
among those who give or interpret messages; members do this. A visitor
to the congregation (i.e. someone not there by invitation of those in
charge) would rarely, if ever, deliver a message or interpretation.

The notion that certain members give and interpret messages points to patterns of stratification among members. These are another discernible means of maintaining order. A stratification mentioned above was between those who pray and those who are prayed for. The implication is that those who pray are more 'spiritual'; hence, male ministers tend to dominate this category. Ranking by power or influence in the congregation yields the following pattern: male ministers, male members, female ministers, female members, adult non-members, children.

A move of the Spirit tends to blur the lines between certain stratifications, while leaving others untouched and still others more defined. Lines between those who pray and those prayed for (which includes the power hierarchy) is blurred. But the line between pastor and people remains intact; the pastor remains the one in charge even during moves of the Spirit. The line between those who give and interpret messages and those who do not is more clearly defined by moves of the Spirit. It is important to note that the blurring of stratification lines is only temporary; their presence is observable in the next service.

Patterns of restraint are observable in the role worship leaders play in the management of charismatic manifestations. On rare occasions they may abruptly stop a particular manifestation if it is disruptive. More common is a pattern of calling the entire congregation to prayer as a means of regaining control during manifestations that would become disruptive if allowed to continue. It was also observed that the worship leader gives cues indicating when it is proper to yield to charismatic manifestations. In the emotionally charged period before such manifestations, worship leaders give cues as to whether such manifestations would be in order. 'Let the Lord have His way' is one such cue. By contrast, if the leader simply moves on with what had been planned, this cues the congregation to the inappropriateness of such manifestations at that time.

Restraint is embedded in a tradition aware of its potential for excess. There is a reluctance, because of the potential for the abuse, either to claim something as the Spirit's leading or to follow one's inclinations without sufficient resistance. This tradition encourages caution in attributing one's impressions to the Holy Spirit and affirms that the Holy Spirit does not hurt or confuse people. When there is confusion, things do not feel right.

Restraint was also obvious in the notion that one should resist impressions if one could. The potential for embarrassment if one's actions turn out not to be led by the Spirit helps restrain certain behavior and claims. Both Ed Rollins and Allison voiced this concern.

> Ed: For example, the Lord had to almost knock me down one time... It was probably a ten to fifteen minute ordeal for the Lord to get me to do that because of the wild fire or self [doing something by one's own direction] that I have seen.

> Allison (on feeling led to 'interpret'): This feeling was here, where the Holy Ghost is so strong and it is like the Holy Ghost is uh... possessing you; all consuming you and you are fighting it or saying, 'No, I know what they will think; they won't believe me' so you don't yield to it.

Conclusion

I have described Pentecostal discernment and decision making noting the kinds of decisions attributed to the Spirit, criteria used to discern the Spirit's leading and the impact these decisions have upon Pentecostals. But certain questions are not addressed by description. How and by what criteria are these practices to be evaluated psychologically and theologically? Is this behavior creative or pathological, divine or demonic? The following chapters address these questions.

Chapter 5

PENTECOSTAL DISCERNMENT AND DECISION MAKING
AS 'CREATIVE REGRESSION': A PSYCHOLOGICAL PERSPECTIVE

Introduction

This chapter explores the psychological nature of Spirit leading, particularly the relationship between Spirit leading and early childhood experiences. It argues that, from a psychoanalytic perspective, Pentecostal discernment and decision making is to be understood as 'creative regression': behavior that taps into certain primal, foundational experiences associated with self formation and is able to draw upon these earliest psychic experiences in creative and revitalizing ways to open up possibilities for growth, strength and guidance in the present, though also presenting opportunities for pathology.

Creative Regression

Origin of the Concept

The concept of non-pathological or 'creative' regression derives from the work of 'ego psychology', an outgrowth of psychoanalysis which sought to define wider, more autonomous functions for the ego. In classical psychoanalytic theory *ego* designated that part of the psyche 'whose function is to direct and control the behavior of the organism while taking into account the dictates of both reality and instinctual impulse' (Fancher 1973: 202). This 'conflict reduction' model (Maddi 1980) was expanded by ego psychology which, by proposing non-conflictual functions of the ego, raised the possibilities of non-pathological regressions.

Regression as pathology. The classical psychoanalytic understanding of regression is that of a pathological reversal of an individual's psychological development. In his 1914 revision of *The Interpretation of Dreams* Freud described three types of regression:

(a) topographical regression, in the sense of the schematic picture of the psi-systems... (b) temporal regression, in so far as what is in question is a harking back to older psychical structures; and (c) formal regression, where primitive methods of expression and representation take the place of the usual ones' (Freud 1900: 548 cited in Holt 1970).

Topographical regression referred to the topographic model of the psyche which had its roots in Freud's abandoned 'Project for a Scientific Psychology' and was a 'reversal' of reflex-like actions in the perceptual system of the brain (Fancher 1973). The topographic model refers to a phenomenological classification of mental life in terms of a realm that is conscious, another that is 'preconscious' (accessible to consciousness), and a third that is unconscious (entirely inaccessible to consciousness). Although Freud revised and retained this model in his book on dreams, it was superseded by the structural model outlined in *The Ego and the Id* (1923). In the two latter types of regression, the central idea is that of a 'figurative temporal retrogression, an undoing or reversal in evolution as an explanation of pathology' (Holt 1970: 265). In temporal regression the ego falls back upon earlier forms of adaptation and gratification when more mature forms are found to be unworkable; in formal regression the secondary process is replaced by the primary process (Holt 1970). Girgis summarizes this classical psychoanalytic understanding of regression.

Regression refers to a return to more primitive patterns of coping (associated with an earlier phase of development) to avoid the challenges of the higher forms of behavior. Regression is a defense mechanism that operates outside of awareness and is used to protect the ego from excess stress and anxiety. When the present appears too overwhelming, the person resorts to behaviors that once gained ego-gratification or provided security (Girgis 1990: 1051-55).

Here regression is pathological behavior and the deeper the regression, that is, the earlier in the developmental process it reaches, the more severe the pathology. Psychoses represented regressions to pre-oedipal stages while the neuroses represented regressions to the later oedipal stages (Girgis 1990).

Ego psychology and the possibility of non-pathological regression. Heinz Hartmann (1958), in his seminal essay, 'Ego Psychology and the Problem of Adaptation', proposed that in addition to the traditional conflict reduction functions of the ego, there are 'conflict free' spheres of the ego in which are located those aspects of development related to growth (ability to react, perception, intelligence and motor skill). Such conflict free spheres of ego influence open the possibility of non-pathological regressions. Ernst Kris (1952), an associate of Hartmann, was the first to speak of 'ego controlled regression' or 'regression in the service of the ego'. By this language Kris sought to elucidate certain aspects of artistic creativity.

> We may view the process of artistic creation as composed of two phases...inspiration and elaboration...The first has many features in common with regressive processes: impulses and drives, otherwise hidden, emerge. The subjective experience is that of a flow of thought and images driving toward expression (1952: 59).

Artistic inspiration may include regressive features such as primary process thinking, but Kris argues further that one must distinguish creativity

> in which the ego controls the primary process and puts it into its service...[from] the psychotic condition, in which the ego is overwhelmed by the primary process (1952: 60).

Kris is here distinguishing two kinds of regression: a maladaptive kind (such as psychosis) and an adaptive kind (as in artistic creativity), and offering the first insight into how the two kinds of regression are distinguished. He contrasts 'ego controlled' regression with regression in which the ego is 'overwhelmed', and he mentions putting that which was gained from the primary process into the ego's service. Thus regression need not always be pathological; certain regressions even promote 'the finest kinds of human achievement' (Holt 1970).

Definition of Creative Regression
Drawing from Kris's two distinctions one can initially define creative regressions as ego controlled returns to earlier states of psychological functioning that permit the recapture of early psychic resources in ways that enhance present functioning. This definition needs further expansion.

Ego controlled returns. Inpathological regression the ego is 'overwhelmed'; there is a loss of the ego 'boundaries' which allow control over instinctual impulses and that distinguish internal and external realities. Hallucinations are a prime example. In contrast, creative regressions are 'ego controlled', that is, such discrete boundaries are maintained. Eidelberg (1969) writes that the ego controlled quality of regressions in the service of the ego is evident in two ways: they are (1) 'circumscribed' (there are boundaries), and (2) 'transient and reversible' (short term in duration).

> The essential quality of these regressions in the service of the ego (total personality) is that they are controlled: they are circumscribed, transient, and reversible. They do not submerge ego function (1969: 372).

The circumscribed limits of such regressions obviously point to maintenance of discrete ego boundaries ('they do not submerge ego function'). If the ego is overwhelmed (as in psychosis [Kris 1952]) such boundaries are lost; the self becomes fragmented.

In an insightful discussion analyzing the regressive nature of mystical experience, psychoanalyst and priest William Meissner (1984) calls attention to two ways that discrete ego boundaries (what Meissner terms self-identity) can be lost: (1) the self is absorbed into the loved object in such a way that self-identity is lost, (2) the self absorbs the loved object into a grandiose self so that object identity is lost.[1]

Meissner writes that mystical union with the divine has characteristics of regressive merger in which self identity is lost through fusion with the loved object. If indeed self identity is lost this would be pathology. Meissner argues, however, that the merger phenomenon of mystical union should not be regarded in this light.

> Nonetheless, it is clear that the sense of fusion with the object in mystical states is not the same as the regressive fusion to primary narcissistic union that might occur in states of psychotic regression. Rather, authentic mystical experience (as distinguished from pseudo-mystical or psychotic experience) not only does not undermine or destroy identity but in fact has a powerful capacity to stabilize, sustain, and enrich identity (1984: 151).

1.   This study follows the definition and distinctions of these terms proposed by Charles Gerkin who sees the 'self' and 'ego' as interrelated but not synonymous.

> There is a sense in which [both] terms point toward the same entity, the central core of individual human life. They are not separate entities, but one. Yet each term points from a different standpoint, a different language construction toward the same entity (Gerkin 1984: 98).

According to Gerkin, ego is best used to refer to 'that core of human functioning' where 'forces' demanding change meet and are mediated. But these forces act upon a 'responding, interpretive core of experiencing being', a self. Self is thus a way to refer to the interpretive, experiencing center of human being, while ego is a way to refer to the center of human functioning in its role of mediating conflict between the forces that shape human experience.

Self-identity is maintained in mystical states despite the experience of merger. Thus mystical states are creative rather than pathological regressions.

But how is a discrete sense of self and object maintained in states characterized as fusion of these? Is not one being inconsistent? Meissner sees an analogy between states of mystical union and Otto Kernberg's (1977) analysis of optimal or mature love relationships where Kernberg describes the phenomenon of union with another in terms of the 'crossing of boundaries'.

> In contrast to regressive merger phenomena, which blur self/non self differentiation, concurrent with crossing the boundaries of the self is the persistent experience of a discrete self, and as well, a step in the direction of identification with structures beyond the self (Kernberg 1977: 95).

Kernberg recognizes an 'intrinsic contradiction' in stating that firm boundaries of the self are maintained at the same time one experiences a transcendent sense of becoming one with the loved person, yet he disagrees with Norman Brown's (1968) assertion that there is an abolition of the boundaries of the self in love, stating that 'there can be no meaningful love relation without the persistence of the self' (1977: 290). To 'remain within the boundaries of the self while transcending them in the identification with the loved object' (1977: 290) is indicative of the highest level of object love. In mature love discrete self–object boundaries are maintained at the same time one experiences union of self and object in love.

The second way discrete self–object boundaries can be lost according to Meissner's analysis is through trying to absorb the object into a grandiose self. Of this he writes:

> In regressive states... the basic mechanism becomes incorporation... by which the distinguishing qualities of the external object are lost. Incorporation blends what has been internalized into an overriding, global sense of primitive narcissistic grandiosity. The transcendent absorption of object love stands in opposition to psychotic self-absorption (Meissner 1984: 153).

Maintenance of discrete ego boundaries in creative regressions means neither self nor object identity is lost. Maintenance of discrete self and object identity is a critical aspect of creative regression; its loss implies a loss in the ability to relate maturely to others.

Loss of discrete boundaries between the self and the non-self also implies the loss of ability to distinguish internal and external reality. In an

article on 'growth groups' Haaken and Adams (1983) define pathological regressions as those that 'undermine ego functioning...to the
extent that reality testing is significantly impaired' (271), noting that

> without an interpretive framework which reconciles affective states with
> objective reality and logical thought processes, such group cathartic
> experiences offer little opportunity for sustained therapeutic change and
> may, in fact, be psychologically damaging (1983: 271-72).

To early ways of knowing and being. Regression means a return to
earlier ego functioning. To understand what creative regressions
recapture, one must first understand something of human development;
how people come to know themselves and their world. What are the
infant's earliest ways of knowing and being? How are self or ego
boundaries initially formed? To understand this process we begin with
'object relations' psychology, an attempt to explain development in the
psychoanalytic tradition in terms of the infant's earliest experiences with
its primary caregiver (generally the mother).

The term 'object' is derived from Freud's early writings where he
designated anything that could serve as focal point for discharge of
instinctual energy as an 'object' (1905). Common objects were the
mother, the mother's breast, and other significant persons; less common
objects might include animals or other things that were 'overvalued'
(fetish objects). 'Object relations' refers to the relationships or attach-
ments one has to these persons or objects as they are experienced
intrapsychically; that is, the 'object' to which one is attached is actually
an internal 'mental representation' of something in the environment.
Object relations theory is concerned with how a sense of self develops as
separate from its objects, how these social relationships are subjectively
experienced, and the consequences of those experiences for personality
development and for psychopathology.

According to Otto Kernberg (1976), a premier object relations theorist, life begins in an 'undifferentiated' state: self and object are not distinguished; infant and mother, infant and world are one and the same in
the infant's experience. This idyllic state is soon challenged (the mother's
face comes and goes) and the process of distinguishing self from object
('differentiation') begins. Kernberg charts this process through three
stages:undifferentiation, toward differentiation, differentiation and
integration.

According to Kernberg, in the undifferentiated state the infant is aware only of relative states of comfort and discomfort. Movement toward differentiation (i.e. formation of mental representations of self and object) begins as the infant 'splits' comfortable ('good') from uncomfortable ('bad') experiences on the bases of differently felt ('affective') states. But because the infant does not initially differentiate itself from its environment, it splits these experiences in ways which suggest that the good experiences come from an all good self-object (Kernberg's term to indicate the lack of differentiation) and the bad experiences from an all bad self-object which the infant attempts to 'expel'.

> The expelling of the 'bad' self–object representations to the 'periphery' of psychic experience originates a motivated conception of the 'out there'. (Kernberg 1976: 63-64).

The conception of an 'out there' that is 'not me' is a first step toward the differentiation of self from environment, a splitting of experience along affective lines that becomes the basis for differentiation of self and object.

> The 'all good' undifferentiated self–object representation is built up separately from the 'all bad' one, and successive experiences of gratifying types elaborate this experience, leading gradually to differentiation of self, object, and affects within the perception (Kernberg 1976: 93).

As development continues, splitting gives way to other processes. The infant comes to realize that good and bad experiences come from the same object (or self); splitting is overcome and positive and negative experiences are fused together in a 'total' or integrated self (or object) image.

These integrations are not achieved without some struggle, however. The loss of the idyllic union gives rise to representations of an 'ideal' self and an 'ideal' object which reflect in fantasy the now lost ideal state of the 'all good' self and object representations. Images of an ideal object provide the basis for a sense of justice in later life while

> The ideal self represents a wishful, ideal state of the self which would make the individual acceptable to, close to, and in the last resort, symbolically re-fused with the ideal object (the unharmed, all loving, all forgiving early mother image) (Kernberg 1976: 68).

In normal development attempts to regain these lost ideal representations give way to a final psychic state characterized by realistic and harmonious integration of internalized object relationships and self-knowledge. Such mature integrations exert an influence throughout life providing a source of strength and guidance.

> Clinical observation shows how much trust in one's self and one's good-ness is based upon the confirmation of love from internalized good objects. In this regard, one aspect of regression in the service of the ego is a reactivation in fantasy of past good internalized object-relations which provide 'basic trust' to the self (Kernberg 1976: 73).

That permit recapture of early psychic resources. Two questions are important here: what are the early psychic resources that are recaptured, and how does the recapture occur?

Kernberg's quotation refers to the 'reactivation... of past good inter-nalized object-relations'. The first thing creative regressions allow is the recapture of various self and object images.

> Although the critical experience of separation and the process of indi-viduation presumably takes place in the first three years of life, throughout the life cycle the human person faces challenges to the cohesiveness and coherence of his or her sense of self. At various times and under various circumstances the human person re-encounters in new and different ways the tensions that characterized the beginning of life: the tension between oneness, affiliation, community, closeness and separateness, individuality, uniqueness, difference (McDargh 1983: 73).

The work of another object relations theorist, D.W. Winnicott (1971), sheds light on how these internalized self and object images can be reactivated. In his attempts to understand how internal, mental objects are connected to external reality, Winnicott introduces the concept of 'transitional objects', objects or phenomena that form something of a bridge to reality as the infant is forming its first understandings of what is 'not me'.

According to Winnicott, psychoanalysis recognizes that a developed person can be said to have an 'inner reality... an inner world that can be rich or poor and be at peace or in a state of war' (1971: 2). This inner, psychic reality is distinguished from the environment which provides a reality external to the person. However, life begins without distinction between these two realities. The infant negotiates the movement from this state of being 'merged with the mother to a state of being in relation to the mother as something outside and separate' from the infant by way of 'transitional objects or phenomena' (1971: 14-15). When Winnicott speaks of transitional phenomena, he says he is arguing for an intermediate area of experiencing, to which inner reality and external life both contribute. It is an area that is not challenged, because no claim is made on its behalf except that it shall exist as a resting-place for the individual engaged in the perpetual human task of keeping inner and outer reality separate yet interrelated (1971: 2).

This 'intermediate area' is the area of transitional objects or phenomena. Winnicott cites the example of a bit of blanket that might get in the infant's mouth during thumb sucking as an example of a transitional object or phenomenon. Other common examples might be the child's teddy bear, or a musical tune or a mannerism. The possibilities are endless. These objects have special value to the infant, particularly in times of anxiety (such as going off to sleep with its attendant separation from the mother figure) because they allow the infant to reestablish continuity in his or her experience. This continuity of experience is necessary to help the infant develop a capacity to recognize and accept reality (Meissner 1984).

Because transitional objects are 'outside, inside, and at the border' (Winnicott 1971: 2) they have a special relationship to fantasy and illusion. But unlike Freud, Winnicott sees illusion as a positive aspect of development. Fantasy and illusion provide a 'transitional space' in which the infant can explore its experience of emerging reality. Ability to use transitional objects and transitional space leads to the infant's ability to 'play', and play is the gateway into the cultural experiences of adulthood.

> I am here staking a claim for an intermediate state between a baby's inability and his growing ability to recognize and accept reality. I am therefore studying the substance of *illusion*, that which is allowed to the infant, and which in adult life is inherent in art and religion (Winnicott 1971: 3).

Because the task of keeping inner and outer reality separate but interrelated is a 'perpetual' task, the creation of transitional space in which object relationships periodically can be recalled or reworked is one way to conceive the recapture of early psychic resources. Even when the influence of early object relations may not be so positive, creative regression opens up possibilities for reworking such images.

> One of the processes of continuous ego or self-synthesis is the summoning up of memories of encounters with objects, whether supportive and loving or disruptive and frightening. These processes serve the individual in the present, helping him to adapt and master his situation. The constant movement from present object and self-representation to past object and self-representation is one of the critical processes which... contributes to our 'becoming a self' (Rizzuto 1979: 57).

Early object relations are not the only potential psychic resource available for recapture in creative regressions; according to Kris (1952), creative regressions allow recapture of the primary process. Freud (1905) distinguished two kinds of thinking: a more primitive, impulse driven ideation based on wish association, immediate gratification and disregard for reality which he called primary process, and a more purposive, realistic, logical kind of thinking which he called the secondary process. While it is this latter type of thinking that characterizes maturity for Freud, it is the former that is recaptured in creative regressions.

Freud pointed out that regression allowed the primary process to break through the rational secondary process, being unbound by rules of logic and reason and thus having the potential for generating creative thoughts and solutions not available through more rational means. Holt's description of the primary process indicates its creative potential. According to him the primary process exhibits

> a general disregard for the usual standards of fidelity to reality and rationality, so that mutually contradictory propositions may stand side by side unresolved, the restrictions of space and time may be flouted, impossibilities be blandly imagined, and normal expectations violated (Holt 1970: 267).

To understand how primary process thinking can be recaptured and made available for current functioning, a return to Kris and his study of artists will be instructive. Primary process thought was understood as an aid to creativity and was thus an illustration of 'regression in the service of the ego'. It is the connection to creativity that helps clarify one way primary process thought can be recaptured.

In an assessment of induced regressions and their relation to creativity, Harrison (1984) argues that regressions that aid creative thinking 'are, for the most part, the commonly experienced self-limited ego regressions normally occurring in everyday life'. He further argues that there is a kind of 'priming work' that should proceed such regressions. For Harrison, the creative process should be conceived as having 'four consecutive, distinct phases' (an elaboration of Kris's two).

> Briefly these phases are: the initial motivation phase, the priming work phase, the ego regression phase, and the elaboration and assessment phase (1984: 82).

Priming work is motivated by the wish to create and is described as

> a consciously focused and often intense study of already known, as well as newly acquired, knowledge, theories, techniques, themes, compositions,

styles, and existing creative products, all of which have been judged to be relevant to the creative aim. Priming work produces and adds relatively strong preconscious and unconscious memory trace constellations or relevant intellectual or emotional subject matter to the total memory (1984: 83).

These memory traces are then available for the ego regression phase and because of the priming work are more apt to be processed in the regressive phase. Harrison further notes that

> The strong wish to create, which is included in the memory trace constellations produced by priming work, stimulates an increase to occur in the frequency or number of self limited ego regressions over that which would take place naturally (1984: 83).

Recapture of primary process thought can be aided by 'priming work', conscious attempts at self-limited ego regressions. One might speak of such self-limiting regressions under the metaphor of 'loosening the ego boundaries'. The concept of loosening of ego boundaries in a healthy self is not far removed from the notion of crossing boundaries in mature object love. In both cases one thinks of the ability of healthy selves to limit ego control without loss of ego identity. Such a metaphor is useful in understanding how creative regression occurs.

Recapture of primary process thinking can occur by other means. Jones (1991), following Loewald (1988), argues that one way this can happen is through the 'symbolic linkages' one experiences through art and religion. For Jones, 'symbols draw us into a psychic realm in which we experience our connection with the primary process...but in such a way that we do not lose our capacity for secondary process (1991: 55).

Thus religion and art, through symbols, are 'primary carriers' of

> return(s), on a higher level of organization, to the early magic of thought, gesture, word, image, emotion, fantasy, as they become united again with what in ordinary nonmagical experience they only reflect, recollect, represent or symbolize...a mourning of lost original oneness and a celebration of oneness regained (Loewald 1988: 81).

Finally one could note that Haaken and Adams (1983) report on several activities used to promote regression in a 'growth training' seminar. These included encouragement of dependence on the group leader to interpret reality, identification with group ideals, minimizing the value of intellectual processes, and exercises that helped one 'get in touch with feelings'. While Haaken and Adams conclude that the regressions they studied were pathological, they note that under certain circumstances, such as military combat, all of the above activities could promote health rather than pathology.

In ways that enhance present functioning. Regarding this aspect of creative regressions Meissner writes:

> Thus the creative regression represents the power of established identity and the mature capacity for relationship to a significant other to recapture the revitalizing sources of psychic potential buried in infantile experience and relate them, in Erikson's terms, to the rudiments of trust. A mature identity also builds on such roots the synthetic capacity to reintegrate infantile residues into ongoing loving experience (Meissner 1984: 152-53).

Reaching back and making early psychic resources available for present use implies an important quality of creative regressions captured in Eidelberg's statement that these regressions are 'transient and reversible' (Eidelberg 1969); one returns to present functioning. An individual's capacity to reverse regression has been identified as a measure of health.

> All of us permit regression... in connection with certain activities, i.e. creativity, sleep, certain forms of psychotherapy, etc. This is sometimes described as regression in the service of the ego...
>
> We permit ourselves to go to sleep and lose contact with reality because we feel we can reverse it. It is equally important to evaluate an individual's capacity to reverse regression... when the need for it has passed (Frosch 1990: 8).

Creative regressions enhance present functioning in several ways. The recapture of primary process thinking taps a dimension of our knowing not normally available through secondary ideation (Ulanov and Ulanov 1982), making more of our total self available for use in decision making. Loewald (1978) writes of the ability of primary process thought to transcend dichotomies and apprehend otherwise unknown unities:

> If we acknowledge the undifferentiating unconscious as a genuine mode of mentation which underlies and unfolds into a secondary process mentation (and remains extant together with it, although concealed by it), then we regain a more comprehensive perspective—no doubt with its limitations yet unknown. Such a perspective betokens a new level of consciousness, of *conscire* on which primary and secondary modes of mentation may be known together (Loewald 1978: 64-65 cited in Jones 1991).

Because 'conscious reason "limits and impoverishes" existence unless it has access to the more unitive and intuitive forms of knowing grounded in the unconscious', returns to primary process thinking are 'sources of creativity and refreshment' (Jones 1991: 53). Primary process thinking taps 'affective' dimensions of knowing connected to early development that are suppressed with the emergence of the secondary process. But initially affect and cognition evolved together in the infant's experience.

> In short, various inborn physiological, behavioral, affective, and perceptive structures are internalized jointly as a first unity of intrapsychic structure. Cognition and affect are thus two aspects of the same primary experience. Although the neurophysiological structures responsible for affective experience and for (cognitive) storage capability of this experience are different, their integration in the earliest affective memory (Arnold 1970a, 1970b) establishes, in my opinion, a common structure (pleasurable or unpleasurable primitive experience) out of which cognition and affect will evolve in diverging directions (Kernberg 1976: 62-63).

A return to early affective knowing without making such gains available in the present might be seen in emotionalism that has no lasting impact or makes no change in the person. The energy of this affective means of knowing is bled off into non-productive activities such as catharsis without insight. Such affective knowing must be made available to and integrated with the secondary process in creative regressions. Creative regressions place the insights from the regressive states within a reality based interpretive framework.

The recapture of early images of self and its significant object relations also enhance present psychic functioning. Once reactivated, energy from these relations can enhance positive feelings about the self or make the reworking of destructive images possible, allowing integration of positive and negative qualities, and thereby increasing the ability of the self to relate more maturely to its objects. Conversely, in pathological regressions the self becomes fragmented and unable to integrate its experiences in enriching ways.

Finally we note that these two ways of experiencing creative regressions (recapture of primary process, or early object relations) seem related to Freud's original distinction between formal and temporal regression as expounded by Holt (1970). Recapture of affective ways of knowing is related to primary process thinking (formal regression) while recapture of early self–object relations is related to early ways of adaptation and gratification (temporal regression).

Discernment and Decision Making as Creative Regression

The remainder of this chapter will argue that Pentecostal discernment and decision making which meets the Pentecostal tradition's own criteria of authenticity also satisfies the definition of creative regression; that is, from a psychological perspective, experiences of Spirit leading that meet Pentecostal religious criteria may be conceptualized psychologically as ego controlled regressions that recapture early dimensions of affective knowing and allow for the reworking of object relations in ways that enhance present psychic functioning.

The expanded definition of creative regression yields three criteria by which one can evaluate discernment and decision making. Ego controlled regressions are circumscribed and reversible; these qualities of control are evident in the ability to

1. give of oneself in object love while maintaining discrete ego boundaries,
2. integrate the insights of primary process thought with the secondary process, and
3. integrate positive and negative aspects of self and object images.

Non-Creative Regressions

Before presenting the case for the creatively regressive qualities of discernment and decision making, pathological tendencies in Spirit leading activities must also be considered. Not all discernment and decision making meet the above criteria. In what ways can loss of discrete ego boundaries, inability to integrate primary process thought with secondary thought processes, or failure to integrate positive and negative aspects of self and object images appear in Spirit leading experiences?

Loss of discrete ego boundaries. Charismatic manifestations are probably the first practices one would identify as connected to loss of discrete ego boundaries, especially in cases where altered states of consciousness are experienced. While altered states clearly involve some sense of ego splitting, whether there is a pathological loss of ego boundaries requires one to look beyond such experiences to subsequent behavior; such states need not necessarily indicate pathology (Meissner 1984). If one returns from the experience strengthened and able to cope in more constructive ways, such temporary or transient splitting would not finally be judged pathological, or the pathological element would be considered transitory. All reports of altered states among those interviewed were connected to discrete, temporary charismatic manifestations and thus cannot be considered to be seriously pathological. These experiences also show that a given behavior may show some but not all features of ego loss.

When charismatic experiences do not involve altered states (cf. Samarin 1969), the possibility of pathological loss of ego boundaries seems even more unlikely. Allison and Fernando both reported charismatic manifestations that did not involve altered states and in both instances a case can be made for the ego controlled quality of these experiences. While Allison uses the language of 'possession' to describe how she discerned the Spirit's leading in giving an interpretation, which might suggest loss of discrete self identity, her complete description of the experience does not in fact support such an interpretation. Referring to other times when she resisted such possessions ('I will have to say there have been times when I felt it and did quench it'), and struggling with whether this is the right word for what she is trying to express, Allison describes her continuing capacity to judge and resist the power of the Spirit even at its strongest:

> This feeling was here, where the Holy Ghost is so strong and it is like the Holy Ghost is, uh, possessing you, all consuming you, and you are fighting it or saying, 'No, I know what they will think; they won't believe me', so that you don't yield to it.

Certainly there is a strong urge to speak, but such urges can be yielded to or quenched. While the language of persistence is used at times to indicate that the person felt compelled to follow, closer examination indicates that the person still retains ego control: the phenomenon described is reported as a *yielding* to these urges rather than being *overcome* by them. In a similar situation Fernando indicated that yielding is the good thing to do; not yielding is considered disobedience.

> But I got such an overwhelming, repeated presence each time I would try to restrain it that it would come upon me so that I had to get up and literally walk to the pulpit. I couldn't help it. I mean I could help it ultimately, but I would have felt like I had really disobeyed.

When Fernando refers to being 'overwhelmed', his admission that he could have resisted this feeling ('I could help it ultimately') indicates that he believed he maintained some sense of control; his experience is there-fore best described not as an overpowering but as a yielding. And while it is possible that Allison sometimes exhibits ego loss, the phenomena described here show no long term ego boundary diffusion or loss.

Evaluating Sheila's behavior is more problematic. (Sheila is the woman who adopted the children and who experienced an altered state of consciousness when she received the baptism of the Holy Spirit in a church youth camp.) Sheila's experience of receiving the baptism of the Holy Spirit seems to have predisposed her to receiving 'special insights' about people's activities and motives that she is not in the habit of evaluating critically. While Sheila claims a special strength from the insights revealed to her, other people are not always certain what to make of her concern. But while failure to evaluate her special insights critically implies a possible failure to integrate primary process thinking with secondary reflection, it does not imply loss of ego boundaries.

However, Sheila's behavior during her baptism with the Holy Spirit suggests dissociation ('when I came to, woke up, or something, I was on the other side of the building. I don't know how I got there') even though this incident was transient; she regained control of her body and thoughts during the extended worship time. Did Sheila's childhood pre-dispose her to cognitive dissociation as a way to relate to the 'two personalities' of her father? She reports that she reacted very differently to her rearing than her siblings. While they seem to have been negatively impacted by the frequent moving and father's behavior, Sheila, on the other hand, found the moves 'adventurous' and her father increasingly manageable.

The suggestion of a relationship between childhood experiences and Sheila's predisposition to dissociative religious experiences can also be drawn from the observation that her behavior toward God is described in terms similar to behavior toward her father. 'I used to talk back to him [her father]. I would tell him, "this is wrong" [hitting her mother].' Her father was described as 'slapping' her mother on several occasions. At the time of her hysterectomy Sheila remembers praying, 'God, this isn't fair. I'm mad at you...I told the Lord everything. It is a wonder He hadn't got mad at me and slapped me down.'

Sheila's incident with the check writing for the groceries might also be understood as an example of being so lost in religious wishful thinking (mild dissociation) that she loses perspective on the seriousness of what she is doing. She gives some indication that she is aware of the potential negative consequences of this behavior but proceeds on the basis of a feeling that things will be all right, which seems rooted in an early object image of God as father comforting her. This incident illustrates the complexity of human behavior. While one might point to the early object image as a source of strength, one must also face the possibility of ego loss through dissociation here. On the positive side, the check cashing incident was reported as a one time event. In light of this, one may cautiously conclude that the loss of ego boundaries evident during these states was not pathological, though calling this behavior creative also would be an overstatement. Such incidents suggest an ambiguous range of ego regressive behaviors whose transitoriness removes the pathological edge, in that there is no obvious continuing personality disorder, but whose creative potential remains conjectural.

Another way that discrete ego boundaries can be lost is narcissistic grandiosity in which object identity is lost as objects are absorbed into a grandiose self. Is there any evidence of this in discernment and decision making? Castelein (1984) has proposed that speaking in tongues be understood as an attempt by Pentecostals to regain the lost ideal self–object union of infancy by means of union with the divine; that is, speaking in tongues compensates for narcissistic injury to the self. Speaking in tongues is a kind of 'spiritual peek-a-boo' that allows

> believing persons who have been too abruptly weaned from the super-natural without 'good enough mothering' [Winnicott 1971] from the mainline denominational churches, to learn to adjust themselves to the apparent absence of God in everyday existence (Castelein 1984: 58).

This suggests Spirit leading might occasionally involve narcissistic object absorption into a grandiose self. Assessing this from the interviews is difficult. While people used language indicating loss of self in merger with the Spirit, no one used language that clearly spoke of the Spirit (object) being lost in such mergers. However, even if one could cite language of object absorption, one should remember that the desire to unite with the divine need not in itself indicate pathology; such unions can be the highest expressions of object love (Meissner 1984). The key to distinguishing narcissistic object absorption from 'crossing the boundaries' in object love is subsequent behavior; is there a positive psychic gain? If speaking in tongues compensates for narcissistic injuries in ways that make one more able to cope, as Castelein claims, speaking in tongues could possibly perform a positive function not unlike the changes achieved by psychotherapy, at least in the short term. The question of therapeutic value, however, also must ask whether these experiences bring about deeper, longer-lasting changes within the structures of the self. While Castelein argues such a possibility, his discussion suggests that glossolalic experiences alone are not sufficient for this.

While pathological regression is too strong a term to explain the practices described thus far, one cannot deny that there are tendencies in discernment and decision making that diminish ego control. Diminished ego control is most obvious in the lack of critical reflection characteristic of many decisions attributed to the Spirit's leading. The Pentecostal practice of 'fleeces' in particular seems to manifest these characteristics. Fleeces diminish ego control by omitting critical reflection. Allison seems very sincere in her use of fleeces, and while aware that one's own desire can masquerade as the leading of the Spirit, she does not seem to grasp the reduction in ego control that is part of the practice of fleeces. Fleeces require little critical reflection; simply set them up and take whatever happens as the Spirit's direction. There is no need to examine one's desires and whether they are Christ-like if the fleece comes to pass.

Rationalization also seems to be a quality of fleeces. A retired minister told of a three part fleece used to make a career change. One of the conditions of the fleece was that the new job provide a salary on which he could live. While the other two parts of the fleece did occur, the salary offered was one half his previous salary. He reasoned that with fewer expenses in the new job, he could probably live on the lower salary. While this does not necessarily show rationalization on the part of the minister (he did survive on the lower salary), it does illustrate the enormous potential for self deception, simply making one's own desires those of the Spirit. Allison's explanation for why the Spirit did not direct her to buy the first house (God had a better one for her) also appears to have the same quality. (In the absence of viewing both houses, one cannot dispute that the second house was indeed a better house.) This is not to argue that following one's desires regarding career moves or buying property is wrong; it is simply to point out the dangers inherent in attributing those actions to the leading of the Spirit if arrived at by means of a fleece.

It also is of interest to note that for Allison fleeces create an emotional distance between her and God that mirrors the emotional distance she felt with her father. She could talk to him about various things, including her other relationships, 'but never about us'. While Allison's Spirit leading experiences are not built entirely around fleeces, when they are used, God is approached in a way that does not require the intimacy of other Spirit leading criteria.

Loss of ego boundaries is also evident in those times when Pentecostals seem driven by impulses not under ego control. Sometimes seeking an emotional escape seemed the order of the day. Brad made references to experiences he had when younger.

> I used to run and shout with the best of them, and if the Spirit moved me today I would do that. But I used to shout when I was young and that felt good. But I wonder, 'What did I take home? A good feeling'.

In similar fashion Ian's remarks in the service seem to promote emotionalism without conscious attention to the creative use of this emotion.

Another person, who had her first exposure to Pentecostalism in college, described this impulsive quality well when she recalled experiences she had had shortly after receiving the baptism of the Holy Spirit.

> I would be in services and I would hold back as long as I could and then I would say, 'I can't stand it! I am so happy', and I would run or shout or whatever.

In time she, like Brad, reported a diminished expression of these outward manifestations.

> I am not outwardly as spiritual as I used to be but I think my relationship with God has deepened. I feel more stability. I don't doubt it [her relationship with God] at all because I know God will not like me or hate me because of how much I speak in tongues or shout. Ten years ago I might have.

Even though these two people report diminished impulsiveness with longer exposure to Pentecostalism (in accord with learning the traditions of order and restraint mentioned in Chapter 4), there remains the need to critique such behavior in terms of motive and outcome. The chief means for distinguishing (healthy) spontaneity from (unhealthy) impulsiveness is subsequent behavior: was the loss of control transient, and was it strengthening of coping skills?

Failure to integrate primary process with secondary reflection. Discernment and decision making does not always meet the second criterion either. Whether one ought to address lack of critical reflection under the criterion of diminished ego control or under the criterion of failure to integrate primary process with secondary reflection becomes blurred with some decisions because of difficulty in judging the influence of primary process thinking on them. Some decisions that lack critical reflection do not seem to involve primary process thinking, but thinking can be influenced by these processes in ways not immediately obvious.

Uncritical reflection in decisions that seemed to be driven by unconscious motives point to possible failures to integrate primary and secondary processes. Sheila's decision to adopt the children shows a lack of critical reflection about the choice and mirrors her own tendency simply to let decisions happen to her. Fernando's decision to write the letter of denominational repentance reflects drives, never fully conscious to him, tied to his own struggle of placating a God ever suspicious of anything human. Although he submitted the actual content of the letter to friends, thus helping to integrate the thoughts that came via the primary process with secondary reflection, he did not fully submit the idea that this was inspired of the Spirit (and not Fernando) to critical reflection. Allison's resistance to interpretation reflects an ongoing struggle over her worthiness and the felt need to be reaffirmed by these opportunities as God's spokesperson.

Another way lack of critical reflection could indicate a failure to integrate primary and secondary processes is attribution of charismatic manifestations to the Spirit without question. Most of those interviewed expressed not only the need to discern such manifestations, but indicated that they did this in practice, but at times there was an automatic equation of such manifestations with the Spirit's leading. Allison illustrates this tendency to hold charismatic manifestations in such high regard that this kind of automatic identification is made.

Inability to integrate positive and negative dimensions into one's self and object images. This criterion produces the most evidence for pathological rather than creatively regressive qualities in common Pentecostal discernment and decision-making practices. For instance, one can point to a struggle to integrate negative aspects of the self in both Brad and Fernando. One can also point to an inability to integrate negative dimensions into the God image of some informants.

In Chapter 4 we noted how Brad's decision to lead the song in the service became an opportunity for the congregation to incorporate certain negative experiences. But did this decision indicate any transformation of self or object images for Brad? Brad recounted personal changes from a focus on doing to being, and from emotionalism to relationship. This suggests some reworking of images of self and God, but these reworkings were incomplete; there was still much emphasis on doing, as the remarks about 'proving' himself reveal. And while the language of relationship over emotionalism indicates some growth in his relationship with the God image, one is not sure that he has been able satisfactorily to incorporate negative aspects into his image of self. He expressed some sense of 'peace' with himself and his failure, but he went on to state that he would title the current chapter of his life as 'Lost. Lost, trying to find out if I have completely wasted a ministry God entrusted me with. That is hard to deal with.' While Brad's decision to remain at King's Avenue to 'prove' himself shows a willingness to face his failure, his report that he does not think about his childhood much 'because it was so negative', also indicates a tendency simply to deny or avoid negative aspects of his experience.

Fernando showed a similar struggle to integrate his 'humanness' into his image of self. His tendency to pride must be split off from his more spiritual motives and actions; he cannot see God having any dealings with this aspect of his nature.

The inability to incorporate negative aspects into object images is evident in the presence of 'primitive idealizations' of the God image by some informants. Primitive idealization refers to the inability to see anything bad in one's objects. Some indication that God was experienced as a primitive idealization was evident in the reluctance or inability of some to answer a question regarding what they disliked about God. Allison indicated some reluctance before giving her answer.

> It is so hard to say what I don't like about God. I guess from a human standpoint I get tired and feel compelled to minister to others. I would like to say, 'I am too tired, God'. I hesitate to say that when He does so much for us.

Others indicate a similar reluctance before going ahead and answering. After voicing that she did not like the fact that God allows children to suffer (naming a friend's child), one person indicated that she does not think about such things much lest she 'really get to not liking' God. Two others, both retired ministers, could not answer the question at all. (While this suggests the presence of primitive idealizations for these three people, it should be noted that others had no difficulty answering this question.)

One concludes that not all discernment and decision making appears to be creative regression. Nevertheless, this study proposes that some discernment and decision making, particularly those means of discernment that rely on things 'feeling right', do generally exhibit the qualities of creative regression.

Evidence of Creative Regression

This section will present two examples of discernment and decision making that appear to qualify as creative regressions. Fernando's decision to write his letter of repentance is an illustration of the recapture of affective dimensions of knowing (primary process thought) that enhances present functioning by attempting to integrate it with the secondary process. And Gwen's decision to remain in her marriage is an illustration of the recapture and reworking of images of God and self in ways that enhance her present functioning. Both of these decisions were made on the basis of a deeply felt sense of rightness.

Fernando and the recapture of primary process thought. Discernment by means of persistent internal feelings (a deeply felt sense of rightness) is a means of accessing the primary process and making it available for decision making. Fernando's inspiration and decision come as he is praying, an activity that exhibits the quality of 'priming work' (Harrison 1984) as he ponders over what he knows, what is yet to be known and done regarding his ministry. He is opening himself to the primary process by this means (Ulanov and Ulanov 1989). Pentecostal worship, along with reflection on various Pentecostal traditions, can be understood as a kind of priming work that precedes the creatively regressive dimensions of discernment and decision making, as well as participating in the ability of religious symbols to recapture primary process thought (Jones 1991). Here Fernando's experience of being led by the Spirit is touching something deep in the core of the human personality, something that cannot be tapped by more rational, verbal expressions. These deeper resources of the human spirit/psyche enrich discernment and decision making beyond strictly rational calculation to include elusive factors of feeling, intuition and unconscious processes.

There is an attempt to integrate the knowledge gained in this state with secondary reflection through consultation with others about his feelings and the letter. Similarly Gwen's consultation with a friend about the feeling she could leave Brad is a way to integrate discernment by things feeling right with secondary reflection.[2]

2.   Sheila's claims to special insight also indicate sporadic and partial attempts at integration of primary and secondary processes. At times her insight seemed confirmed, but the fact that it came after the alleged events makes it hard to assess the true nature of the claimed insight. At other times she would share her concern generated by such insights but she did not always reflect upon the person's reception of

Gwen and the reworking of self and object images. The recapture and reworking of self–object images is seen in Gwen's changing understanding of God and how the leading of the Spirit is discerned. Her movement away from fleeces to discernment that is more ego controlled, more inner directed, is growth for her. This increase in ego control is evident in the awareness of choices she can make.

The recapture and reworking of self and object images recalls Winnicott's notion of transitional space, a psychical area in which one can retrieve past relationships for strength or reworking. In this space one's relationship with God and God's world can be transformed in creative and healthy ways. For Gwen the need to discern and decide attendant to her marital problems creates a 'challenge to the cohesiveness and coherence of...her sense of self' (McDargh 1983) that opens up a transitional space in which images of God and self undergo change. Gwen's image of God changes from one in which God is quick to punish and does not really like her to one in which God is experienced as more loving and forgiving.[3] This new image of God is instrumental in

her concern. Following a dream about a minister and a woman other than his wife, Sheila went to talk with him after seeing him and the woman together in town.

> So I went to the minister's house one day and asked if I could tell him something. I said, 'I have been praying for you because I feel Satan is out to ruin your ministry, your family and your marriage'. He looked at me with the oddest look and then said, 'Thank you'. [Interviewer: Did you tell him anything specific?] No, I just told him I had felt prompted to pray for him. He knew when I said, 'ministry, family, and marriage'. It is weird, it makes you feel strange.

Going to the minister shows courage and a capacity to subject her insights to some degree of social verification.

The case of Sheila's check writing for the groceries also is interesting at this point despite the problems elaborated above. Here Sheila seems to have an insight not arrived at by normal secondary processes but known at some deeper level. There appears to be a kind of internal dialogue that tries to make this available to secondary reflection. Her willingness to trust this insight is aided by recapturing strength from an earlier object image.

> It was like the most gentle calming (pause). It was like when you are little and you fall down and your dad picks you up and says, 'Honey, it is going to be all right'. But it was almost like an audible voice. It was warm, gentle. I said, 'Okay, fine' and I went and got what I needed.

3.   It is of interest to note that Gwen's changing image of God came after a time in which her relationships with her parents had undergone significant change. This is exactly the order Jones (1991) outlines: changes in relationship with one's parents precedes changes in one's image of God.

changes in her own self image that allow her to incorporate negative aspects of herself into that image and still feel loved.

> One thing I have learned recently is that you have to be totally honest with God and in being totally honest and in getting away from the facade where you hide from yourself, the image of 'this is how I am' [i.e. as an excusing destructive behavior], and get out from behind that and to be brutally honest with God in what you have done. 'God, I did that and I blew it and you will have to forgive me and pick me up and let's go on from here.' I guess that is part of learning the father image of God; that He is not the old man in the sky with a stick and that He really loves you and it is okay when you mess up.

Her increased dependency on God is a regressive behavior that returns her to the present more able to cope. She finds a strength in this image not present to her before. She is cast back on the 'ground of her being' (Tillich 1951) and is empowered to challenge church doctrine or, as it turned out, to work toward restoration with Brad.[4]

But could Gwen's decision to stay in her marriage as God's best for her be a rationalization rather than growth in self-understanding? Certainly the denominational teaching on divorce would provide strong, perhaps unconscious impetus to interpret the Spirit's direction as one of confirming the church's teaching. The need to rationalize her decision would also be more apt to arise in a context in which she felt she had no other choice; Spirit leading would then provide the excuse for staying. In this instance, however, Gwen's description indicates that she believed she had real choices; that a sense of being trapped by denominational teachings had passed. Her struggle to discern and decide shows evidence of opening up possibilities rather than closing them off. Her recognition of the pain in staying (there would have been pain in leaving also) is a realistic assessment of her conditions. While no human behavior is without some ambiguity, and growth in one area may be coupled with lapses

---

4. The notion that the Spirit empowers is also a way that Spirit leading influences and changes the way in which people see themselves and their world; 'shy' people feel empowered to speak, 'weak' people feel empowered to resist pressure to conform. Brad indicated this type of change ('before I received the Holy Spirit I was introverted, shy . . . The Lord gave me a boldness . . . where I had been afraid') as did Ed Rollins, the minister of music:

> I was involved in sports and music and in those you have different forces coming against you; friends who want you to drink and such and it [the Holy Spirit] was a stabilizing force and also a directing force.

in another (Moseley 1991), on the whole there seems to be growth in her understandings of God, her self, and her relationship with Brad. She shows evidence of incorporating negative images of her self as emotionally distant and controlling in relationships into her self-understanding and of being opened to a world beyond her previous limits.

Before concluding this chapter, it will be instructive to note further connections between transitional phenomena (Winnicott 1971) and discernment and decision making as creative regression. This connection can be seen in several ways. First, one might say that Spirit leading creates transitional space by means of rituals that loosen boundaries between God and self, creating an atmosphere or space in which negative self and object images can be dealt with. In an attempt to move beyond the impasse of whether speaking in tongues is pathological or non-pathological behavior, Castelein (1984) argues that speaking in tongues should be understood as a transitional phenomenon, creating a liminal space (Turner 1969) in which a person can experiment and 'play with the sacred to see how close or how distant one wishes to remain' (Castelein 1984: 58). Castelein sees speaking in tongues as analogous to laughing and crying in that all three are non-semantic utterances that allow creation of the liminal state in which life can be re-oriented toward meaning and greater value. Another observer of Pentecostal behavior (Baer 1976), although not working from an object relations perspective, has similarly concluded that speaking in tongues functions to contribute to a playful dimension in worship that

> permits the analytical mind—the focused, objectifying dimensions of man's intellect—to rest, thus freeing other dimensions of the person, what we might loosely refer to as man's spirit, for a deeper openness to divine reality (Baer 1976; 152).

Baer sees Catholic liturgy and Quaker silence as other religious behaviors that permit a similar freedom. Certain rituals connected with Spirit leading allow experiences of a transitional space in which images of God and self can be recaptured and reworked without threat.

Loewald's (1978, 1988) argument about the power of religious symbols to open one up to the unitive sensibilities of the primary process makes a similar point also derived from Winnicott's concept of transitional phenomena. While Loewald does not accept Winnicott's notion that the infant moves from subjectivity to objectivity aided by transitional objects (he argues that the infant moves from a state prior to the differentiation of subjectivity and objectivity to a state when these come into being), he does see transitional objects as helping bridge the gap from 'the ineffable to the effable'.

Rizzuto (1979), in a study exploring the process by which one comes to have a personal belief in God, indicates another way that transitional phenomena are related to Spirit leading by means of the image of God that guides and informs these experiences. Rizzuto shows how 'God' images may be understood as a special kind of 'object representation', images in the psyche of significant people with whom one has had relationships ('interlocked memories of others and oneself'), made up of bits and pieces of memories of relationship with real parents, wished for or feared parents, or other significant relatives or persons. Unlike Freud, who saw the wish for God arising out of the oedipal conflict with the jealous father simultaneous with the desire for a caring father, Rizzuto posits that the representation of God has its beginnings in the pre-oedipal stages of development along with other representations the child is constructing. This is the time of transitional objects and spaces; thus 'God' begins as a transitional object. Most transitional objects are 'gradually allowed to be decathected, so that in the course of years [they] become not so much forgotten as relegated to limbo' (Winnicott 1971: 5). God, too,

> may seem to lose meaning, paradoxically, on account of being rejected, ignored, suppressed, or found temporarily unnecessary. Nonetheless, as is true of all other objects, God cannot be fully repressed. As a transitional object representation he is always potentially available for further accept-ance or further rejection... In summary, then, throughout life God remains a transitional object (Rizzuto 1979: 178-79).

This retrieval of the God representation provides a continuity with reality enabling one to return to the present enriched and strengthened.

Meissner's (1984) argument that 'religion' broadly conceived is transitional reinforces the idea of a relationship between Spirit leading experiences and transitional phenomena since all religious experience has a transitional quality. Meissner builds upon Winnicott's notion that transitional phenomena lead to the capacity to share cultural experience.

> Winnicott notes that there is a direct development from the appearance of transitional phenomena to the capacity for play and from isolated play to shared playing, and hence from shared playing to the capacity for cultural experience (Meissner 1984: 170).

The connection comes in the infant's ability to use transitional pheno-mena to lay the basis for an emerging capacity for symbolism.

Basic to the cultural experience is the manner in which man transforms or transfigures his environment and the objects it contains by attributing to objects, shapes, and figures in the real world a symbolic value and meaning. Through culture, man introduces the external realm into the inner world of personal significance (Meissner 1984: 173).

Meissner argues that religion partakes of the character of transitional phenomena and like all transitional phenomena achieves its psychic reality in the potential space of illusory experience. But here illusion is understood as something which nourishes the human spirit; illusion allows life creative expression.

The man without imagination, without the capacity for play or for creative illusion, is condemned to a sterile world of harsh facts without color or variety, without the continual enrichment of man's creative capacities (Meissner 1984: 177).

In this way, Meissner sees many aspects of religion as transitional in nature.

Bollas (1987) further elaborates the relationship between transitional phenomena and religious experience. According to Bollas, following Winnicott, the child's first awareness is not of an object but of a relationship, the mother–child dyad. In providing the infant the catalyst for integrating its experiences (of body, pain, pleasure, sensory data), 'the mother helps to integrate the infant's being (instinctual, cognitive, affective, environmental)' (1987: 14), and this relationship paves the way for religious experiences. Bollas terms this relationship a 'transformational object' because from it the child learns to transform its experience into knowledge of self and world. This powerful relationship influences one throughout life and its relationship to religious experience is seen during times of crisis when people look for a transformational object to comfort them and help them integrate new experiences. The discovery of new transformational objects 'in another person, or an overpowering piece of music, or an evocative poem or novel, or the awesomeness of nature' are experienced as 'moments of ecstasy, what Bollas calls the "aesthetic"' (Jones 1991: 119-20).

Conclusion

This chapter has shown that while not all discernment and decision making are creative regressions some are, providing warrant for understanding these practices in non-pathological ways. In particular, discernment by means of 'things feeling right' is shown to exhibit qualities of creative regression. The connection of the discernment criterion of things 'feeling right' to early self development suggests that one need not automatically distrust this criterion as some have suggested (see Chapter 2), though neither can it be understood to legitimate a non-critical criterion of 'if it feels good or feels right, it must be the Spirit'. The analysis of creative regressions also provides some criteria by which such practices can be evaluated; namely, (1) whether they lessen ego control by blurring the boundaries between self and object, and (2) whether they enhance present psychic functioning, either through making affective dimensions of knowing available for decision making or permitting the recapture and reworking of early, formative, and hence powerful, object relations.

This chapter has also pointed out relationships, sometimes unconscious, between early childhood and Spirit leading experiences, both in terms of image of the God who leads and the types of Spirit leading experiences people have. Allison's use of fleeces and the emotional distance she experienced with her father, Fernando's primary discernment criterion of retrospection and the God who kept his distance, Sheila's tendencies to dissociative behavior and her 'two personality' father, Gwen's changing relationships with her parents and new images of God, and Brad's struggles to incorporate negative aspects of his self and his tendency to forget his negative childhood all illustrate relationships between childhood experiences and experiences of Spirit leading.

Chapter 6

PENTECOSTAL DISCERNMENT AND DECISION MAKING
FROM THE PERSPECTIVE OF PAUL TILLICH'S THEOLOGY

Introduction

This chapter uses the theology of Paul Tillich (1951, 1957, 1963) to provide theological resources for understanding and evaluating Pentecostal discernment and decision making. Tillich's theology becomes the vehicle by which these practices are brought into a mutually critical dialogue with the 'Christian fact' (Tracy 1975). This articulation of elements from the Christian tradition provides a theological 'vision' (cf. Browning 1991) for evaluation of these practices. This chapter argues that certain types of discernment and decision making are 'revelatory', times in which one experiences a sense of awe and empowering connection to the source or ground of all being. More specifically, this chapter argues that the discernment criterion of things feeling right is a mediating symbol of the divine Presence, a revelatory moment in which one is 'shaken, transformed, and grasped by ultimate concern' (or that which confronts one unconditionally). It thus adds to the psychological evaluation of the previous chapter a theological assessment of the value of these practices for the individual and the church.

Overview of Tillich's Theological System[1]

Tillich saw the task of theology as one of relating the message of Christian truth to each generation. There was a particular need for this in modern culture which he saw as suffering from a dualistic view of reality

1. This section draws widely from Tillich's *Systematic Theology* (1951, 1957, 1963) as well as his *The Courage to Be* (1952). The following sections in the *Systematic Theology* undergird this summary: Vol. I (1951): 11-14, 163-201; Volume II (1957): 29-47, 165-68; and Volume III (1963): 30-43.

exacerbated by certain trends in technology and philosophical rationalism.[2]

> For Tillich, one of the most disastrous characteristics of the modern cul-
> tural situation is its dualism, its universal and apparently self-evident
> assumption that reality is split into fundamentally unconnected blocks or
> areas. There is a dualism between us and God: we are ourselves, and God
> is a vast personal self; a dualism between us as personal selves and
> 'nature', the inorganic world around us and in us; a dualism between body
> and psyche; and in culture between natural science and the humanities
> (Gilkey 1990: 24).

In such a world there is little or no perceived connection between
knowledge and eros, matter and spirit, reason and its divine ground.
Rational thought and control ('technical' knowledge) are overvalued and
non-cognitive, affective (eros) dimensions of existence are mistrusted.[3]
By means of the language of 'ontology' Tillich sought to overcome the
dualism between knower and known, between self and world by pene-
trating below the differences to grasp the essential unity of all things
(Gilkey 1990: 25).

Ontology and the Unity of All Things

For Tillich theology has to do with what concerns one 'ultimately', and
that which is of ultimate concern for humans is their existence, their
'being or non being'. The basic question of existence (the ontological
question), 'Why is there something instead of nothing?', arises in some-

---

2.   Tillich is not the only one to note such dualisms (cf. Bernstein 1983), but
Tillich is the point of entry for this chapter since he will also be used to suggest ways
for overcoming the dualism. The more general reasons for choosing Tillich were
outlined in Chapter 3.

3.   Gilkey (1990) summarizes Tillich's argument regarding the relationship
between the knower and the known:

> Without commitment or eros to truth, scientific objectivity is impossible; without clear
> and valued ends, means destroy themselves; without presuppositions held by intuitive
> vision or faith, thinking cannot even begin much less persevere. The problem is not, for
> Tillich, that modern culture has separated *reason* as logical and scientific thinking from
> emotions and ends; it is rather that reason has been defined as purely the former, as
> what he terms 'technical reason' (*ST* I: 53-54, 56, 72-74). Thus, stripped of commitment
> and valuing, reason is estranged from itself. There can be no objective thought, no
> scientific inquiry, without commitment to that mode of thinking, a commitment that
> neither the promise of grants nor even of fame can dissolve: objectivity itself depends
> upon the love of it, that is to say, on intense subjectivity. Creative thought...thus
> combines emotive and decisive elements with logical and empirical elements. This is
> what Tillich calls 'ontological thought' (1990: 36-37).

thing of a 'metaphysical shock', the existential recognition that one could not be; there could be nothing.

But such a question already presupposes an asking subject and an object asked about. This self-world structure is part of the givenness of human existence and part of what is to be transcended if humans are to grasp the essential unity of all things. The self–world structure is experienced both negatively and positively. Negatively, existence is experienced as estrangement while positively it is experienced as freedom or selfhood. These positive and negative poles of existence are illustrated by the biblical story of the fall for Tillich. Existence (actuality) is contrasted with essence (the ideal or possibility). Tillich sees a three step movement in the formation of the self that begins with a state of 'dreaming innocence', not an actual or historical state, but a way to refer to an ideal state ('essence'). However, one's actual state ('existence') is experienced as estrangement and for Tillich, the story of the fall is a paradigm for understanding estrangement. In the state of dreaming innocence there comes the point of decision for humanity; a choice whether to actualize one's potentialities in freedom or to maintain one's state of innocence. With the decision comes the awareness of one as a decider and a recognition that one could not be. Thus the choice to actualize one's potential becomes a choice against the possibility of non-being; the self is formed in the process of decision making. For Tillich, the fall is therefore fortunate and also necessary for existence.

Having made the transition from essence to existence, the question becomes one of how to respond to this existence and the questions that arise out of it. Estrangement is experienced 'negatively' because one senses that one is estranged from that to which one essentially belongs and to which one seeks to reunite, that is, to 'essential being'. All things participate in being but humans participate in being in a self-conscious way.

This capacity to stand outside oneself and observe oneself and one's world (self-transcendence) is what distinguishes the human from other modes of being. Being a self means being separated in some way from everything else so as to look at it. When Tillich says that 'man has a world' (1963: 38), he refers to the human's ability to transcend particular environments and see a unity of these converging in oneself as a center of initiative and decision making. Yet to be truly a self is to be aware that one also belongs to that at which one looks; there is no self-consciousness without world consciousness and vice versa.

Human's experience being through certain structures of the mind called 'categories'. These categories are indispensable prerequisites without which there could be no awareness of being. They include 'time', 'space', 'causality', and 'substance'. In addition, Tillich distinguishes 'elements' for the expression of being. The elements are dialectical relationships which Tillich terms dynamics/form, freedom/destiny, and individuation/participation. The poles of each element define the quality of the other. Form refers to structure and actuality while dynamics indicates possibilities. Freedom/destiny refers to the relationship between expressions of the self as agent and those unchangeable aspects of the self given by one's birth into a particular time and place. For Tillich, humanity is a combination of freedom and destiny. Forces have shaped each person, yet humans are free because they can stand outside of themselves and observe themselves. Insofar as humans are able to transcend any limiting aspect of the world through conscious thought, they are free from determination by it; humans are freed from their finitude by being aware of it. Thus, for Tillich, having a destiny does not contradict freedom, because humans can realize their destinies. Individuation/participation expresses the dialectical relationship between individual selves and the communities in which they live; that is, between autonomy and social relationships. All being expresses itself in these three polar elements in greater or lesser degrees according to Tillich.

But because humans have the ability to see beyond the present, finite limits to other possibilities, they experience anxiety, a threat that their being may cease. The threat can be manifest in death or in meaninglessness. One's response to the threat of non-being involves what Tillich (1952) calls courage. Courage can be manifested in several ways. It can be manifested as the courage to be as a part, attaching oneself to something greater than oneself (e.g. ideals, or one's country) while recognizing that there are no guarantees that these commitments are the right ones; or it may be manifested in the courage to be as a self, acknowledging oneself as a center of initiative and decision and taking responsibility for one's decisions; or it may be manifested in the courage to be as acceptance, affirming being in spite of the threat of non-being. Here courage is related to faith, which is accepting that one is accepted by Being despite the gulf between finitude and infinitude. Said another way, faith is being grasped by ultimate concerns (1963: 130). As Jones (1991) summarizes:

To experience God, then, is to move from the experience of ontological shock—the dread that comes when we confront the precariousness of life—to the realization of the power of being itself, the experience of the source that sustains existence in the face of nothingness and provides the basis for the courage to live in the face of life's inevitable uncertainty (1991: 127).

The Method of Correlation

Tillich's contribution to the task of relating theology and culture was one of correlating theological 'answers' to the 'questions' posed by modern culture. His three volume *Systematic Theology* (1951, 1957, 1963) is the most extensive illustration of his method of 'correlation'.

In using the method of correlation, systematic theology proceeds in the following way: it makes an analysis of the human situation out of which existential questions arise, and it demonstrates that the symbols used in the Christian message are the answers to these questions (1951: 62).

By expressing the message of traditional Christian symbols in contemporary language Tillich sought to provide theological answers to the 'existential' questions that arise from the limits of human existence. To achieve his goal Tillich organized his work around five major correlations: reason and revelation, being and God, existence and Christ, life and the Spirit, and history and the Kingdom. Unhjem (1981) has summarized these relationships:

Questions about the powers and limits of man's reason prepare him for answers given in revelation; questions about the nature of being lead to answers revealing God as the ground of being; questions about the meaning of existence are answered by the New Being made manifest in Jesus Christ; questions about the ambiguities of human experience point to answers revealing the presence of the Holy Spirit in the life process; and questions about human destiny and the meaning of history find their answers in the vision of the Kingdom of God (1981: 409).

Revelation in Tillich's Theology

Since discernment and decision making are concerned with how one can know the Divine Presence and its guidance, the correlation most suggestive for understanding these practices is that of reason and revelation, particularly as this correlation is enlarged by the correlation of life and the Spirit.

Revelation Defined

Revelation is a richly nuanced term for Tillich. He defines it initially as the 'manifestation of that which concerns us ultimately' (1951: 110), by which he means to point to its connection with the basic question of existence. Revelation is commonly understood to be the making known of something that has been hidden. For Tillich, however, what becomes known in revelation is not ordinary knowledge, not knowledge about things, even if such knowledge was believed to have come by divine impartation. Rather what is known in revelation is awareness of one's relatedness to the source or ground of all being. Such occurrences are characterized by both awe and elation and are said to unite 'mystery' and 'ecstasy'.

Mystery is the 'objective' or 'giving' side of revelation; that which revelation makes manifest in reality. The quality of mystery which is made manifest in revelation is an awareness that 'being is and nonbeing is not'; that is, the power of being is at work overcoming the power of nonbeing. This is of 'ultimate concern' for humans.

> The genuine mystery appears when reason is driven beyond itself to its 'ground and abyss', to that which 'precedes' reason, to the fact that 'being is and nonbeing is not' (Parmenides), to the original fact (*Ur-Tatsache*) that there is *something* and not *nothing*. We can call this the 'negative side' of the mystery... The positive side of the mystery—which includes the negative side—becomes manifest in actual revelation. Here the mystery appears... as the power of being, conquering nonbeing... as our ultimate concern (1951: 110).

But that which is manifest must be received. There must be a receiving state of reason within the person that corresponds to the giving side of revelation; without someone to receive revelation in experience, no revelation has occurred. This receiving state Tillich describes as 'ecstasy', a term he insists is worth redeeming from its misconception as referring simply to emotional excess. Citing its root meaning as that of 'standing outside', he uses the term to refer to a state of reason in which the subject–object dichotomy of knower and known is transcended or overcome.

> 'Ecstasy' ('standing outside one's self') points to a state of mind which is extraordinary in the sense that the mind transcends its ordinary situation. Ecstasy is not a negation of reason; it is the state of mind in which reason is beyond itself, that is beyond its subject–object structure. In being beyond itself, reason does not deny itself. 'Ecstatic reason' remains reason (1951: 111-12).

Ecstatic reason is a way to speak about the mind grasping the unity of all things as it transcends the subject–object dichotomy of cognitive reason. Tillich's distinction between 'technical' and 'ontological' reason is another way he speaks of the disjuncture versus unity between knower and known. Technical reason is knowledge for the sake of controlling and ordering reality. It reduces reason to its cognitive dimension and relegates the non-cognitive dimensions to 'the irrelevance of pure subjectivity' (1951: 73). Tillich rejects this one dimensional understanding; reason is not to be limited to the exercise of control. Ontological reason, the 'structure of the mind which enables the mind to grasp and shape reality' (1951: 75), expresses the relationship between knower and known in more holistic terms. Ontological reason unites cognitive, aesthetic, practical and technical ways of knowing. It is not a 'subjective' knowing in contrast to the 'objective' knowing of technical reason but a grasping of the relationship between reason and its ground,[4] of understanding the 'depth of reason'.

> The depth of reason is the expression of something that is not reason, but which precedes reason and is manifest through it. Reason in both its objective and subjective structures points to something which appears in these structures but which transcends them in power and meaning (1951: 79).

This 'something' that 'precedes' reason is spoken of metaphorically as the 'ground of all being'.[5] Ecstatic reason grasps one's relatedness to

---

4. From a different perspective, Gerkin (1991) speaks of pastoral wisdom as the ability to assess 'the particular at hand by its relationship to the whole of things'. Drawing upon the work of Gadamer (1975), Gerkin argues for an 'aesthetic hermeneutics' in which

> the exercise of judgment involves a kind of mutually critical dialogical relationship between the particular instance of human experience at hand and an aesthetic knowledge of the whole. It is not fully governed by principles of logic and reason, but entails the exercise of what Gadamer, following the pre-Kantian humanistic tradition—a tradition originating in Greek culture that had powerful influence on early Christian history—speaks of as taste. To exercise taste is to have the imaginative capacity to discern what is fitting in relation to the whole of things as that whole has been seen by the best wisdom of a community's tradition (1991: 69).

In this aesthetic hermeneutics, the good, the true, the right, are discerned through a knowing that transcends the rational alone. Of course, the biblical narratives form part of the 'whole' of a Christian community's tradition and thus, contribute to its aesthetic judgment.

5. Tillich notes other metaphors that could be used to speak of the relationship of reason to its ground:

this ground and the concomitant relatedness of all things. Again, ecstasy is not a negation of reason but an overcoming of the limits of the subject–object dichotomy of 'reason' so that the 'mystery of being' which is manifested may be received. What one receives in the ecstatic state is not knowledge about things or a body of supernaturally conveyed information, but 'revelation', a special kind of knowing concerned with ultimates. One experiences the reality of being overcoming non-being.

But something more is received in this experience: one's relationship to the mystery becomes a matter of experience as well.

> Something more becomes known of the mystery after it has become mani-
> fest in revelation. First, its reality has become a matter of experience.
> Second, our relationship to it has become a matter of experience. Both of
> these are cognitive elements. But revelation does not dissolve the mystery
> into knowledge. Nor does it add anything directly to the totality of our
> ordinary knowledge, namely, to our knowledge about the subject–object
> structure of reality (1951: 109).

Tillich further elucidates the human response to mystery through the terms 'spirit' and 'Spirit'. In revelation one experiences one's connectedness to the Spiritual Presence or divine Spirit.

> The spirit, a dimension of finite life, is driven into a successful self-tran-
> scendence; it is grasped by something ultimate and unconditional. It is still
> the same human spirit; it remains what it is, but at the same time, it goes
> out of itself under the impact of the divine Spirit. 'Ecstasy' is the classical
> term for this state of being grasped by the Spiritual presence (1963: 112).

Tillich notes that the relationship between spirit and Spirit is usually defined 'metaphorically' along the lines of the divine Spirit indwelling and working within the human spirit. This encounter is experienced as both 'shock' and 'uplifting'.

> It could be called the 'substance' which appears in the rational structure, or 'being-
> itself' which is manifest in the *logos* of being, or the 'ground' which is creative in
> every rational creation, or the 'abyss' which cannot be exhausted by any creation or by
> any totality of them, or the 'infinite potentiality of being and meaning' which pours
> into the rational structures of mind and reality, actualizing and transforming them. All
> these terms which point to that which 'precedes' reason have a metaphorical character.
> 'Preceding' is itself metaphorical. This is necessarily so, because if the terms were used
> in their proper sense, they would belong to reason and would not precede it (1951: 79).

While 'only a metaphorical description of the depth of reason is possible', such a multiplex of metaphors also make it difficult to know if Tillich is always referring to the same phenomenon (cf. Thatcher 1978).

In revelation and in the ecstatic experience in which it is received, the onto-logical shock is preserved and overcome at the same time. It is preserved in the annihilating power of the Divine Presence (*mysterium tremendum*) and is overcome in the elevating power of the Divine Presence (*mysterium fascinosum*) (1951: 113).

Metaphorically speaking, in the ecstatic reception of the divine indwelling, the ontological shock, the sense of threat to one's existence, is overcome by this experience of elevating power. In this way revelation is salvational (Tillich 1957: 166-67). Stated differently, what one receives in revelation is an empowering awareness of one's relationship to the ground of being, an awareness that brings healing and wholeness.

The Role of Experience in Revelation
If revelation is not the disclosure of knowledge about things but the elevating sense of one's relationship to the ground of being, Kelsey (1967) has observed that it would seem to be indistinguishable from religious experience. Yet Tillich vigorously resists equating religious experience with revelation. He wants to establish a mediating position between the extremes of Schleiermacher's claim that experience is the source of theology and the neo-orthodox assertion that experience has no role in theology. To do this, he proposes that experience is a 'medium' but not a 'source' of theology (1951: 46).

There are good reasons for maintaining the relationship of experience to revelation, insisting that the receiving side is an integral part of true revelation as Tillich does. Otherwise, as Kelsey (1967) notes, if revelation refers only to the giving side, one has the absurd possibility of something being revealed which no one knows anything about. Revelation comes to one through his or her experience, but the experience does not become a source for knowledge (except in a restricted, dependent sense to be described below).

Yet Tillich is not always consistent in his explanation of the relationship of revelation to knowledge. This inconsistency leads in turn to confusion over the relationship of religious experience to revelation and to knowledge. There also are good reasons for maintaining the distinction between revelation and religious experience. Tillich insists that there is more to revelation than just the 'receiving side' of human experience; there are events that are other than human experience, given from the divine side. Without such a distinction Tillich could not defend the uniqueness of the Christ-event. This was precisely the reason for distinguishing experience as a medium but not a source of revelation: to safeguard the uniqueness of the Christ-event as revelation. The uniqueness of this event in turn safeguarded Christian theology from claims to new knowledge based on the experience of believers.

> If experience is called the medium through which the objective sources are received, this excludes the reliance of the theologian on a possibly post-Christian experience. But it also denies the assertion that experience is a theological source. And, finally, it denies the belief in experiences which, although remaining in the Christian circle, adds some new material to the other sources. Christian theology is based on the unique event Jesus the Christ, and in spite of the infinite meaning of this event it remains *this* event and, as such, the criterion of every religious experience. This event is given to experience and not derived from it (1951: 46).

At this point Tillich's critics have noted a fundamental problem. By maintaining Christian theology's footing in an historical event, as this quotation indicates ('the unique event Jesus the Christ'), Tillich becomes inconsistent in his claim that revelation is not tied to historical or empirical knowledge. As one of his critics observes:

> We noted at the start of this discussion of the relation between revelation and religious experience that Tillich uses the term 'revelation' inconsistently. Usually he uses it to refer to the entire revelatory occurrence, but sometimes he uses it to refer only to the giving side of that occurrence. This inconsistency leads to a serious muddle when Tillich applies his distinction between revelation and religious experience to the occurrence of the original Christian revelatory event (Kelsey 1967: 37).

In connecting ecstatic reason with the historical event of Jesus of Nazareth, Tillich acknowledges a connection, however precarious, between revelation and empirical knowledge.

> If revelation is a constellation of which one element is a particular event [e.g. the life of Jesus of Nazareth] the knowledge of that event by technical reason cannot be completely independent of the knowledge of revelation (Thomas 1963: 54).

The question of the role of experience in theology is an important one and has significant implications for how one understands certain aspects of Pentecostal discernment and decision making. Tillich's proposal that experience be considered a medium but not a source of theology sought to guard against claims that experience conveyed 'knowledge' incompatible with the revelation of Jesus as the Christ. But in the end such a proposal reduces to the question of which traditions are authoritatively allowed to interpret experience.

Gilkey (1990) concludes that what lies at the heart of Tillich's inconsistency is that what appeared to be an attempt at a general theory of revelation, not tied to specific contents, was actually a Christian model of revelation in philosophical clothing. Tillich's attempt to preserve the uniqueness of the Christian revelation is not fully compatible with his attempt to exclude any kind of historical or empirical knowledge from revelation. Emmet (1952) summarizes this frequent criticism of Tillich:

> If it is true that the utterances of the ecstatic reason are simply expressions of 'numinous astonishment' (more like, 'oh, how wonderful!' than like 'Ceasar crossed the Rubicon'), it is true that they do not entail factual assertions. But I cannot help feeling that Tillich is trying to have it both ways... The 'ecstatic' reason finds numinous astonishment and a kind of creative elation and devotion in contemplating certain events. If the events did not occur, the elation can only be a kind of mystical aspiration. If they did occur, then there is more reason to say that the 'ecstatic reason' is not simply expansive feeling, but is a recognition of possibilities concerning what we believe to be ultimately important, linked with events which really happened (Emmet 1952: 212-13).

Tillich's attempt to 'have it both ways' leaves him inextricably mired in inconsistency. If experience is the medium by which revelation comes, then experience of necessity becomes a source for theological reflection along with any knowledge it conveys, however limited. As will become evident, Tillich's inconsistency regarding the relationship of revelation to empirical knowledge has implications for how one understands certain aspects of discernment and decision making.

Criteria for Evaluating Revelation
In spite of this inconsistency, Tillich's understanding of revelation suggests two criteria for evaluating purported instances of revelatory experiences and for distinguishing true from false occurrences: (1) true revelation conjoins ecstasy and reason, and (2) true revelation does not confuse finite media with their infinite ground. The discussion below indicates the specifically Christian origins and overtones of the second criterion. Tillich's lack of consistency over what is revealed in revelation leaves some question as to whether this last criterion ought to be considered a criterion only for Christian revelation rather than for revelation in general.

Conjoining ecstasy and reason. The reception of the mystery in ecstasy does not destroy reason, according to Tillich; ecstatic reason remains reason. By contrast demonic possession is said to be a destruction of reason.

> While demonic possession destroys the rational structure of the mind, divine ecstasy preserves and elevates it, although transcending it (1951: 114).

In a remark that recalls the argument that creative regressions show no loss of discrete ego boundaries and makes primary process thinking available to the secondary process, Tillich further states that 'divine ecstasy does not violate the wholeness of the rational mind, while demonic possession weakens or destroys it' (1951: 114). In true revelation, reason or rational control (cf. ego control) is not negated but joined to ecstasy (cf. integrating primary process with secondary reflection) in more holistic knowing. Such ecstatic experiences are not to be confused with experiences that simply provide 'subjective intoxication' either. In contrast to intoxication, 'an attempt to escape...[the] burden of personal centeredness and responsibility and cultural rationality', ecstasy manifests a 'spiritual productivity and Spiritual creativity' (1963: 119). Moreover,

> The criterion which must be used to decide whether an extraordinary state of the mind is ecstasy, created by the Spiritual Presence, or subjective intoxication is the manifestation of the creativity in the former and the lack of it in the latter. The use of this criterion is not without risk, but it is the only valid criterion the church can employ in 'judging the Spirit' (1963: 120).

Tillich's comments on the nature of this creativity focus on the ability to grasp the unity between all things under divine ecstasy. 'A union of subject and object has taken place in which the independent existence of each is overcome; new unity is created' (1963: 119).

Not confusing the finite with the infinite. True revelations do not confuse finite media of the Divine Presence with the actual Divine Presence. Tillich's insistence that experience be treated as medium and not source is one way by which he tries to avoid such confusion in his own system. The substitution of anything finite for the infinite is idolatry and demonic.

> Idolatry is the perversion of a genuine revelation; it is the elevation of the medium of revelation to the dignity of the revelation itself... The claim of anything finite to be final in its own right is demonic (1951: 133-34).

This criterion draws from two arguments in Tillich. One is his concern that 'God', that which stands behind all symbolic representations of the divine ground, never be equated with its symbols. This is the meaning of Tillich's oft quoted reference to the 'God above the God of theism' (1952). The second argument behind this criterion is Tillich's understanding of the Christ-event as a final revelation. A revelation is said to be final if it has the power to negate itself without losing itself. In a final revelation the medium surrenders itself to point to that which is beyond itself and in which it is grounded. Jesus as the Christ is said to be such a revelation, but Christianity is not.

> Christianity, without being final itself, witnesses to the final revelation. Christianity, as Christianity is neither final nor universal. But that to which it witnesses is final and universal (1951: 134).

Thus Tillich derives from a specifically Christian model of revelation a criterion that is proposed as a criterion for evaluating general revelation. While this creates some problem in terms of whether this criterion may validly be applied in contexts other than Christian revelation, the rooting of this study in such a context points to its usefulness here.

At the practical level, revelation that does not confuse the finite with the infinite is said to point beyond the individual receiving it. As an evaluative guide true revelation embraces the whole community. Although revelation is always received in the 'depth of a personal life, in its struggles, decisions, and self-surrender', Tillich states,

> No individual receives revelation for himself. He receives it for his group, and implicitly for all groups, for mankind as a whole (1951: 127-28).

Before moving to an analysis of Pentecostal discernment and decision making as revelatory, one further comment needs to be made regarding the question of how Tillich distinguishes a revelation as specifically Christian. His answer to this question introduces a distinction between 'original' and 'dependent' revelation. Original revelation refers to constellations of ecstasy and mystery that have never appeared in conjunction before; Jesus as the Christ is considered such a revelation. Other correlations of mystery and ecstasy may be dependent on such original revelations and the church's continuing experience of Jesus as the Christ over the centuries illustrates such dependent revelation. Dependent revelation, like original revelation, conjoins mystery and ecstasy to shake and transform individuals and communities and to make unconditional claims. It is not enough to point to the testimony of Jesus in the

Scriptures and call it dependent revelation for Tillich; there must be a receiving side here as well. One might say that for Tillich, 'Christian' revelations are those in which one's tradition-based knowledge of Jesus as the Christ becomes existentially real for persons and communities.

To summarize, a revelatory experience may be defined as one in which one is grasped by one's relatedness to the ground of being and the concomitant relatedness of all things, a relationship experienced as ecstatic and transforming and thus as empowering and healing. The two criteria for distinguishing true revelation, the conjoining of ecstasy and reason and the distinction between finite media and their infinite ground, are seen to include further evaluative elements: a negative element that forbids the avoiding of reason and responsibility, and a positive element that embraces others beyond the individual receiving the experience and ultimately God.

Discernment and Decision Making as Revelatory Occurrences

This section examines reported Spirit leading experiences in the light of the above criteria. The case material is important in this regard because it raises certain issues critical to a better understanding and evaluation of these practices: (1) What is the relationship between Spirit leading experiences and early childhood experiences, particularly those experiences that help form the God image and shape a person's character? (2) What is the significance of the psychological origins of Spirit leading behavior for determining the value imputed to these experiences? Human behavior is complex, especially when it is also 'religious'; case material helps one grasp the richness of this complexity.

To call Pentecostal discernment and decision making revelation would require that what is being conveyed in these experiences is not a special kind of knowledge concerned with things, but an awareness of one's relationship to the source of all being. The deeply felt sense that things are right would be interpreted as such a moment of being grasped by ultimate concern. Insofar as revelation makes the unconditional power of being to overcome nonbeing a reality in one's personal experience, the human spirit is empowered or elevated; the Pentecostal Christian is not merely made to *feel* good, but is strengthened and sustained for daily living through these experiences. The remainder of this chapter proceeds by returning to the case material to examine the revelatory and non-revelatory aspects of these practices and to answer the above questions.

Allison

How do Allison's experiences of Spirit leading measure up to the criteria for revelatory occurrences? As noted earlier, her chief means for discernment and decision making were the use of fleeces and certain feelings associated with charismatic manifestations. Is there a conjoining of ecstasy and reason in these practices such that reason and responsibility are affirmed and a clear distinction is maintained between the finite media of revelation and their infinite reference?

Fleeces are an intriguing phenomenon from the perspectives of this study. Are fleeces an 'ecstatic' abandonment of technical control and a transcending of practical reason such that they provide the opportunity for a revelatory experience in Tillich's sense? And does their use illustrate a primal trust that taps the kind of psychic resources outlined in Chapter 5? There was an obvious sincerity and trustfulness connected to their use in Allison's self reports, and in her willingness to accept the fleece's answer regardless of outcome which may initially suggest such an interpretation.

One must begin by acknowledging that fleeces cannot be condemned outright as excluding the possibility for revelatory occurrences; any experience, according to Tillich, has the potential to mediate revelation, to bring a sense of one's connectedness to the ground of being. However, the use of fleeces is not without problems. Chapter 5 has noted the possibility, if not probability, of certain rationalizations in the use of fleeces. A remark by Allison on the usefulness of fleeces for 'times when we weren't sure even when we wanted it', points to occasions when reason did not play a prominent role in the decision-making process. The use of fleeces seems to sidestep the responsibility for rational reflection incumbent upon decision making. In light of Tillich's criterion, this would not be a conjoining of ecstasy and reason.

Fleeces also seem to fail the criterion of not confusing finite media with ultimate concerns. At least in all cases reported, fleeces were limited to inquiries regarding specific, finite personal decisions (e.g. whether to buy a particular house or take a particular job) that would appear to have no applicability beyond one's immediate needs. True revelation, however, reaches beyond the one receiving it to shake and transform one's group as well. Identifying the decision to buy a particular house or take a particular job with the divine will is thus to confuse the finite with the infinite. The problem does not lie wholly in the method but in the ends to which it is directed.

Nor is the question of control unrelated to this evaluation of fleeces. While certain aspects of fleeces seem to abandon the need for control, one could also understand the use of fleeces as an attempt to bring some control to the multiplex ways God might answer by limiting the means and options. One would conclude therefore that fleeces are not an example of transcending the limits of technical reason to grasp the unity of things through a more ecstatic reason, at least not as they were used here, but are rather to be viewed as uncritical attempts to harness the Divine Presence for finite ends.

A second way that Pentecostals like Allison risk confusing the finite with the infinite is to consider charismatic manifestations holy in and of themselves. This tendency is evident in the uncritical acceptance of such manifestations as the Spirit. Tillich would point to this tendency to reify charismatic manifestations as another place where Pentecostals risk the 'idolatry' of making particular finite mediations of revelation unconditional within themselves.

How then ought charismatic manifestations be viewed? What is the relationship between such manifestations and the Spiritual Presence? In the New Testament the work of the Spirit is clearly connected to charismatic manifestations (Acts 2). Is one then to understand these as empirical signs of the Spiritual Presence? Tillich would pull back from such an equation, preferring to speak of 'mediating' signs.

> But holy objects are not holy in and of themselves. They are holy only by negating themselves in pointing to the divine of which they are mediums. If they establish themselves as holy, they become demonic. They are still 'holy', but their holiness is antidivine...All things in a way, have the power of becoming holy in a mediate sense. They can point to something beyond themselves. But, if their holiness comes to be considered inherent, it becomes demonic (1951: 216).

Further insight into how Tillich viewed charismatic manifestations can be gained from his discussion of the power of language to mediate revelation. Tillich makes an oblique remark that has some application to speaking in tongues. Arguing that language is less a medium of revelation alongside other mediums than a necessary prerequisite for humans to receive revelation, he comments that 'man is man through the power of the word, nothing really human can be so without the word' (1951: 124). Moreover,

> nonsensical combinations of words do not indicate the presence of the divine, although they may have an expressive power without any denotative function (1951: 124).

Clearly Tillich believed that phenomena like glossolalia should not be considered signals of the Divine Presence in and of themselves. While speaking in tongues has 'expressive power', allowing the person a non-rational expression of experience, one should hesitate to identify them as mediums of the Divine Presence.[6]

This may be too severe a judgment, however. By Tillich's own principles, any experience has the potential to mediate revelation. Dempster (1983) uses Tillich's concepts to argue that charismatic manifestations may help one realize that in the Divine Presence human understanding (with its rational categories) is transcended and transformed; that is, tongue speaking transforms rational thinking into imaginative thinking that transcends empirical language with symbolic language and keeps one from absolutizing human understandings of God or substituting them for God. While Dempster's analysis does not give due consideration to the negative potentials of charismatic manifestations, it does make the point from the perspective of Tillich's theology that speaking in tongues, like anything else, may become a medium of the Divine Presence. Thus, by Tillich's own principles there is no reason to exclude *a priori* the potential of speaking in tongues to mediate the Divine Presence; however, it should not simply be equated with the Divine Presence. Tillich's theology underscores again the need to join reason to ecstasy lest one end up substituting a finite medium for the infinite ground to which it points.

In addition to evaluating the revelatory aspects of fleeces and charismatic manifestations, the relationship of Allison's childhood experiences to her Spirit leading experiences and the impact of this relationship on the value of these experiences must be examined. The relationship between Allison's childhood experiences and discernment and decision making practices appear at several points. Her image of God shows the influence of several important people in her early childhood (Rizzuto 1979). The image includes aspects of her maternal grandmother, 'a godly woman' who always had time to listen' to Allison, and aspects of her relationship with her parents. Allison's most pleasant memories of childhood center around conversations with her grandmother. Her long conversations with God, talking as she would to her best friend, recall images of the long conversations with this woman. Allison's struggles

---

6. Pointing to the 'expressive' versus 'denotative' power of speaking in tongues is a common approach among those who explore the relationship of this behavior to ordinary language (cf. Samarin 1968, 1969, 1973; and Maloney and Lovekin 1985).

with her acceptance by God, her worthiness to be used by God, and her repeated confessions of failure appear to be rooted in early experiences with parents whom she felt she was never able to please satisfactorily. (Allison's repeated assurances by God show the blending of these images from her parents with that of the grandmother.) Are Allison's experiences of Spirit leading a compensation for the early emotional deprivation of her childhood? And what relation does this have to the value to be assigned to these experiences?

That Allison's experiences did not meet the criteria for creative regression, showing evidence of possible ego loss, would suggest that her experiences are indeed compensatory. This in itself does not mean that the experiences are valueless or that they have been unhelpful for Allison. One cannot dismiss the idea that by compensating for early childhood deprivation her experiences of the Spirit have provided alternative sources of strength. Allison certainly claims as much. This is not to say that such compensation also may have reduced the impetus for healing conversations with her parents, which have only recently taken place. Allison did not give sufficient information to determine the full role of the Spirit leading experiences in either inhibiting or encouraging these conversations. However, one can anticipate that changing relationships with her parents will bring about changes in her image of God and the relationship that ensues from this (Jones 1991).

Sheila

What is one to make of Sheila's Spirit leading experiences? Do they meet Tillich's criteria for revelatory occurrences? Sheila's chief means for discerning the Spirit were certain feelings that she had which were accompanied on occasion by altered states of consciousness and claims to special knowledge about people's activities and motives. Do such experiences conjoin ecstasy and reason or confuse the finite with the infinite?

Experiences, such as Sheila's, that claim to receive special knowledge, constitute an area in which Pentecostals risk confusing finite media with their infinite ground in light of Tillich's understanding of revelation. Tillich would argue either that such experiences are not revelatory or that what is important in such experiences is not receiving special knowledge. According to Tillich, the knowing of revelation is not ordinary knowledge, even if supernaturally given, as Sheila's claims are said to be. As noted in Chapter 5, her report of these incidents makes it hard to verify any of them as true incidents in which 'nothing' was known beforehand. Her claim to know about the youth minister's move prior to its formal announcement was not shared until much later than she said it had come to her, and public disclosure of this knowledge came after the minister's plans for a second visit to the area in which the church he moved to was located was known to her. The insight about the attempted molestation of her daughter was confirmed 'after the fact' and Sheila herself admits to the difficulty of sorting out such knowing prior to such confirmations. The insight into the minister and the woman who was 'trying to destroy his ministry' was confirmed when she saw these two people visiting together after the dream in which she claims to have gained this understanding. Even in the incident with the groceries she acknowledged that she knew there would come a time when she would receive some money for one of the girls. According to Tillich, such knowing is better understood, not as revelation, not as experiences of being grasped by ultimate concern, but simply as reconfigurations of already known information. While some argue that revelation in Tillich is seeing what was already known in a different way (cf. Hammond 1966), what makes this new knowing revelatory is the quality of being grasped by ultimate concern in these knowings (Emmet 1952). Tillich's theology would suggest that Sheila, through processes of intuition, coincidence, and concern, had formed a new information gestalt from things already known, but had not received revelatory knowledge because the dimension of ultimate concern is lacking from this experience; there is nothing here that reaches beyond the benefit to Sheila and, on occasion, the person she knows about.

Is this the best way to understand such claims? Tillich himself is not consistent in his insistence that revelation entails no finite knowledge and has been criticized precisely at this point, leaving open the possibility that one can speak of revelation as conveying knowledge. Such a position is not without problems, however.

If one admits the possibility that ordinary knowledge is conveyed in revelation, one must inquire as to the nature of such revelations and the criteria by which they are to be evaluated. The nature of such claims is not immediately obvious. If seen as a type of dependent revelation, claims that empirical knowledge is revelatory would means that the original revelation from which such claims were derived was also a revelation based in empirical knowing. This clearly is more than Tillich wants to say. He argues that empirical knowledge has no power to shake, grasp and transform and is therefore not revelatory, although he himself tied the original revelation of Jesus the Christ to historical events. Tillich's inconsistency certainly clouds the issue as to whether Pentecostal claims to special knowledge can be revelatory.

As noted earlier, Tillich's inconsistency is rooted in his attempt to build a general theory of revelation upon the unacknowledged foundation of Christian revelation (Gilkey 1990). His disavowal that empirical knowledge is received in revelation was an attempt to protect the uniqueness of the Christ-event while allowing a role for experience in theological reflection. The way out of Tillich's dilemma lies in finding a more adequate way to articulate the role of experience and the uniqueness of the Christ-event for theology.

In Chapter 3 Tracy's method of mutually critical correlation was described as embracing both the 'Christian fact' and 'common human experience' as sources for theological construction that are put at risk. This articulation of the role of experience moves beyond Tillich's inconsistency but it does so by putting the uniqueness of the Christ-event at risk along with experience. To read Tillich through Tracy is clearly to prefer the interpretation, latent in Tillich, that experience is not only a medium but a source for theology and thus empirical knowledge can be revelatory. What is then needed are criteria to evaluate such claims to knowing that arise out of experience. Tillich actually provides some guidelines for such cases under his concept of dependent revelation. If the knowledge claimed is said to be of a Christian nature, it would be evaluated against the historically mediated tradition about the Christ. A crucial problem, however, is that one must ask whose 'Christ' serves as the criterion (Chopp 1987)? In the end one is left with some sort of Protestant version of the *magisterium* in which the church and its traditions provide the criteria by which such revelations are judged. Judgments as to the Christian character of Pentecostal experience, or Mormon experience, or the experience of the victims at Jonestown are determined by comparing all such experiences with the historic, ecumenical Christian tradition.

If evaluated by the criterion that revelation extends beyond the person receiving it, a more general criterion for discerning true revelation, claims to special knowledge can be scrutinized in terms of the wider applicability of such knowledge. Is the knowledge said to be received for personal gain or for the benefit of others? This is not always an easily answered question. Sheila's claim to knowledge about the minister was shared with him, ostensibly for the sake of saving his ministry and not to show Sheila to be some great spiritual giant. Her own struggles over whether such insights come from God or merely express her ordinary concern for others indicate the complexity of judging these actions even for her.

In light of Tillich's inconsistency, one must allow the possibility of empirical knowledge being received in dependent revelations and to judge them by the longer Christian tradition and the criterion of their wider applicability to humanity. However, one can appreciate why Tillich resisted the possibility that revelation included the reception of empirical knowledge; to claim that revelation includes this kind of knowing (even if 'supernaturally' received) runs a grave risk of confusing finite knowledge with the unconditional knowledge that heals and transforms (despite Tillich's own inconsistency on this point).

While claims to special knowledge could be revelatory in light of the above analysis, one would not judge Sheila's experiences as revelatory. Her claims to special knowledge show evidence of confusing the finite with the infinite; they do not extend to grasp and transform the larger community. Furthermore, other Spirit leading experiences rely on uncritically accepted feelings that indicate failure to conjoin ecstasy and reason. Certain aspects of the psychological analysis in Chapter 5 reinforces this position; her dissociative behavior showed some loss of ego control in these experiences. While her behavior was not judged especially pathological, it was not seen as creative regression either.

The relationship between Sheila's early childhood and experiences of Spirit leading is evident in both her image of God and her tendency to produce dissociative religious experiences. Sheila's image of God appears to be drawn from fragments taken from her parents and an older step-brother. Chapter 5 has suggested relationships between Sheila's dissociation and her relationship with her father. Her image of God as the caring father/protector is evidently drawn partly from her experience of her father and is partly an idealized father image. This ideal image seems conflated with memories of the older step-brother who lived in the home until Sheila was seven. She reports that she 'idolized' him and tells of two occasions when he protected her, once from an angry neighbor and once from her father who was trying to spank her, possibly under the influence of alcohol ('I don't know if my father had been drinking or what'). On the other hand, when God takes on the passive attitude of her mother, being silent and unfelt, Sheila voices grave concerns.

One is again pushed to ask the value of such experiences for Sheila (and Pentecostals like her). Early childhood experiences certainly influence the manner and options by which Spirit leading experiences occur for a given person, but this is not to suggest a negative value for such experiences. One must ask about their outcome. Is Sheila better or worse for them? The dissociative experiences probably keep Sheila from facing issues that she needs to face, yet one cannot dismiss the possibility that through such experiences she receives a strength for coping that may not otherwise be available to her (as it does not seem to be for her brother or sisters).

Brad

What of the revelatory quality of Brad's Spirit-leading experiences? Brad judges by persistent feelings coupled with a sense of order in worship contexts; in the context of his call to ministry he struggles with images of 'being' versus 'doing' and the 'father' image of God. Do Brad's experiences show evidence of conjoining ecstasy and reason and not confusing the finite with the infinite?

Certain of Brad's comments indicate that Pentecostals speak at times as though they simply wish to feel good or to avoid decisions ('I used to shout with the best of them...but what did I take home? A good felling'). This points to a failure to conjoin ecstasy with reason and to confuse excitement with Spiritual Presence. The potential to confuse the finite with the infinite seems to be a problem inherent in the nature of Pentecostalism as a spirit movement. Tillich contrasts overexcitement with genuine ecstasy and warns Pentecostals of the dangers of confusing the two:

> The so-called ecstatic movements are in continuous danger...of confusing overexcitement with the presence of the divine Spirit or with the occurrence of revelation. Something happens objectively as well as subjectively in every genuine manifestation of the mystery. Only something subjective happens in a state of religious overexcitement, often artificially produced. Therefore, it has no revelatory power. No new practical or theoretical interpretation of what concerns us ultimately can be derived from such subjective experiences. Overexcitement is a state of mind which can be comprised completely in psychological terms. Ecstasy transcends the psychological level, although it has a psychological side. It reveals something valid about the relation between the mystery of our being and ourselves (1951: 112).

Ian's remark in the service also seems to confuse excitement with Spiritual Presence without critically evaluating their connection. Others have noted that despite the excitement of Pentecostal worship, Pentecostals often show no evidence of changes in behavior or social consciousness (Anderson 1979).[7]

Failure to submit to scrutiny decisions made on the basis of internal feelings is also a way by which Pentecostals fail to unite reason with ecstasy. While Tillich is appreciative of the emphasis that spirit movements have brought to the church, especially in their resistance to calcified forms of religious life and thought (e.g. not restricting the Spirit to the affirmation of the known truth of the biblical message, as Reformed theology tends to do), he is quick to point out that spirit movements, such as Pentecostalism, need certain safeguards placed on the enthusiasm to prevent practices based in subjective emotion only (cf. 1963: 118, 126).

Certainly some of the things Brad mentions as leading of the Spirit would not be judged revelatory. But what about Brad's decision to lead the song at the end of the service? Was this a revelatory experience or overexcitement brought on by the heightened emotional atmosphere of the worship service. In light of Tillich's criterion that revelation reaches

7.   A recent study by Land (1993) raises interesting questions at this point. Land interprets certain charismatic manifestations such as shouting, laughing, crying and speaking in tongues as proleptic enjoyment of the kingdom of God, signs of one's participation in and with God in a kingdom in which race and class barriers are broken and the disenfranchised are empowered. In such an interpretation, emotion is not escapism but a celebration that God is with the poor, the oppressed and the underclassed in a special way.

It is critical to Land's interpretation that one realize that his study is restricted to the first ten years of the Pentecostal movement when its adherents were more apt to be restricted to the poor. The 'redemption and lift' phenomenon (Wagner 1988) that accompanies religions of the poor, moving their adherents up the social ladder, coupled with the charismatic revival among the denominations, means there are significant numbers of Pentecostals no longer among the 'poor'. One wonders of such groups whether Land's analysis still holds. Is shouting among those who also have social power the same behavior as it is among the powerless? It is of interest to note that some of those interviewed in this study still spoke of the importance of the Holy Spirit in the kinds of language Land quotes from the early years of the movement ('power for service', 'made me more bold to share my testimony', 'a closeness to [or possession by] God'). However, the work of McGuire (1982) suggests caution in assuming that charismatic manifestations have the same meaning for the powerful as they do for the powerless.

beyond the person receiving it to the group, one should recall that this incident was the beginning of Brad's reintegration into a leadership role in the congregation. To some extent then one could say that the impact of this Spirit leading incident extended beyond Brad to bring positive consequences to the congregation. The leading of the Spirit that Brad experienced in the context of the more general move of the Spirit in the worship brought a reintegration and healing both to Brad and the congregation. The possibility that Brad may have simply been forcing his way back into the congregation, in ways not fully conscious to him, cannot be excluded although the conversations with Brad did not seem to indicate this motive. However, the psychological analysis developed in Chapter 5 indicates how unconscious motivations often influence actions so that self reports of intention and motives are never sufficient for resolving such questions. The question may not be fully resolvable, but if Brad's subsequent behavior is indicative of the positive or negative value of this behavior, it seems to have been beneficial to both in that it aided integration of negative elements within the life of the congregation and brought Brad back into fuller fellowship.

The revelatory aspects of this behavior could be judged further if Brad had discussed this leading of the Spirit with others in the congregation, but he did not indicate that such had been done. This suggests that the ecstatic dimension of this experience (the sense that it is right to lead this song that grew out of prayer) appears to have been only tentatively conjoined to structure or reason; the action was not judged out of order, at least observation of the congregation's reaction did not indicate this. Thus, this incident shares some qualities of a revelatory experience, though not all.

Like Allison and Sheila, the relationship of Brad's childhood to Spirit leading experiences is seen in his God image and the types of Spirit leading experiences he has. Brad's God image appears to be an idealized father image. His own experience of a father too old and passive to spend time with his youngest son yields little positive material for his image of God, so God becomes an idealized father, an image that continues to undergo revisions for Brad and that seems to contend with an image drawn from his mother, who could be quite angry and displeased with her son. Brad speaks of growing beyond an image of God as having a big stick and 'out to get him'. It is again easy to suggest that Brad's Spirit leading experiences and idealized father image of God are compensation for childhood deprivation, but these relationships also show the complexity of human motivations. In a positive way this image calls Brad into a more mature self-understanding that grasps the ambiguities of life in which there is not a particular God-ordained job he must hold, yet one can also see his continued struggle with this issue; he is not free of thinking that maybe there is a particular job and that he has irrevocably messed up his ministry. His struggle over 'being' versus 'doing' indicates a similar ambivalence.

Brad's experiences of Spirit leading in which the criterion of order is added to the persistence of feelings also mirrors the need to bring order out of a very disorderly childhood. His intense struggle over incorporating the negative aspects of his recent behavior further mirrors the struggle to incorporate the negatives from his childhood, experiences he does not dwell upon, and hence cuts himself off from the potential growth that could be gained from a critical understanding of how these early childhood experiences, and his disavowal of them, motivate his current behavior. In a similar way, the self-understanding that emerges following the incident of infidelity seems to lack appropriate depth. While the new understanding of God as forgiving and loving even when he fails frees Brad from feeling the need to be 'perfect', it is not quite clear whether this image also frees him to evaluate himself critically or excuses the need for such evaluations. This incident illustrates the importance of subsequent behavior for adequate evaluation of some claims to Spirit direction.

Fernando

Up to this point the assessment has tended toward the non-revelatory nature of the experiences reported. Are there Spirit leading experiences that can be identified as revelatory with more certainty than the hints thus far encountered? The study turns to Fernando and Gwen to explore this question.

Fernando's experiences of Spirit leading were primarily through retrospective judgments and feelings of the rightness of a given situation. His decision to write the denominational letter of repentance shows some qualities of conjoining ecstasy with reason. His initial inspiration is received in prayer, which Tillich identifies as the exemplar of ecstasy, and is then submitted to the judgment of friends. That this experience has something of revelatory quality to it also is seen in the fact that the purpose of the letter extends beyond Fernando to seek to address his denomination and from there to speak to the Christian world more broadly. Fernando's willingness to submit his letter to the judgment of friends also indicates his awareness of the potential of confusing his finite understandings with their infinite ground, and further suggests the revelatory character of this decision.

However, this incident also indicates the complexity of human motivations in that one cannot dismiss the connection between Fernando's image of God as always requiring self-abasement from him and the fact that the revelatory experience was about the need to repent. One is pushed to ask, could Fernando have received any other kind of revelation? Given his God image and childhood experience, one is tempted to say, 'Of course Fernando would receive a revelation about the need to repent'. It seems obvious that Fernando's God image is drawn from his parents. God, like his father, is emotionally distant and severe in rebuke. But like his mother, God's care for him is seen in God's desires for his constant improvement. In Chapter 5 a connection between Fernando's experience with his father was seen to influence his preferred style of judging leadings of the Spirit through retrospection, and a more emotionally distant form of discernment and decision making that reflects the more emotionally distant relationship he had with his father.

How is one to evaluate experiences of Spirit leading so obviously influenced by early childhood relationships and the personality they shaped? It should be clear by now that the 'origins' of one's Spirit leading experiences do not invalidate these experiences. One can have no experiences, including religious experiences, not colored by these early relationships. It is subsequent behavior that becomes the means for evaluating these practices. What an awareness of origins does allow for, however, is a more critical assessment of such subsequent behavior. In Fernando's case, when one recalls his comments about this being a 'unique historical event' and remembers the driving ambition that had energized Fernando's many accomplishments before becoming a minister, one must ask whether this is simply a sanctified version of his earlier, 'secular' ambition to do things no one else had done? While such questions could only grow out of an understanding and appreciation for Fernando's early experiences, these connections between his early and current experience do not predetermine the answer. As Tillich has argued, one can have a destiny because one is free to choose. The kinds of critical correlational analyses that this study works toward ideally enables such choices to be made in more freedom than one would have without them.

Gwen

What of Gwen's experiences? Do they satisfy the criteria for revelatory occurrences? Are ecstasy and reason conjoined in her decision to remain in her marriage? Or does Gwen's claim that staying in her marriage is God's best for her violate Tillich's second criterion by confusing finite knowing with its infinite ground?

Gwen's experience in trying to discern the Spirit's leading in relation to her marriage may be taken as a possible example of a revelatory occurrence. This situation and the need to know what and where the Spirit was directing created a 'limit' experience in Gwen's life, a time in which the old ways and means no longer seemed applicable. At a time when she felt everything had been 'knocked out from under' her, she found deep within her a peace and 'quiet knowing that He was there'. She discerned the Spirit's leading by means of a deeply felt sense that the action she chose was right. In describing this event as one that changed her thinking about God, Gwen used language reminiscent of Tillich:

> To say it another way, when the things you thought were the most stable things in your life are knocked out from under you, you realize that God is all there is ultimately.

Gwen describes here (and in her earlier remarks) what might be interpreted as an awareness of her connection to the ground of being. At a time when her coping skills were pushed to the limit, when her personal life seemed to be disintegrating, she found a peace and connectedness to God in ways new to her. Fleeces and any overexcitement that might be confused with the Divine Presence are gone. She feels sustained and empowered, and possibilities and choices emerge which dissipate her sense of being trapped. Insofar as the data permit one to judge, Gwen seems to be describing the receiving side of a revelatory experience. The conjoining of ecstasy and reason is seen in her consultation with friends over the various feelings, positive and negative, she was having and in her continued willingness to evaluate these feeling derived decisions. As argued in Chapter 5, the regression that attended this decision was creative or constructive in the final analysis; it gave Gwen strength for coping and recovery.

Whether the second criterion has also been met is harder to determine. Gwen's conviction that staying with a particular marriage partner was right for her may be confusing a claim to finite knowing with the infinite. This conviction grew out of newly emergent choices Gwen believed she had which included staying or leaving. However, her sure conviction that staying was 'God's best' for her may be to confuse the finite and infinite. It would have been better had she said more clearly, that 'right or wrong' she knew that God was all there was ultimately, but her statement is not this clear. In Tillichian terms the best interpretation is to say that within this finite knowing, Gwen was grasped by something greater, a sense of her connectedness to the ground of being, and in this her experience was revelatory.

As with everyone else, the relationship between Gwen's childhood and her experiences of Spirit leading is seen in the types of Spirit leading experiences she has and in her God image. Gwen's Spirit leading experiences have mostly to do with a strong sense of things feeling right which is sometimes submitted to the judgment of others. Gwen's image of God is forged out of memories of her parents, both actual and idealized (Rizzuto 1979). God, like her father, must have his way, but unlike her father, God is an ideal companion so that part of the image of God is an idealized father. When God is silent like her father, when God 'doesn't reveal himself in some way I get very frustrated...Lord, I'm trying to live for you...where are you?' Gwen also speaks of 'wounding' her relationship with God, language which recalls her mother's feelings during times when Gwen's relationship with her changed (such as the time in junior high school when she quit kissing her mother good-bye before going off to school or the more recent time as an adult). These early images of wounding her mother created in Gwen the desire to be a very obedient daughter. It is also of interest to note that Gwen's changing image of God occurs after her changing relationship with her parents. As Jones (1991) has observed, changes in parental relationship open up the possibility for changes in one's image of God. Gwen feels freer not to be so obedient and passive with her parents, aspects of her personality also reflected in her changing relationship with God.

Summary Conclusions

This chapter has explored important issues and connections raised by the case material in light of Tillich's theology. This material points out the importance of the relationship between early childhood and experiences of Spirit leading. It shows how the former influence the latter both in terms of the kinds of Spirit leading experiences a given person might be anticipated to have and the image of God that guides those experiences. The nature of one's childhood experiences seem to predispose one to experience the leading of the Spirit in certain ways and preclude the Spirit being experienced in other ways. The personality characteristics of a person also were evident in the types of Spirit leading experiences they reported. The question of the roots of Spirit leading experiences and the impact of this on how such experiences are to be valued was explored. This study concluded that the value of an experience cannot be judged by its 'roots' but must be judged by its 'fruits' (cf. James 1902). The case material has shown how complex human behavior is, especially those behaviors that claim to have been led by the Spirit.

Tillich's theology has added to the psychological implications of Spirit leading a value criterion that points beyond the constructive relevance of these practices to the individual alone to include their relevance and value to the larger community. In turn the psychological evaluation has made it obvious that the complexity of human behavior requires an understanding of how the unconscious dimensions of this behavior guide the church's activities.

Tillich's theology provides Pentecostals a way to understand discernment and decision making theologically as revelatory occurrences. This understanding provides a role for experience consonant with the Pentecostal emphasis, but redirecting any tendencies to overvalue experience. Tillich provides a theological vision to help answer the question of how one discerns the leading of the Spirit in a tradition that tends to confuse overexcitement with the Spiritual presence. Tillich's insistence that experience is best treated as a medium but not a source of theology was modified. His motivation to guard against the dangers of privatization and esoteric interpretations that can occur when experience is treated as a source was retained, but without denying experience a role in theology as neo-orthodoxy and Evangelicalism are prone to do.

Tillich also offers two criteria by which revelation can be judged. True revelation always conjoins ecstasy with structure; ecstatic reason remains reason. If the tendency in non-Pentecostal churches is to emphasize structure over ecstasy, the tendency of Pentecostals is to emphasize ecstasy over structure. Tillich reminds one that both elements must always be conjoined. It is also worth noting that Tillich's concept of ecstatic knowing includes what was called affective knowing in the previous chapter. Ecstatic reason recognizes dimensions of knowing that are less technically rational and more holistic in that both affective and cognitive dimensions of knowing are involved. Without the conjoining of structure and ecstasy one only has access to a technical reason that can never know fully the things of the Spirit. Hammond (1966) speaks of the union of ecstasy and reason in language reminiscent of Kernberg's (1977) description of 'crossing boundaries' in mature love, giving further nuance to the relationship between Tillich and object relations theory: 'Just as in love the person is beyond himself without losing his integrity, so in revelation reason transcends itself without being destroyed' (Hammond 1966: 61).

Finally, one might note that Tillich's theology forces one to recognize the ambiguities of existence and the unavoidability of choice. This is what an 'existentialist' framework means. Neither Pentecostals nor anyone else can avoid such ambiguities or choices. While some have suggested that certain Pentecostal practices may avoid these kinds of existential ambiguities and choices (Hunter 1984), attempts to rid oneself of all ambiguity and responsibility for choice through claiming the 'leading of the Spirit' is neither healthy nor true to the nature of the Spirit. Pentecostal attempts to avoid ambiguity through appeal to charismatic manifestations or fleeces are misguided; the divine Spirit cannot be forced or coerced by the human spirit (Tillich 1963: 112). Even a rigorous application of the criteria drawn from Tillich cannot determine unambiguously whether particular experiences are revelatory (though they provide helpful guidelines for such determinations). While this is due partly to the ambiguity in Tillich, it should be noted that it also is due to ambiguity in the experiences themselves. This means there will always be some claims to Spirit leading that will be difficult to judge regardless of the criteria to which one appeals.

In a similar manner one should note that although this study has sought to elucidate certain connections between early childhood experiences and their impact on Spirit leading, and to make consideration of such experiences more valuable and meaningful by doing so, one must conclude that these experiences cannot be exhausted by the categories that have been used to bring a better understanding. After all the analyses, there is still 'mystery' here.

Chapter 7

TOWARD A PRACTICAL THEOLOGY OF PENTECOSTAL DISCERNMENT AND DECISION MAKING

Introduction

This chapter concludes the mutually critical correlation of perspectives necessary for constructing a practical theology of Pentecostal discernment and decision making. It looks at the issues each perspective has generated in the dialogue and summarizes the chief learnings that emerge from this study. It also offers guidelines for evaluating these practices in an attempt to re-envision discernment and decision making. In doing this, the study follows Tracy's (1975, 1981) model for practical theology in which the 'theoretical moment' of correlating various interpretations of the practices of a local congregation is followed by a return to 'praxis'; practical theology must present the results of these correlations, this theoretical moment, in ways that can guide the further practice of the congregation studied.

Summary of what Has Been Learned

This section summarizes the chief learnings and related issues that have emerged from this study under the following headings: (1) recognition of holistic ways of knowing, (2) the nature of self formation, (3) community formation in these practices, and (4) the relationship of the deeply felt 'sense that things are right' to these other three foci. It critically examines points of convergence and difference on these issues among the Pentecostal, psychological and theological perspectives.

Recognition of Holistic Ways of Knowing
One area where all three perspectives converge concerns the need to recognize holistic ways of knowing in acts of decision making. In all three perspectives there is a recognition that human knowing is not

bounded by reason alone. That God breaks into human knowing apart from rationality is a deeply held belief in Pentecostalism. The Pentecostal reliance on things 'feeling right' points to a conviction that true decision making involves more than rational reflection alone. Tillich's way of recognizing the need for holistic ways of knowing is his criterion of conjoining reason and ecstasy. For Tillich, ecstatic reason includes both cognitive and affective dimensions of knowing and apprehends the unity between knower and known, in contrast to technical reason which seeks simply to control 'objects'. From the psychological perspective, object relations theory also points to the intertwining of cognitive and affective dimensions of knowing growing out of early childhood experiences. It sees these early ways of knowing as more realistically reflecting a universe where knower and known, subject and object are perceived as mutually interactive (Jones 1991). Ego psychology's appeal to the creative potential of primary process thinking also recognizes that decision making includes more than rational thought alone.

But this focus on holistic knowing in decision making must be critically evaluated. Does talk of holistic knowing obscure more negative or malevolent processes? From a psychological perspective, might these practices just as well represent abandonment of reason to the irrational impulses of primary process thinking without a creative dimension? Or when viewed from the perspective of Tillich's theology, might this be confusion of overexcitement with Spiritual presence, 'subjective intoxication' void of revelation? From a Pentecostal perspective, might these experiences represent people who are 'in themselves' and not actually led by the Spirit?

This study presents ethnographic data that pushes for realism concerning the claims made for Pentecostal discernment and decision making. It shows both positive and negative aspects of these practices; the 'ideal' interpretations of the theological (and psychological) perspectives are not always the reality one encounters. The analyses presented in Chapters 5 and 6 show that some decisions made on the basis of feelings are clearly unreflective and unable to satisfy the criteria for creative regression or revelation while other decisions made on the basis of feelings satisfy the criteria for both of these interpretations. In addition, the person's willingness to submit these decisions to discussion with others indicates that inclusion of intuitive, affective means of knowing in decision making need not mean that more rational means must be given up. The previous chapters illustrate that blanket pronouncements about the positive or negative effects of these practices are problematic; some-times the same example contains both positive and negative elements to greater or lesser degrees.

In probing the relationship between discernment and decision making and the focus on holistic knowing it will be helpful to explore more directly the correspondence between the psychological and theological explanations of these practices. What convergencies are there between these two perspectives and are there significant differences between them? Tillich's emphasis on conjoining ecstasy and reason appears simi-lar to the psychological emphasis on integrating primary process thinking with secondary reflection: both processes are characterized by a more holistic knowing that apprehends the 'unitive' (Jones 1991) qualities between knower and known. However, conjoining ecstasy and reason and integrating primary process thinking with secondary reflection are not identical processes. In Tillich, ecstatic reason is not an experience in which reason is abandoned and subsequently regained; reason is always present. In primary process thinking, by contrast, one has a temporary abandonment or subversion of reason so that earlier, less rational ways of knowing becomes accessible. In addition, ecstatic reason grasps that which is of ultimate concern while primary process thinking simply grasps certain unities not recognized by normal secondary processes.

These differences create the possibility of creatively regressive expe-riences which would not be revelatory. If making primary process thought accessible to secondary process is a form of creative regression, and yet this process is not the same as Tillich's criterion of conjoining ecstasy and reason, then one concludes there are some experiences that are creatively regressive, yet not revelatory. On the other hand, it is difficult to imagine a situation in which a genuine revelatory experience is not also creative since Tillich points specifically to creativity as a crite-rion for accessing the revelatory quality of an experience, although he does not elaborate on this criterion (cf. 1963: 120).

Formation of the Self
A second series of questions arises around the issue of self formation. Chapter 5 argues that discernment and decision making makes the recapture and reworking of early self and object relations available in ways that enhance present psychic functioning, and presents case mate-rial to illustrate this. It also shows that not all discernment and decision making satisfies the criteria for these 'creative regressions'. Some

experiences of discernment and decision making show evidence of ego loss and inability to integrate positive and negative images of the self sufficiently. Other experiences were clearly compensatory for emotional deprivation. But there are also times when it is not so clear whether healthy or unhealthy, Spirit led or self motivated activities are taking place. As with holistic knowing, blanket judgments are problematic. There are subtle complexities in the relationship between discernment and decision making and self formation to which the previous chapters try to attend. Chapter 6, for instance, points out the influence of early childhood in shaping religious experience and discusses the value to be assigned these experiences. Chapter 5 looks at the positive and negative influences of these experiences on present psychic functioning. Two further issues not covered in the previous chapters need to be addressed in the mutually critical correlations of perspectives on this relationship. What are the significant similarities and differences in the psychological and theological explanations of selfhood? And what is the telos of the self proposed by the various perspectives (that is, what type of self is being formed and how is it to be judged?).

One of the most interesting points of convergence on this topic is between Tillich and object relations theory regarding the formation of the self through the ability to make choices and through resistances met in the environment, a hint toward the social dimensions of self formation. Tillich's notion that the self is formed via the anxiety that arises in decision making is analogous to the object relations position that self formation takes place amid the anxiety of separation and attachment to the mother figure (Kernberg 1977). Tillich (1951, 1957) sees anxiety arising from the estranged state of existence; decisions must be made in courage, and made in the face of anxiety against the threat of nonbeing. Psychologically, the first post-partum time infants experience a sense of being cut off from that to which they belong is the separation anxiety attendant to the comings and goings of the mother. Self formation requires overcoming the anxiety of separation experienced by the infant as it differentiates from its environment.

The three step movement to self formation that Kernberg (1976, 1977) outlines is also similar to Tillich's description of self formation. According to Kernberg, infants begin life in an undifferentiated state, followed by movement toward differentiation, in which the infant sorts out its experiences on the basis of affective states, and then by movement to a state in which the self experiences itself as fully differentiated from its environment. The undifferentiated state in infants could be seen as similar to the state of 'dreaming innocence' in Tillich (1957: 33-36): in neither state can one be described as fully a self. The movement toward differentiation, according to Kernberg, involves a separation from what one experiences as a primal unity. This movement seems analogous to the 'fall' in Tillich, the movement from essence to existence which is experienced as estrangement (1957). Finally, the differentiation of the self from its environment involves the infant in its first, rudimentary struggles regarding its own agency, a process of emerging self-con-sciousness (Winnicott 1971). This accords with Tillich's notion that selfhood is discerned in self-awareness and choice (1951).

The notion that the self is shaped through resistances encountered in the environment is another place where Tillich and object relations theory converge and where both point to the social dimensions of self formation. For Tillich, this resistance comes in the form of 'other' selves; that is, the self finds its existence in coming up against the limits of another. 'Personal life emerges in the encounter of person with person and in no other way' (Tillich 1963: 40). The limit to one's attempt to draw all content into oneself is met in another self which is continuously and inescapably encountered in community (Tillich's individuation–participation polarity). In object relations theory formation of the self through environmental resistance is seen in the infant's coping with the comings and goings of the mother-figure. Winnicott (1971) speaks of the importance of the 'good enough' (versus perfect) mother. In meeting some but not all of the infant's needs the good enough mother helps the infant establish a continuity with reality: '*if all goes well* the infant can actually come to gain from the experience of frustration, since incom-plete adaptation to need makes objects real' (Winnicott 1971: 11 his emphasis). Gerkin (1984) points out how this notion of the good enough mother means that formation of the self occurs in tension with others.

> Winnicott's psychological analysis of early infant–mother relationships suggests that it is in a crucible of a degree of suffering and sacrifice on the part of both mother and infant that such right relationships are born (1984: 88).

It is worth noting that Tillich's focus on the other's role in develop-ment of selfhood is addressed primarily under the concept of limit. The focus for Tillich is clearly on individual selves whose 'dependency' on others is rather narrowly conceived. Here, the object relations under-standing that the other (the mother primarily) is not only 'limit' but essential to one's survival as a human being embraces a more realistic understanding of the self–other relationship than Tillich's individualism.

Regarding the telos of the self, all three perspectives offer a normative vision of what the self should be. For Tillich, the Christian tradition provides criteria for evaluating the telos of the self by focusing on Jesus Christ as the ultimate norm for judging visions of the self. The Christian understanding of self is shaped by this original (and final) revelation and the traditions associated with it. For Tillich, Christ's self-negation, pointing to God and not himself, becomes a final revelation that critiques all claims that would absolutize any finite understandings of symbols of God. The traditional theological category for treating norms that are not ultimate as though they were is 'sin'. For Tillich, the self must point beyond itself to the God who transcends both self and its world.

The psychological perspectives provide a normative vision of the self that focuses on such psychological operations as maintenance and enhancement of ego functioning, valuing unity of self and openness to the world and its present reality and future possibilities, over fragmentation and isolation as indicators of positive transformation. The Pentecostal vision of the self views it as receiver, instrument and dwelling place of the Divine Presence. Discernment and decision making are understood as divine encounters in which the Holy Spirit directs the self, especially through a 'sense of things feeling right', into activities that enhance individual and community functioning. A fuller comparison of the similarities and differences in these normative visions requires engagement of the next issue, that of community formation and its relationship to discernment and decision making.

Community Formation
This study argues that Pentecostal discernment and decision making also participate in community formation by opening up possibilities, aiding reconciliation, restoration and incorporation of negative elements into the life of the congregation. The issues that arise from this topic include the tension between individual autonomy and community relationships, the role of tradition in community formation, and the need for the critique of whole communities.

One dimension of self formation is the tension between individual and communal or relational dimensions of growth. This is an area in which the psychological and theological perspectives mutually critique each other. Object relations theory often posits separation–individuation as the goal of infant development, normatively viewing the developed individual as ideally separate from others and arguably not giving sufficient attention to the relational or communal nature of the self. Jones's (1991) argument that object relations theory of the self needs to balance autonomous dimensions with relational dimensions mirrors Tillich's theological concern to balance the poles of individuation and participation. When the goal of growth is autonomy, religion, with its emphasis on participation in a larger reality is easily seen as a threat. When the goal of growth includes relationship with others, then religion is seen in a more favorable light (Jones 1991).

Pointing to the communal nature of the self also raises the question of the role of tradition in self formation and experiences of Spirit leading. The role of early childhood experience in shaping the types of religious experiences one has has already been noted. One's first experience of the world is relational or social; one's experiences are intertwined with the existing language of the caretaker which conveys certain realities and values. This is the beginning of the influence of tradition on one's interpretation of experience, including those experiences that will later be attributed to the Spirit. All are influenced by the traditions of the community into which one is born. The task of practical theology is to correlate these traditions critically with other traditions and perspectives. A practical theology of discernment and decision making must look at the role of traditions in determining and guiding Spirit leading experiences. The impact of tradition is already seen in, for instance, the role of leaders and membership stratification in keeping down charismatic excesses, the use of music to guide worship, and stories about the character of the Holy Spirit (see Chapter 4). 'Testimonies' also participate in and expand traditions regarding what it means to be a Spirit led people, offering a kind of reflection on Pentecostal practice in the process.[1]

One should note that 'tradition' embraces more than the Scriptures; it also includes the particular interpretations a community gives to them, borne in their songs, sermons, testimonies, prayers and stories as a

---

1. Land (1993) argues that testimonies provided opportunities for 'theological reflection' among early Pentecostal communities.

> Testimonies were given constantly in order to develop in the hearers the virtues, expectancy, attitudes and experiences of those testifying... Healings, trials, temptations and victories could be reflected upon by the body. By listening to and giving testimonies the congregation was involved in a praxis of theological reflection which though open-ended produced great uniformity and carried built-in relevance (1993: 80).

people of God. Pentecostals share this understanding of tradition with all Christians. Land (1993) shows how such traditions worked in the worship of early Pentecostals to mold and form a people.

> The whole congregation was involved in the process of formation. The singing, preaching, witnessing, testifying, ordinances (Baptism, Lord's Supper, Foot Washing), altar calls, prayer meetings, gift of the Spirit—all elements of corporate worship prepared people for and called them to new birth, sanctification, Spirit Baptism and a life of missionary witness. These ways of remembering the biblical Word mediated the biblical realities in a kind of Pentecostal sacramentality in which there was a constant, mutually conditioning interplay between knowledge and lived experience (1993: 75).

This concept of tradition raises another issue, particularly for Pentecostals influenced by Fundamentalist thought. It might be phrased as a question regarding how closely Pentecostal traditions (in the above sense) adhere to biblical traditions. From a Fundamentalist perspective this means how closely they adhere to the literalist biblical interpretation of Fundamentalism. But the question is also valid and important in the larger context of Christian tradition affirmed in this study (see Chapter 6).

The relationship of Pentecostal experience to Scripture is a close one. Pentecostals believe in and seek charismatic manifestations because the Scriptures speak of them. Land (1993) has noted this typical relationship among early Pentecostals:

> New experiences would often be the occasion for finding new insights into Scripture. Familiar Scriptures would take on a new meaning. But the beliefs, affections, and practices would all have to be tested by the Word.
> Thus, the point of Pentecostal spirituality was not to have an experience or several experiences. The point was to experience life as part of a biblical drama, a participation in God's history (1993: 74).

The close relationship between Pentecostal experience and Scripture points to the influence of the biblical narratives in shaping Pentecostal practice. A practical theology of Pentecostal discernment and decision making needs to correlate critically the Pentecostal identification and appropriation of these narratives with the understanding of these narratives in the wider, ecumenical Christian tradition. Because of the normative quality of the biblical narratives and their appropriation, the role of these traditions in guiding Spirit leading practices will be taken up again in the section below on a model for Pentecostal discernment and decision making.

One further question regarding the role of tradition and discernment and decision making needs to be addressed. Is it the work of the Spirit when one is led to deviate from one's tradition? Gwen felt empowered to deviate from the denominational tradition concerning divorce, yet reaffirmed it in the end. John Avery also deviated from the denomination's tradition on leaving a congregation before one's time has officially expired. Gwen's action was judged to be Spirit directed because it brought strength, possibilities and a sense of her connectedness to the ground of being, while Avery's was not judged to be Spirit directed because it appeared to cloak personal desires in ways that closed off dialogue with others. Thus evaluation of Spirit leading is not simply a question of whether one's actions affirm or deviate from one's tradition, but involves attention to the fuller criteria being summarized in this chapter.

Might it also be the work of the Spirit to challenge and attempt to reform some traditions? This raises the question of the need to critique entire communities and their traditions; to ask what kind of community is being built by these traditions and the practices they encourage. Certainly not all communities are to be judged positively (Nazism, Jim Jones's followers). How is one to evaluate the community formation that takes place through Pentecostal discernment and decision making? Judging the 'health' of whole communities from a psychological perspective is problematic because of psychology's tendency to make communities themselves the reference point for measuring health: 'it is the psychologist's job...to return the person...to 'normal'—as defined by the society in which the person must live and function' (McConnell 1983: 535). In this understanding, the ability to adjust to and function within a group, as contrasted with isolation or withdrawal from the group, is generally considered positive psychological behavior. But judging whole communities calls for more encompassing criteria than whether such communities provide a sense of belonging for their individual members.

This study proposes that a mutually critical correlation of multiple perspectives is the best way to identify these more encompassing criteria.[2] Whole communities tend to be judged positively if they find

2.   Regarding the source of these more encompassing criteria, one should note that at times critique of a community and its practices comes from within the community itself, the so-called 'prophetic' function in which values from the community's larger tradition are highlighted in ways that call current practices into question. At

some balance between the needs of the individual and those of the community. Tillich articulates this as the need to balance the polarity of individuation and participation. On the other hand, communities tend to be judged negatively if they become oppressive of human freedoms, either among their own members or of others (e.g. totalitarian communities) or allow individual expression to become so dominant that collective authority is lost. Mutually critical correlation of multiple perspectives assures, to the fullest extent possible, that such biases are unmasked and accounted for, and that adequate attention is given to all relevant factors necessary for making a judgment. Multiple perspectives provide a safeguard against idolatrous claims of any perspective. For instance, inclusion of the psychological perspective provides a

other times, however, what calls the values of one community into question is conflict with the values of another community. But can one community's values be judged better than another's? And, if so, on what grounds?

This raises the question whether there are 'transcendent' norms that can be derived apart from historical communities that embrace those norms. This question generates complex philosophical, theological and ethical problems that cannot be fully explored or resolved within the limits of this study. However, a few comments on the position taken by this study are in order. This study agrees with Bernstein (1983) that while there is no 'Archimedian point' in ethics, some claims to rightness are more sustainable than others; all norms are not equally valid although all are historically mediated. Bernstein argues that one must give the 'best possible reasons' for one's evaluations while retaining a humility about them because of 'the finitude of human rationality' (1983: 68-69). Since everyone is subject to historical conditionedness, even philosophers like Bernstein, the best one can do is to acknowledge this, and make one's values available for mutual, comparative conversation. He further acknowledges that his own historical conditionedness is part of what makes him see this approach as the 'best possible' way for philosophy and ethics to proceed. But as Bernstein concedes, at some point his philosophy must be willing to turn back upon itself and acknowledge, by its own argument, that its own best reasons may prove 'wrong' later; there is no escape from the historical conditionedness of all evaluations. This study proposes that a mutually critical correlation of multiple perspectives is the best method to address the problem of the historical conditionedness of all norms.

At this point one might ask whether such a position brings this study inexoribly into conflict with Pentecostal practice. Is the Pentecostal claim to Spirit leading a claim to have found a point for making judgments outside historically conditioned norms? While some might find this attractive, such a position cannot be defended in light of this study. Although the Pentecostal experience of the Spirit conveys a sense of the numinous, of being grasped by something greater from beyond oneself, this experience is only given content and form through a historically mediated tradition about the Spirit.

'hermeneutic of suspicion' regarding 'ultimate norms', even if drawn from the example of Jesus Christ as the gauge for the new humanity. From the psychological angle, such norms can never be separated entirely from finite human origins and expressions. Said differently, psychology helps identify the finite conditionings of a person's ultimate concern, continuously revealing the ambiguity of those claims. Hence, there is always the question of 'whose Christ' provides the norm for judging, the Christ of the victors or the victims (cf. Chopp 1987). The method of mutually critical correlation calls attention to the fact that those who evaluate and critique are themselves not exempt from historical conditionedness and need for evaluation. What one is willing to pronounce as the work of the Spirit depends on one's understanding of the Spirit's work drawn from the longer Christian tradition, and such traditions are always mediated through historically conditioned power structures (Metz 1980). Thus, whether one understands the work of the Spirit to be that of bringing a sense of peace and harmony, so that one feels more integrated and whole, more adjusted to oneself and the world or of bringing a sense of disharmony so that one feels as a 'pilgrim' not at home in the world is determined in large part by one's own position in the socio-political power structure. The reciprocal relationship between norms and those in power is seen in McGuire's (1982) observation that 'discerners' were the most powerful people in the Pentecostal groups she studied.

The critical correlation of the practices of the Pentecostal community with the theological vision drawn from the larger Christian tradition provides one means for evaluating its health as community. The congregation described in Chapter 4 did not show evidence that the community took precedence over the individual and therefore would not be judged negatively in this regard. In fact, the opposite tendency, toward too much individualism, seems more the case in Pentecostalism. Although some investigators (cf. Abell 1982; McGuire 1982; Williams 1974) have found that some Pentecostal groups claim inordinate amounts of time and allegiance from their members (a finding that might suggest a tendency toward giving the group precedence over the individual), this was not the case in the congregation studied. Furthermore, even with inordinate claims to time and allegiance, the activities in which Pentecostals are involved also give much attention to individuals. The question of whether Pentecostal experience is made an ultimate concern (a kind of spiritual elitism) is harder to answer. Remarks that might indicate a tendency to spiritual elitism (the Holy Spirit gives one 'something more' than other Christians have) did not appear to be a general feeling among the congregation and some individuals stated plainly that they saw no difference between Pentecostal and other Christians. This is certainly a change historically (cf. Anderson 1979).

The Deeply Felt Sense that Things Are Right

How is one to understand the deeply 'felt sense that things are right' in light of these issues? From a psychoanalytic object relations perspective, judging on the basis of this sense is rooted in the more affective, relational knowing characteristic of early psychic experience. These experiences or ways of knowing shape or distort all later experiences and knowing. In Chapter 6 the qualities of these early relationships, particularly their affective tone, are seen to influence and shape the type of religious experiences one can have.

Religious experiences, according to this perspective, allow access to formative experiences at the heart of selfhood; it is this that gives them their transformative power.

> The power of the sacred is, in part, that it carries the potential of recapturing the psyche's moment of creation, and with it the promise of present and future moments of re-creation...
>
> Something is denoted as sacred, then, if it evokes the matrix out of which the self originates (Jones 1991: 121, 125).

The connection between experiences of the sacred and early childhood experiences is also noted by Tillich who pointed to the similarity between his concept of revelation and depth psychology's focus on the 'healing powers' of insight, 'meaning, not a detached knowledge, but a repetition of one's actual experiences' (1951: 96). Thus, the reworking of early childhood images and relationships impacts the ability to experience the elevating encounters Tillich describes as revelation. In a discussion of the transitional quality of religious experiences Jones (1991), drawing upon Bollas (1987), also notes this parallel between Tillich and object relations theory:

> Religious moments are transitional not only because they transcend subjectivity and objectivity (Meissner) or invoke imagination (Rizzuto) but also because they allow us to enter again and again into that timeless and transforming psychological space from which renewal and creativity emerge. And what makes such experiences continually renewing? Perhaps, as Bollas suggests, in the presence of a transforming object relationship,

we gain access again to the formative (and reformative) experience at the heart of selfhood, the experience Tillich calls the power of being (1991: 134).

From an ego psychological perspective, the deeply felt sense that things are right is rooted in the holistic, unitive ways of knowing characteristic of primary process thought. Judging by this criterion is a means of enriching discernment and decision making beyond strictly rational calculation to include elusive factors of feeling, intuition and unconscious processes.

Theologically, one can describe the means of judging based on a deeply felt sense that things are right as rooted in the elevating, empowering experience of revelation in which awareness of one's connectedness to the ground of being brings healing, wholeness and transformation (cf. Tillich 1957: 166-67). Said this way, however, one has little more than a re-worded philosophically conceived psychological perspective; the focus is still on an experience. A theological interpretation of this experience also must consider its relationship to the narratives of the Christian tradition and the specific claims made there concerning the world and its relation to God.

In a discussion that has relevance to what is being proposed here, Charles Gerkin (1991) points out that to share in the 'common sense' of a community, its aesthetic sense of rightness, is to have one's own story molded by the community's story. He has characterized the relationship between one's ability to 'exercise sound judgment' (what could be called discernment) and one's grounding in the normative traditions of a community from a Gadamerian perspective.

> I would here propose that beneath the content of all notions of common sense, sound judgment, and aesthetic taste—in the sense that Gadamer uses these concepts—lie the images, themes, evaluative suppositions, and ideal understandings of a commonly held story or complex of stories that have shaped that community and its tradition. To share in the common sense of that community is to have had one's own mythic life story shaped to fit the images, themes, evaluations, and ideals of the communal story. To exercise sound judgment in that community is to embody the normative images, themes, evaluations, and ideals found in the communal story. To be a person of good taste in that community is to express in one's life and behavior the aesthetic vision contained in the deepest images and metaphors of that communal story (1991: 59).

Chapter 4 noted that the aesthetic quality of this feeling was rooted in certain Pentecostal traditions. One could say that the deeply felt 'sense that things are right' is the result of a perceived congruence between the world as constructed by Pentecostal tradition and then experienced by the Pentecostal within that tradition. Like all people, it is assumed that Pentecostals create meaning and experience 'reality' through a dialectical construction involving individual appropriation of categories given through culture (Berger and Luckman 1966). One's world emerges through interactions with the shared symbols given by one's earliest caregivers; 'we take over the narratives of the people we love' (Browning 1991: 242). In a similar manner, the stories Pentecostals tell about Spirit leading establish an ethos for discernment and decision making that influences the way decisions are understood. For instance, 'testimonies' that create expectations that the Spirit does and will lead, often in ways that can be 'felt', along with reports of actual Spirit leading experiences, become contributions to a larger shared story. Stated differently, the deep sense of things feeling right is the result of a perceived harmony between the world and one's self.[3] Such experiences are energizing and empowering.

This is very close to an argument advanced by Stromberg (1986). Drawing upon the work of Bourdieu (1977), Stromberg argues that religious traditions create certain 'cultivated dispositions', understandings or approaches to life, in their adherents. The experience of events that confirm these dispositions are felt as particularly powerful instances of 'grace', or what might better be termed here a sense of felt harmony between self and world.

> Bourdieu (p. 14) points out that we may observe that a group of people continually resort to characteristic ideas about preserving honor, for example, but that it is a distortion to conceive this fact as though the

---

3.   In reference to the idea that embeddedness in a tradition governs the sense of things feeling right, it is of interest to quote a remark by Williams (1990). In discussing how the Spirit guides believers into truth he states that what is imparted by the Spirit is not

> detailed knowledge of all aspects of Christian truth; indeed, there is often confusion and error in the attempts at expression and articulation. But a deep resonance with the truth exists whether, for example, it is the truth about God and the world, Christ and salvation, or the Holy Spirit and the gifts. They [Spirit guided believers] feel fully 'at home' within the essential framework of Christian truth (1990: 242).

While Williams is arguing here for a deep resonance with 'truth' that transcends specific traditions, there is a hint that even when the particulars of a Spirit led person's beliefs are inadequate, there is a deeper sense of things feeling right that is true to something foundational in the way things are.

'abstract principle' of equality in honor were itself ordering the behavior of group members. To do so would be to displace agency from actors and locate it in principles; in such a conceptualization the persons concerned with honor are but puppets manipulated by an abstract principle. Instead, suggests Bourdieu, honor should be seen as the emergent creation of a community of persons who share a sense of honor embedded in habitual dispositions and postures...

In my own observations, these embedded understandings may be manifested as extraordinarily consistent patterns of conception in the believer's thought, patterns of which the believer is not aware... In this sense such a pattern could be called a *posture*, a stance in experience. It may be useful to think of such a pattern not as a phenomenon of the mind but of something that operates on a more basic level than the mind because it *organizes* the mind (Stromberg 1986: 64-65).

Stromberg discusses the case of Anders, a man whose 'disposition' is characterized as one in which 'meaning emerg[es] from inside'. That is, for Anders, events have an inner meaning that emerges when approached in faith. When asked when he felt the need to pray, Anders cited 'stuff that happens in the world and society'. These prompt him to pray as a means of understanding the inner meaning of events that may appear meaningless on the surface. This disposition is a 'pre-articulate constituent of Anders's identity'.

In other words, the style that has been located in Anders's thought is self-reinforcing. When Anders observes some phenomenon which might plausibly be interpreted along the lines that have been outlined, he is likely to seize the opportunity. Doing so, he is likely to be struck by a deep and profound sense of significance, for his observations will resonate with pervasive patterns in his thought...

One can understand how such an experience, which is both an example of and a symbol for a fundamental disposition that is constitutive of Anders's very uniqueness and identity as a person, may very well strike him as a manifestation of divinity (Stromberg 1986: 67-68).

In a related work that touches on this issue, Land (1993) has identified certain Pentecostal 'affections' (which include dispositional qualities) and has written of their impact on beliefs and practices. He shows how the apocalyptic, eschatological expectations of early twentieth-century Pentecostalism shaped a spirituality of gratitude, love and courage that had as its focus the consummation of all things in God. The 'signs' that accompanied the Pentecostal revival both confirmed and created a 'passion for the kingdom'.

Guidelines for Evaluation:
Revision of Discernment and Decision Making

Pentecostal discernment and decision making is a complex process that defies easy summation. This section offers a model, extracted from the practical theological method employed in this study, which identifies necessary elements that discernment and decision making must include. However, these elements should not be considered rigid 'steps' to follow; as an 'aesthetic practice' (Gerkin 1991), Pentecostal discernment and decision making cannot be reduced entirely to a step-by-step logic. In addition, this section draws upon the foregoing chapters to provide several guidelines for evaluating these practices. The model and the guidelines give form and content to a constructive practical theology of discernment and decision making.

A Model for Ideal Pentecostal Discernment and Decision Making
This study moves through several steps in order to understand and evaluate Pentecostal discernment and decision making. It begins by listening to and thickly describing claims to Spirit leading. These claims are then subjected to multiple analyses from various perspectives, including psychological, theological and Pentecostal ones, in an attempt both to enrich a positive understanding of this behavior and to identify negative elements that emerge from these practices. Then, evaluative judgments are made about these claims by means of criteria found in each perspective. Finally, these assessments, along with evaluative guidelines for future practice, are offered to concerned Pentecostals for further discussion by means of this summary. Although partial and incomplete versions of these elements are observable in the illustrations of discernment and decision making reported in Chapter 4, this study proposes that ideally Pentecostal discernment and decision making should consciously and intentionally include all of the following elements or moments:

1. A time for attending to the intuitive, affective dimensions of discernment and decision making. These dimensions are recognized as a valuable and necessary part of all decision making and time and space are given for attending seriously to them. 'Feelings' connected to issues under consideration are understood, not as 'things that get in the way' of decision making, but as important and necessary to good decision making. In Pentecostal terms, this element is a recognition that the Spirit

transcends the strictly rational processes of decision making to work at the affective, intuitive level as well. This does not mean that the Spirit is not at work in the rational processes, although the anti-intellectual bias that characterizes much of Pentecostalism (cf. Anderson 1979) might lead Pentecostals to think this. As will become obvious in the articulation of the other elements in this model, Pentecostal discernment and decision making provides a means for attending to both of these dimensions. The moment described here is one in which the affective dimensions are attended to particularly.

One could point to the decision of the minister of music to halt temporarily the progression of the service, or to the serious (tears by some) and expectant prayers concerning the selection of the new youth pastor as evidence of this element in the examples reported in Chapter 4. The importance of this step, from a Pentecostal perspective, is that it creates a 'space' in which the Spirit can move. From the psychological perspectives, one could say that it creates a transitional space in which the creative potential of primitive psychic resources of primary process thinking and early self and object images can be recaptured in ways that enhance present psychic functioning. From Tillich's perspective one could say that it creates a space for the ecstatic reception of revelation. This is not meant to imply an engineering of such experiences, but simply an attitude of openness and expectancy, in contrast to an attitude that might preclude such processes as a place for the Spirit's work.

2. A time for attending to and describing claims to experiences of Spirit leading. This element basically involves the sharing of experiences, moving discernment and decision making from an individual experience to a communal endeavor in the process. In a rudimentary way it initiates reflection upon experiences of Spirit leading when participants describe what they thought the Spirit to be saying or doing. Attending to the affective dimensions of decision making continues as participants describe impressions and decisions that feel right to them, including preliminary statements as to why they feel as they do. This will often include some remark as to how they connect this experience to the normative biblical narratives and interpretations of these narratives that are dominant in this congregation. This moment would also be a time for sharing the nature of any charismatic manifestations that may have accompanied these experiences. This element of discernment and decision making helps to unfold the more personal and group-specific dimensions of experience that are later correlated with general cultural dimensions of

experience and the 'Christian fact' (cf. Whitehead and Whitehead 1980).

This element of sharing one's experiences of Spirit leading is present in much Pentecostal practice, though not always so consciously or intentionally. Its presence may be seen in the sharing of people's thoughts and feelings about the selection of the new youth pastor following the prayer or in 'testimonies' that often occur after a move of the Spirit. The senior pastor's decision to let the former youth minister speak after such a move of the Spirit indicates a kind of first level report about the Spirit's leading for him. Many of the individual reports of Spirit leading showed something of this element in that anytime such experiences are shared, a certain reflection has begun simply in the way these shared experiences are selected and told. Discussing such experiences with church leaders is also evidence of this step; Allison discussed certain experiences involving charismatic manifestations that concerned her with Pastor Smith. Thus this idea is not absent from Pentecostal practice.

This study argues for more conscious attention to and incorporation of this element in discernment and decision making; time needs to be made for intentional discussion of Spirit leading experiences. These discussions could be done by the entire congregation if the purpose was to share experiences from a common worship event. On other occasions they could be conducted in small groups and would ideally occur within a reasonable period of time following the Spirit leading experiences. Such groups need not be led by the pastor and should include people from all generations.

3. Enriching the description of Spirit leading experiences from multiple perspectives. This element deepens the reflective aspect of discernment and decision making and begins an evaluative moment as well. It expands the descriptive functions that began above to include descriptions of what is happening in these practices, both positively and negatively, from perspectives both within and outside the group's own traditions. For instance, evaluation of the ambiguous ego regressive behaviors mentioned in Chapter 5 would come under scrutiny during this element. Inclusion of this element brings the most noticeable revisions to current Pentecostal discernment and decision making and so more attention is given to describing this element of the model.

The presence of this element in Pentecostal practice is more sporadic than the previous elements. Although it is not completely absent, its presence is more subtle and informal and its use less rigorous. It is seen in descriptions and discussions of Spirit leading experiences that occur at later times, for instance. 'Interpretations' of these experiences can emerge in sermons, as leaders help shape the valuation of given experiences, or Pentecostals may simply inquire of each other as to thoughts or feelings about certain experiences. I am aware of many such informal discussions that occur after services in which some claim to Spirit leading was present, especially if there was some confusion as to whether it was actually the Spirit at work. Conversations about whether someone was trying to 'stir up a shout' is one way Pentecostals voice concerns about manipulation of people's actions or emotions; inquiries of whether someone 'got in themselves' (or 'in the flesh') voice questions about self-deception, mildly conceived. This study argues for a more conscious, intentional use and expansion of this element of discernment and decision making in two ways.

First, Pentecostals should expand and enrich from within their own practice and tradition the times and occasions when this step is used. This expansion and enrichment is to elevate to a more conscious level both the positive and negative elements to be found in these experiences. Creative reappropriation of its own traditions and formative narratives can do much to enrich the positive description and assessment of these practices. The careful, thoughtful scholarship of Pentecostals such as Dempster (1983) and Land (1993) show how the original, biblical Pentecostal community can provide rich sources of images, metaphors and values to guide and evaluate current Pentecostal practices. For instance, Dempster argues that the experience of glossolalic worship can create a 'sense of experiential solidarity' with the original Pentecostal community of the Bible and to the God made known to this community. Speaking in tongues is viewed as an act of worship that evokes a 'symbolic reordering of experience' (cf. Bellah 1970) that can redefine the self and transform motives, commitments and values through encounter with the *mysterium tremendum*.

> In the influx of creative power experienced in the glossolalic encounter, the individual can be induced to experience a fresh symbolic identification with the original eschatological community of the new humanity. When such a sense of solidarity is aroused, the mundane symbols of self-identity are challenged and a renewed symbolic identification occurs with the God of Pentecost, who is also the God revealed in Jesus Christ, the God of captivity and future hope and the God of the exodus. Personal reflection in the post-worship experience upon the glossolalic encounter and upon the

normative convictions embodied in the pertinent biblical stories can induce
in the believer a transformation of motivation, commitment and value, and a
revitalized understanding of his/her moral identity (1983: 19).

Such an interpretation is very much in line with the psychological and
theological analyses offered in this study. Dempster also makes it clear
that glossolalia, in and of itself, does not interpret one's experience. Such
interpretation is done in post-worship reflection which points to the role
of a community's traditional stories for shaping moral understandings.
While Dempster's argument concerns the ability of a charismatic manifestation to signify a sense of solidarity with certain biblical traditions,
one should note that it is not simply the charismatic manifestation that
accomplishes this. It is the interpretation of the experience by way of a
tradition concerning the Holy Spirit's work and character that
contributes to the sense of experiential solidarity (cf. Macchia 1992).

The same argument would hold for non-charismatic activities; it is the
interpretations given to these practices that contribute to the sense of
experiential solidarity. In a similar way Land (1993) presents Pentecostal
worship as a means by which Pentecostals identify with the biblical
Pentecostal community and are shaped by narratives about this community. Citing testimonies, sermons, pamphlets and songs by twentieth-
century Pentecostal pioneers, Land shows how crying is understood as
identification with Christ's death and crucifixion, laughter as identification with his resurrection (p. 146), speaking in tongues as evidence of
communion with God (p. 130), and shouting as rejoicing over the demise
of racial and class barriers and the empowering of the disenfranchised
(p. 123).

But Pentecostals also recognize that claims to Spirit leading may
involve overexcitement or a confusing of personal desire with the Spirit's
direction. Such comments indicate the beginnings of negative descriptions and assessments of their practices. Another way Pentecostals can
deepen the descriptive and evaluative element of discernment and
decision making is by elaborating and discussing the evaluative criteria
implicit in the kinds of safeguards outlined in Chapter 4. Making these
patterns of restraint and order a more explicit part of Pentecostal
reflection would encourage the kind of religious reflection that Tillich
described as religion with the energy and freedom of the spirit movements but without the excesses. The spirit movements themselves provide the best starting place for such a realization because there is already
in their practice various implicit critiques in such matters as membership

stratification, resistance to urges, and recognition that there are different kinds of tongues speaking (some for praise only, others for 'messages and interpretations'). Elaborating the loosely defined criteria by which Pentecostals evaluate their own practices such as the presence of excessive emotion, complete loss of motor control, tonal quality of tongues, deferential preferences to certain 'interpreters' of tongues would not only make such criteria more obviously available for evaluative use but would open up dialogue regarding the sufficiency of such criteria and possible ways to enhance (or modify) them.

Secondly, Pentecostals should enrich the description and assessment of these practices by expanding this element to include perspectives from outside the Pentecostal tradition. In this study this was done through perspectives from the larger Christian tradition and ego and object relations psychology. Enlarging the meaning of tradition to include conscious appropriation of criteria drawn from the longer, ecumenical Christian tradition does not require loss of the deep structures of Pentecostalism as the work of Dempster (1983) and Land (1993) shows, but is necessary because not all traditions are good ones. Traditions need to be mutually critically correlated. Pentecostals have not always been quick or willing to acknowledge the role of the larger Christian tradition (or even the role of their own tradition[4]), thinking the immediacy of the Holy Spirit sufficient for their decision. Yet, as this study has shown, their own traditions and the wider Christian tradition are both important to their practices, and a chief source of norms for judging these practices. This study draws from the larger Christian tradition, as represented by the theology of Paul Tillich, not only to provide ways to enrich the positive understanding of these practices as revelatory, but also to provide some evaluative criteria for judging these practices.

The argument to include psychological perspectives in their discernment and decision making may sound strange to most Pentecostals. In

---

4. The ahistorical tendency in Pentecostalism is largely traceable to its beginnings as an 'apocalyptic restorationist' movement. Early Pentecostals interpreted their experiences as a sign that the last days had come and the task was to restore the Church to its pristine, New Testament form so that it would be ready for the second coming of Christ. Intervening centuries, at least since Constantine, were seen as years of apostasy, with nothing that need be retained in a 'last days church'.

However, Pentecostal practice and belief did not in actuality discard all tradition. In fact, Pentecostal beliefs and practices are traceable to a variety of Christian traditions (Dayton 1987).

defense of this, it may again be noted that neither the element of enriched description nor evaluation is absent from discernment and decision making. This is simply an argument to expand the perspectives from which such descriptions and evaluations will be made. But more compelling is the fact that Pentecostals already include something of this perspective, if only superficially and informally, in their discernment and decision making. This is not surprising given the social impact of psychology in this culture (cf. Reiff 1966). One of the interviewees in this study told of a disturbing experience early in her Pentecostal pilgrimage in which a woman disrupted a worship service by 'barking like a dog'. When the interviewee later discussed her distress with the minister in charge, the minister indicated that this person was known to have 'mental problems' and that the interviewee should not be confused by thinking the woman's behavior to be from the Spirit.[5] I am aware of other nascent psychological evaluations that form parts of discussions of Spirit leading experiences. Since this perspective is not totally absent from discernment and decision making, this study is simply arguing that its use be more conscious, intentional and sophisticated.

As with the other perspectives, enriching the descriptive and assessment elements from the psychological perspective would be for purposes of understanding both the positive and negative aspects of this behavior. Chapter 5 shows how the positive understanding of discernment and decision making can be enriched by pointing to examples of creative regression in these practices. Chapter 6 illustrates connections between early childhood and various types of Spirit leading experiences. Illuminating such connections is not done merely to show that a given experience may be dismissed as not of the Spirit's leading, but rather to enrich discernment and decision making through understanding the personality dynamics that people bring to it. For instance, awareness that a church member's heightened sensitivity to handicapped persons comes out of a history of having been a handicapped child, and even may involve insensitivity to other issues because of this particular history, does not mean that the Spirit may not use the person to lead a congregation

---

5.   Interestingly, this report also indicates the Pentecostal tendency to tolerate a certain amount of aberrant behavior, even when the person has obvious problems. Some have cited such tolerance among the reasons Pentecostal worship attracts a disproportionate share of such people (Maloney and Lovekin 1985). It should be noted, however, that part of the reason for the tolerance is the ambiguity that attends certain experiences also judged (often later) to have been of the Spirit.

into activities involving a special sensitivity to the handicapped.

In addition to enriching the positive assessment of discernment and decision making, psychology can also raise questions about manipulation, deception, rationalization and pathology. It is this aspect of the psychological perspective that will probably create the most resistance among Pentecostals. Is not such a suggestion too foreign to the way the work of the Spirit is commonly conceived? As noted above, however, Pentecostals already raise some of these issues in their questions about 'stirring up a shout', or whether people 'got in themselves', or taking known 'mental problems' into consideration. Adding a conscious psychological element is simply to extend and deepen this type of inquiry, and need not be seen as completely irreconcilable with Pentecostal practice.

One's psycho-developmental history cannot be divorced from one's experience of the Spirit. But this does not mean that a knowledge of psychological dynamics is sufficient in itself for deciding the Spirit's leading; the Divine Mystery uses 'earthen vessels' (2 Cor. 4.7) with imperfect developmental histories. By the same token it does not mean that psychological perspectives need be adopted uncritically; psychological critiques of religious practices can be morally or philosophically biased against religion and specifically against Pentecostalism. Therefore, each perspective needs to critique the others in order to 'unmask distortions' (Tracy 1983) that may arise from any one perspective.

4. Evaluation of these experiences. Here one should note that there is not a strict division between the elements being enumerated, they are not 'steps', but they involve considerable overlap or interpenetration. The previous element has already expressed evaluative dimensions by describing both the positive and negative aspects of an experience; the element of attending to affective dimensions also includes reflective dimensions in the way experiences are selected and told. The purpose in listing evaluation as a separate element is to highlight the fact that at some point judgments are made as to whether a given experience was the Spirit's leading. Discernment and decision making is not an endless exercise in enriching description; at some point judgments are made, sometimes tentatively, sometimes with finality. In actual practice these judgments are made on the basis of criteria that arise from the perspectives by which this behavior has been described.

A Pentecostal would be most aware of this element in those times when a judgment is made on the basis of norms drawn from within the Pentecostal tradition. These norms are based in Scripture but also include more loosely defined traditions from shared Pentecostal experience. Pentecostal norms concerning the orderliness of the Holy Spirit's work are of this nature. They have their foundation in Scripture (cf. 1 Cor. 14), but stories of experiences when things got out of order also inform current judgments. Pentecostals should also recognize this evaluative element in judgments about the 'spiritual maturity' (or lack thereof) of certain people who claim the leading of the Spirit. Pentecostals speak of people who are 'more spiritually mature', more sensitive to the Spirit, better able to discern the Spirit's leading, than others. These comments imply evaluative judgments made from within the Pentecostal tradition. Gerkin argues that judgments of a person's spiritual maturity are judgments regarding how well the person 'embod[ies] the normative images, themes, evaluations, and ideals found in the communal story; (1991: 59). This deep rootedness in the traditions about the work of the Spirit produces a kind of 'practical wisdom' (Browning 1991) that others recognize.

Ideally, discernment and decision making expand the evaluative element to include criteria drawn from other perspectives. This study presents criteria drawn from ego and object relations psychology and Paul Tillich's theology as perspectives for enriching judgments about Spirit leading. In this model, assessment of a person's spiritual maturity would include consideration of criteria for positive transformation drawn from all three perspectives: spiritual maturity would involve psychological health, theological soundness, and faithfulness and continuity with normative Pentecostal narratives and traditions.

At some point the evaluative criteria by which Spirit leading experiences are judged must be made publicly accessible. Whether or not this is considered a separate moment from the evaluation itself, this element of the model needs to be noted. These public criteria then become contributions to ongoing dialogue that both frames and shapes future discernment and decision making and enlarges the tradition about the leading of the Spirit. In this study, this element is included by presenting the summary of evaluative criteria below.

This revised model of discernment and decision making is an 'ideal' one. I am aware of no congregation or denomination that uses all these elements in their discernment and decision making (but I do not deny the potential for its existence). Although partial and incomplete versions of it appear in given examples of discernment and decision making, it may be that the entire model will never be used. A certain amount of ambiguity within Spirit leading may mean that fragmentary use is the best that can be expected. Nevertheless, the model is offered in the hope of reducing the amount of fragmentation.

Normative Guidelines for Practice

There must be a moment for making evaluative guidelines for future practice public if practical theology is to be constructively critical. This section summarizes certain evaluative guidelines that have emerged from this study.

Holistic knowing. The first guideline by which these practices can be evaluated is whether they seek to integrate reflective and affective dimensions of knowing. Integration means that one dimension of Pentecostal decision making does not subsume the other; there is a legitimate place given to both the affective, intuitive dimensions as well as the rational, reflective dimensions of decision making. In trying to give attention to both dimensions the ideal model described above rejects two misconceptions about Spirit leading. First, it rejects the idea that discernment and decision making is divisible along 'rational versus spiritual' (or non-rational, intuitive) lines (cf. McGuire 1982). In the integrative model, finance committee decisions would allow new concerns, insights, visions and alternative perspectives to rise to consciousness that would have been overlooked in discussions that omit this dimension. Conversely, attending to rational dimensions in 'spiritual' decisions also would allow new ideas, thoughts and insights to emerge.

Secondly, an integrative model avoids two extremes among Pentecostals: those convinced the Spirit leads only through what is here called the affective dimension, and those who wish to exclude the affective dimension as the root of Pentecostal excesses.

An integrative model recognizes the need for attention to both reason and affection. Failure to attend to the dimension of reason has sanctioned much abuse in Pentecostal practice; selfish desires, power struggles, spiritual elitism, and emotional escapism have all been hidden under claims to the Spirit's direction. An integrative model of discernment and decision making recognizes that reason and the Spirit are not inextricably opposed to each other. The larger Christian tradition has defended reason as a gift of God. Even its technical, controlling dimensions are useful for theological investigations concerning the finite dimensions of religious experience (cf. Tillich 1951: 40). This does not mean, however, that reason alone is sufficient for discerning the Spirit's direction. Reason alone, especially in its technical, controlling sense, can be deceptive and destructive. The recognition that 'reason' can degenerate into deception and rationalization guided by the interests of those in power is partially overcome by a more critical rationality (Habermas 1971). In this study, the appeal to multiple perspectives is a similar way to deepen rationality. But in addition to deepening the critique of reason via a more critical reason, Pentecostal discernment and decision making would argue that attention to more holistic dimensions of knowing (in which the subject–object dichotomy of technical reason is transcended) offers its own critique against a rationality rooted in control and destruction.

Partial use of this guideline is seen in those times when the ecstatic dimensions of Spirit leading (insights from prayer, the deeply felt sense that things are right) are discussed among members of the congregation. In the case material, Gwen's and Fernando's willingness to submit decisions made on the basis of feelings to review by others are cited as illustrations of trying to integrate the rational and affective dimensions of knowing. The selection of the new youth minister also illustrates attempts to include both these dimensions in decision making. In that event the congregation discussed what it desired and needed in a youth pastor, but the discussion was combined with serious and expectant prayer and its affective dimensions. Describing how these dimensions are combined in actual practice brings to mind Paris's (1982) comparison of Pentecostal worship with jazz composition; there is both structure and freedom for improvisation, but sometimes only the players know when it has been 'done right'!

Integrating needs of self and community. The second guideline by which discernment and decision making can be evaluated is whether it seeks to integrate the needs of the individual and the community. Decisions bring about moments for becoming a self or shrinking back in anxiety. Spirit led decisions participate in healthy self formation; that is, they promote an openness to God and others, an integration of positive and negative aspects of the self, and an opening up of imaginative and creative possibilities that empowers one to undertake constructive action. But Spirit led decisions also build community. Earlier chapters pointed to instances of reconciliation and reincorporation into the community through these practices. A concern for both the needs of the self and the needs of others characterize Spirit led decisions since, as Tillich (1963) notes, individuals always exist as individuals only within the context of a specific community.

The model described above tries to take this tension into consideration. It gives attention to both individual needs, recognizing that such needs are met through various experiences of Spirit leading and by attending to the individual recounting of such experiences, and by encouraging dialogue among members of the congregation. At the same time it attends to the role of tradition. Through conversations regarding experiences of Spirit leading it might also ask, within the context of worship, whether a particular claim to the Spirit's leading ministers to the congregation or only to the individual. Chapter 4 described certain charismatic manifestations that created tension or uneasiness in the service when only one person was involved. Such times would be the object of reflection in light of this criterion. Tillich argues that genuine revelation reaches beyond the individual who receives it to touch and transform others in positive ways (cf. 1951: 127-28). From the case material, the Pentecostal tradition that the Holy Spirit does no harm physically or emotionally is affirmed as useful for distinguishing the Spirit's direction because it is rooted in concerns larger than the individual.

Ultimate versus finite concerns. The third guideline for evaluating discernment and decision making is to ask if these practices focus on issues of 'ultimate concern'; that is, are they activities that truly mediate the Spiritual presence by pointing beyond the finite media themselves. Judging discernment and decision making by this guideline would involve asking if the nature of these experiences is such that one is grasped by ultimate concern, claimed by something greater than oneself (or group), 'shaken' and transformed in positive and creative ways? Discernment and decision making that focuses more on the medium than on what is mediated would not meet this guideline.

Tillich defines the demonic as 'the elevation of something conditional to unconditional significance' (1951: 140). There are many ways this can happen. When either the self or the community is valued absolutely, something conditional has been substituted for the unconditional. Such elevation leads to identifying one's own will or perhaps nationalistic feelings with the will of God. Similarly, overvaluing either the affective or technical dimensions of knowing is another way of confusing finite media with their infinite ground. In the case material, claims to special knowledge and use of fleeces were evaluated negatively in light of this criterion.

The guideline to distinguish finite concerns from their infinite ground does not come with guarantees. Humans are fallible and the best of their commitments, even those they think to be to God, can be wrong. This study proposes that dialogue about those commitments one believes to be from the Spirit is a useful way to help discern between the finite and infinite, in that it helps identify areas of finite conditionedness that underlies one's experiences of the infinite. Such dialogue has the potential to transform the larger group. Conversely, claims to the Spirit's direction that one is not willing to have evaluated by others is suspect.

If one takes the 'prophetic' role seriously, however, the call for willingness to have one's Spirit leading experiences submitted to evaluation by others presents a dilemma. But even if one concedes the prophet's right simply to announce his or her revelation without submitting it to public evaluation, the one who hears the prophet speak must still decide whether to receive this revelation as from the Spirit. Such judgments inevitably link the listener with a larger community who provide a tradition and context for judging such experiences. That such communities risk rejecting the voice of the Spirit in rejecting such prophets is part of the ambiguity (and *mysterium tremendum*!) of discernment and decision making. While dialogue among people with a reputation for sensitivity to the Spirit is a safeguard, it is not a guarantee for hearing the voice of the Spirit, for knowing with certainty that one has distinguished the finite from the infinite. With this guideline, one can but be aware and ask the question.

Ambiguity. Human behavior is extremely complex; there always remains a quality of ambiguity to claims of Spirit leading. This then is the fourth guideline for evaluating discernment and decision making. This guideline emerges from Tillich's understanding that the divine mystery always remains (or retains elements of) mystery. 'The Spirit blows where it will' (Jn 3.8) and one simply cannot generate a list of guidelines that chart the ways the Spirit can and will move. The immediate access to the Spirit that Pentecostals claim should not be thought to eliminate all ambiguity (Dempster 1983). In particular, charismatic manifestations should not be used to avoid the hard questions of life. Discerning the divine will always involve risk; there is no way to know for certain that one's choices or allegiances are ultimately the right ones. One must be willing to look at decisions at a later time and admit that they were wrong. Human fallibility suggests that all decisions, even those made under the leading of the Spirit, need periodic review. In this regard, one should not misinterpret the nature of these guidelines. They are not unmediated or absolute, but simply those that appear more sustainable for understanding and evaluating this behavior when traditions and perspectives on the behavior are critically correlated. Even experiences that meet the guidelines can still be ambiguous; closing off possibilities in one area even as they open them up in another. The guidelines should not be understood as somehow explaining the work and mystery of the Spirit in ways that substitute for a vital relationship to the Spirit.

Pentecostal discernment and decision making must retain some ambiguity (and humility) about leadings of the Spirit. One's humanness (or selfhood) is seen in the choices he or she makes (or refuses to make). It is not the role of the Spirit to remove one's humanity and one cannot and should not try to escape all ambiguity through appeal to the Spirit's leading. Such thinking only leads to avoidance of responsibility for one's decisions. With freedom comes anxiety and no absolute guarantees that one's decision are correct. Not even through the Spirit.

Summary Conclusions

The purpose here is to summarize what a practical theology of Pentecostal discernment and decision making accomplishes both for Pentecostals and for the wider Christian community.

What this Study Does for Pentecostals

While acknowledging that Pentecostal discernment and decision making is not always 'creative' or 'revelatory', this study points out the value of the way Pentecostals make decisions, offering a constructive analysis of these practices, while warning against their abuses. These methods of decision making can build self formation, open up new possibilities for understanding self and God, empower people to action, and build community. These means of decision making retain a proper, though restricted role for charismatic manifestations in decision making and remain true to the Pentecostal emphasis on experience. Intuitive means of decision making, while not without dangers, are not to be automatically distrusted or abandoned. Such processes are part of the decision making of all groups (cf. Gerkin 1991). While such dimensions tend to be found only in minor or recessive forms in non-Pentecostal groups, they are especially valued in Pentecostal decision making.

Not all Pentecostal discernment and decision making is judged equally valuable, however. The criterion of judging by a deeply felt sense of things being right satisfies more of the criteria for creative regression and revelation than other forms of discernment and decision making. Arguments for the inclusion of these dimensions do not imply that any good feeling is necessarily to be identified as a leading of the Spirit.

This study also offers suggestions to enhance discernment and decision making. Pentecostal theology has been said 'to convey that an arid, rationalistic, formalistic, unemotional, non-experiential and non-charismatic approach to religious life is unacceptable' (Wheelock 1983), but Pentecostals nevertheless need to integrate reason more effectively with the more intuitive, affective ways of knowing characteristic of their tradition. The fact that valuable things are going on in the ecstatic ways of discernment and decision making should not be taken as an excuse to minimize or eliminate rational discussion; the language of Spirit leading is not to be used to hide a lack of critical thought. Pentecostal discernment and decision making seeks to integrate rational and affective dimensions of knowing and the needs of the individual and the community. It points beyond itself to issues of ultimate concern, realizing that, at best, there will always be ambiguity in this endeavor.

What this Study Does for the Wider Christian Community

This study explores the deeper structure of Pentecostal discernment and decision making in order to reflect on what this deeper structure points to and how it may be applicable in non-Pentecostal settings without simply adopting Pentecostal practices (as mainline charismatics and neo-Pentecostals have done, for instance).

At the heart of Pentecostal discernment and decision making is a way of judging based on a deeply felt sense that things are right. This study shows that there is a warrant for trusting this kind of 'felt' discernment because these practices tap resources that can contribute to the formation (and transformation) of self and community. This study shows the relationship between this means of discernment and decision making and early psychic resources that included more holistic ways of knowing. Valuing this deep structure in non-Pentecostal settings would involve finding ways to tap the affective, intuitive dimensions of knowing in a more conscious manner. Perhaps music or liturgy could be understood to create a kind of 'transitional space' in which an openness to the primal resources of primary process thinking or a recapturing of early self and object images is encouraged. Baer (1976) argues, for instance, that the repetitive nature of liturgy 'permits the analytical mind—the focused, objectifying dimension of man's intellect—to rest, thus freeing other dimensions of the person, what we might loosely refer to as man's spirit, for a deeper openness to divine reality' (1976: 152). In other contexts, allotting time for 'priming' exercises and activities (Harrison 1984) could be a way of attending to affective, intuitive dimensions of decision making. The finance committee of the mainline church might find that a time of inner reflection in which members attend to their 'feelings' as well as 'thoughts' about the proposals being considered may open one to new insights about the budget. Allotting time to share these reflections may further open access to affective dimensions of knowing. In similar manner, having someone pray aloud about each matter under consideration may open up new insight or understanding of an issue; hearing an issue prayed about publicly may lead to a feeling of rightness about the proposal, or may reveal its pettiness or incongruity with the convictions and norms of the community. Integrating these affective insights with rational ones would require conversation about one's experiences during these times and activities (and would then be followed by the critical analyses recommended in the model above).

Finally, one must note that Pentecostal discernment and decision making cannot be separated entirely from the deeply held conviction that God is at work in these activities; decision making is not a human endeavor only. This is not meant to imply that one can or should try to engineer divine intervention, but it does constitute an acknowledgment that Christian decision making participates in realities wider than the egos of the decision makers themselves. This conviction creates an openness and expectancy in Pentecostal decision making. Attending seriously to affective dimensions of knowing as mediators of the Divine Presence in non-Pentecostal contexts would require embracing this belief to some extent but it need not require adopting specific responses to accompany the conviction; openness and expectancy to divine involvement in decision making can take more restrained forms than those generally associated with Pentecostals.

Appendix I

VARIATIONS IN PENTECOSTALISM

Synan (1987) distinguishes the following five major streams within Pentecostalism:

1. *Classical Pentecostal movements*. These refer to groups that arose around the turn of the century and owe their origins to the teachings of Charles Parham and William Seymour. These movements hold that speaking in tongues is the 'initial evidence' of the baptism of the Holy Spirit and tend to be institutionalized in their own denominations.

2. *Mainline Protestant charismatics*. The charismatic movement in the mainline churches began in the early 1960s. It has historical connections to the classical Pentecostals (Bruner 1970) but the people in this grouping elected to stay within their own denominations. They tend to reject the idea that speaking in tongues is the initial evidence of the baptism of the Spirit, arguing that the Holy Spirit baptism is evidenced by charisms other than speaking in tongues. They were sometimes called 'neo-Pentecostals'.

3. *Catholic charismatics*. These are groups that also emerged in the 1960s and have chosen to remain within the Catholic church.

4. *Independent groups*. These groups can have roots in either the earlier classical Pentecostal groups or to the later charismatic movements. They may have broken away from these earlier groups or may have simply started independently around some 'magnetic' leader. They tend to hold beliefs on the theological fringes of the movement and often proliferate through the use of television and radio ministries.

(5. *Indigenous 'third world' groups*. Some third world Pentecostals may be associated with one of the historical Pentecostal groups and are much more indigenous to their region. Their classification as Pentecostal may be on the basis of 'superficial similarities in worship and the practice of glossolalia'. These groups are among the fastest growing Pentecostal movements in the world (Synan 1987). Wagner (1988) points out that in Latin American countries Pentecostalism is second only to Catholicism in its number of adherents.

Synan also lists four major theological groupings among Pentecostals:

1. 'Wesleyan' Pentecostals emphasize instantaneous sanctification and usually have more centralized or episcopal forms of government. This group is sometimes called the 'holiness-pentecostal'; movement. Representative bodies from this group include the Church of God (Cleveland, TN) and the Church of God in Christ (Memphis, TN).

2. 'Baptistic' Pentecostals emphasize sanctification as a gradual work and tend to be more congregational in terms of government. They are also considered less legalistic than the Wesleyan Pentecostals. The Assemblies of God (Springfield, MO) is representative of this grouping.

3. 'Oneness' Pentecostals deny the orthodox doctrine of the trinity and teach that one must experience speaking in tongues as a necessary part of salvation. This group is sometimes called the 'Jesus only' or 'Jesus Name' movement. Representative groups are the United Pentecostal Church and several groups that use 'Apostolic' in their church name.

4. 'Charismatic' Pentecostals. These Pentecostals remain in their previous denominations and so embrace theologies that are part of that denominational heritage. They tend to emphasize all the charismata, not glossolalia alone. Most also reject the classical Pentecostal teaching that glossolalia is the necessary 'initial evidence' of Spirit baptism.

Appendix II

INTERVIEW GUIDE QUESTIONS

Questions in parentheses were asked only if not answered in the major question.

Questions about Spirit Leading Experiences

1. Tell me about how you received the baptism of the Holy Spirit.
2. Before you received the baptism of the Holy Spirit what were your thoughts or feelings?
3. After you received the Holy Spirit, what were your first thoughts? What was the first thing you did?
4. Have you ever tried to help someone else get the baptism of the Spirit? Tell me about that. (What did you do?)
5. If someone were to ask you why you think being baptized with the Holy Spirit is important what would you tell them?
6. What differences do you see in the lives of people who have the baptism of the Holy Spirit and those who do not?
7. How has the baptism in the Spirit changed your life? (Have there been occasions when the Holy Spirit helped you in your job/school? Tell me about this.)
8. What kind of personal manifestations of the Spirit have you experienced? Witnessed?
9. On what occasions have you been 'moved' by some manifestation of the Spirit? (What was the occasion? church services? other times?)
10. What is the importance of such manifestations for you? (What do they mean to you?
11. How would you describe your thoughts or feelings before such times (Can you tell they are coming?) How would you describe your thoughts or feelings after these times?
12. Have you ever been in a situation when you felt the Holy Spirit was directing you (or the church) to some action or decision? (That is, have you ever felt led of the Spirit to do something?) Tell me about this (How it came about; how you felt; what it involved; how you knew that it was the Spirit).
13. How would you describe your feelings during this experience of Spirit leading?
14. What was done following this experience? Have you ever taken any action (changed an attitude) as the result of what you felt to be the leading of the Spirit? What kinds of actions (changes)?

15. What difference (if any) would you say that experiencing God's guidance made in this situation?

16. Have there ever been times when you perhaps 'felt led' but were not sure whether it was the Spirit's leading or not? Tell me about those experiences. What did you do in those instances?

17. How do you know that what you experience is the Spirit and not 'being in self'?

18. Have you ever witnessed occasions of 'wild fire' (occasions when charismatic manifestations were disruptive)? Tell me about this. (How was the situation handled? How could you tell it was 'wild fire'?)

19. What kind of things do you think the Spirit leads people to do? (What kind of things do you think the Spirit would never lead people to do?)

20. Have you ever had occasion for 'second thoughts' about decisions you made based on the conviction that it was the Spirit's leading? How have you resolved this?

21. If a minister told you the Lord led him to move to another congregation during the middle of the appointment year, what would you think?

22. If someone told you that their pastor had been selected after a message and interpretations in tongues, what would you think?

23. If you were asked who you feel is best at discerning the spirit in this congregation (or anyone else you know), who would you name? Why do you think that person(s) is a good discerner? (What characteristics or qualities do they exhibit?)

Questions Concerning One's Relationship with God

24. What are your first memories of God?

How would you complete the following sentences:

25. I feel close to God when... because...

26. I do not feel close to God when... because...

27. The time in my life I felt the closest to God was when... and I was ____ years of age.

28. The time in my life I felt the most distant from God was when I was... because...

29. I feel that what God expects most from me is... because...

30. In general, I think God is pleased (or dissatisfied) with me because...

31. What I like (or don't like) the most about God is... because...

32. Emotionally, I would like to have the _____ God has because...

33. The most important thing I expect from God is... because...

34. I think God rewards (punishes) people if... because... He does this by...

35. An event that caused me to change my thinking about God was... because...

36. According to my experiences I would describe God as... because...

Appendix III

QUESTIONNAIRE ON PERSONAL AND FAMILY BACKGROUND

Current Information

1. Name and date of birth.
2. Marital status. If applicable, date of marriage, children's ages, previous marriages, and children by other marriages.
3. Give a brief résumé of your educational and occupational history.

Growing Up

4. What do you remember of your earliest child rearing? (Were your parents Christians? Members of the church?)
5. Please indicate your birth order and sex of your siblings.
6. What was your father's occupation? Tell me about your father (What was the worst [best] experience you had with your father?)
7. Tell me about your mother (Was your mother employed? Was she your primary care giver? What was the best [worst] experience you had with your mother?)
8. How was affection shown in your family? By your father? Your mother? You and your brothers and sisters?
9. Who was the 'boss' in your family? The disciplinarian? The provider? Because...
10. How were disagreements handled in your family?
11. What 'groups' were there in your family?

. Your Life in Stages

12. Tell me the single most significant event of the following time periods or stages in your life. You may want to think of things like geographical moves, illnesses, marriages, births, deaths, sexual development, times of particular growth or turning points in your life.

    Small Child
    Pre-Teen (Elementary school years)
    Mid-Teens (Junior High)
    Late-Teens (High School)
    Young Adult
    Middle Adult
    Late Adulthood

13. What was your best experience growing up? Your worst?

Family Relationships

14. Who in your family are you most like emotionally? In what ways?
15. Who was the member of your family that you felt the closest to? Most distant from? Because...
16. Who in your family did you like (admire) the most? The least? Because...
17. Who in your family would you say your father was closest to? Your mother? Because...
18. If you could change yourself to be like anyone in your family who would you like to be? Because...

Self Reflections

19. If you could be any historical or fictional figure in the world, who would you like to be? Because...
20. If you could change to any kind of thing or object in the world what would you want to be? Anything you would never want to be? Because...
21. When do you feel 'really alive'? Because...
22. Can you recall a dream that has had a significant impact on you and why?...

DESCRIPTIVE DATA

Although information on the age of each member was not available, a record of the Sunday School enrollment gives some information on age distribution. The Sunday School enrollment includes those who attend Sunday School regularly and is about equal to the 225 members and 125 friends and children the pastor estimates as attending at least once a month. The Sunday School enrollment with approximate age groupings shows the following distribution:

Age Group	Total Enrolled	Number Who Are Members	% of Members in this Age Group
0- 1	10	2 (teachers)	1
2-3	7	1 (teacher)	0
4-5	7	0	0
6-7	16	2 (teachers)	1
8-9	14	3	1
10-11	16	3	1
12-13	24	8	3
14-17	23	11	5
18-22	19	11	5
20-30	15	11	5
30-35	38	28	12
35-50	69	65	28
50-65	62	50	22
65+	42	35	15
Totals	362	230	99

One can note that an approximate median age would fall in the upper 30s.

Based upon the above distribution, the sample of interviews should be distributed as follows:

Age Group	Ideal Number Number	Actual
Below 14	1.0	0
14-17	0.8	0
18-22	0.8	0
20-30	0.8	2
20-35	2.0	3
35-50	4.8	6
50-65	3.7	4
Over 65	2.5	2

These figures exclude the initial three interviews with co-workers done to refine the questions and the two ministers, both of whom fit in the 35-50 category. With the exception of the lower age groups, the sample approximates the age composition of the congregation.

Regarding other factors of social makeup described in Chapter 4, the following comparative table is provided:

Category	Group Percentage	Sample Percentage
Female	53	41
Male	47	59
Black	5	6
Hispanic	4	0
Denominational Officials	4	6
Denominational Workers	17	29
Ministers	13	18
Retired Ministers	7	12

With the ministerial staff and three co-workers again excluded from these figures the sample roughly approximates the social makeup of the congregation. Given the nature of this study and the types of information sought, such differences may be assumed to have minimal impact.

SELECT BIBLIOGRAPHY

Abell, T.
1982   *Better Felt than Said* (Waco, TX: Markham Press).
Alland, A.
1962   'Possession in a Revivalistic Negro Church', *JSSR* 1: 204-13.
Ammerman, N.
1987   *Bible Believers* (New Brunswick, NJ: Rutgers University Press).
Anderson, G.
1992   'Pentecostal Hermeneutics', in *Drinking from our Own Wells* (Papers presented at 22nd Annual Meeting of the Society for Pentecostal Studies, Springfield, MO).

Anderson, R.
1979   *Vision of the Disinherited: The Making of American Pentecostalism* (New York: Oxford University Press).

Arnold, M.B.
1970   'Brain Function in Emotion: A Phenomenological Analysis', in P. Black, *Physiological Correlates of Emotion* (New York: Academic Press): 261-85 (cited in Kernberg 1976).

Arrington, F.
1988   'Hermeneutics', in S. Burgess, B. McGee and P. Alexander (eds.) 1988: 376-89.

1994   'Use of the Bible by Pentecostals', *Pneuma* 16 (1): 101-107.
Baer, R.
1976   'Quaker Silence, Catholic Liturgy, and Pentecostal Glossolalia—Some Functional Similarities', in Spittler (ed.) 1976: 150-64.

Basham, D.
1971   *A Handbook on Tongues, Interpretation and Prophecy* (Monroeville, PA: Whitaker Books).

Bellah, R.
1970   *Beyond Belief: Essays on Religion in a Post-Traditional World* (San Francisco: Harper & Row).

Benson, F.
1975   'A Story of Division', in Hamilton (ed.) 1975: 185-94.
Berger, P., and T. Luckman
1966   *The Social Construction of Reality* (New York: Doubleday).
Bernstein, R.
1983   *Beyond Objectivism and Relativism* (Philadelphia: University of Pennsylvania Press).

Bloch-Hoell, N.
1964   *The Pentecostal Movement* (New York: Humanities Press).

Bollas, C.
1987   *The Shadow of the Object* (New York: Columbia University Press).
Bourdieu, P.
1977   *Outline of a Theory of Practice* (Cambridge: Cambridge University Press).
Brown, N.
1968   *Love's Body* (New York: Vintage Books).
Browning, D. (ed.)
1983   *Practical Theology: The Emerging Field in Theology, Church and World* (San Francisco: Harper & Row).
Browning, D.
1991   *A Fundamental Practical Theology* (Minneapolis: Fortress Press).
Brumback, C.
1947   *What Meaneth This? A Pentecostal Answer to a Pentecostal Question* (Springfield, MO: Gospel Publishing House).
Bruner, F.D.
1970   *A Theology of the Holy Spirit* (Grand Rapids: Eerdmans).
Burgess, S.
1976   'Medieval Examples of Charismatic Piety in the Roman Catholic Church', in Splitter (ed.), 1976: 14-27.
1988   'Holy Spirit, Doctrine of: Ancient Fathers and Medieval Churches', in Burgess, McGee and Alexander (eds.) 1988: 417-44.
Burgess, S., G. McGee and P. Alexander (eds.)
1988   *Dictionary of Pentecostal and Charismatic Movements* (Grand Rapids: Zondervan).
Cargal, T.
1993   'Beyond the Fundamentalist–Modernist Controversy', *Pneuma* 15 (2): 163-88.
Castelein, J.
1984   'Glossolalia and the Psychology of the Self and Narcissim', *Journal of Religion and Health* 23: 47-62.
Chopp, R.
1987   'Practical Theology and Liberation', in Mudge and Poling (eds.) 1987: 120-38.
Conn, C.W.
1955   *Like a Mighty Army* (Cleveland, TN: Church of God Publishing House).
Cross, T.
1993   'Toward a Theology of the Wind and the Spirit: A Review of J. Rodman Williams, *Renewal Theology*', *JPT* 3: 113-35.
Cutten, G.B.
1927   *Speaking in Tongues Historically and Psychologically Considered* (New Haven: Yale University Press).
Dayton, D.W.
1987   *Theological Roots of Pentecostalism* (Grand Rapids: Zondervan).
Dempster, M.
1983   'Soundings in the Moral Implications of Glossolalia', in H. Hunter (ed.), *Pastoral Problems in the Pentecostal-Charismatic Movement* (Papers presented at the 13th Annual Meeting of the Society for

Pentecostal Studies, 3-5 November, Church of God School of Theology).

1993   'Paradigm Shifts and Hermeneutics: Confronting Issues Old and New', *Pneuma* 15 (2): 129-36.

DeVol, T.
1974   'Ecstatic Pentecostal Prayer and Meditation', *Journal of Religion and Health* 13: 258-88.

Dollar, G.W.
1963   'Church History and the Tongues Movement', *BSac* 120: 316-21.

Dominion, J.
1976   'Psychological Evaluations of the Pentecostal Movement', *ExpTim* 87: 292-97.

Dunn, J.D.G.
1970   *Baptism in the Holy Spirit* (Philadelphia: Westminster Press).

Eidelberg, L.
1969   'Regression', in L. Eidelberg (ed.), *Encyclopedia of Psychoanalysis* (New York: Free Press).

Elbert, P. (ed.)
1985   *Essays on Apostolic Themes* (Peabody, MA: Hendrickson).

Emmett, D.
1952   'Epistemology and the Idea of Revelation', in C. Kegley and R. Bretall (eds.), *The Theology of Paul Tillich* (New York: Macmillan): 198-214.

Ervin, H.
1968   *These Are not Drunken as ye Suppose* (Plainfield, NJ: Logos International).

1984   *Conversion Initiation and the Baptism in the Holy Spirit: A Critique of James D.G. Dunn's* Baptism in the Holy Spirit (Peabody, MA: Hendrickson).

1985   'Hermeneutics: A Pentecostal Option', in Elbert (ed.) 1985: 23-35.

1987   *Spirit Baptism: A Biblical Investigation* (Peabody, MA: Hendrickson) (revision of *These Are not Drunken as ye Suppose*).

Fancher, R.
1973   *Psychoanalytic Psychology: The Development of Freud's Thought* (New York: W.W. Norton).

Farley, E.
1983   'Theology and Practice outside the Clerical Paradigm', in Browning (ed.) 1983: 21-41.

Faupel, D.
1989   'The Everlasting Gospel' (PhD dissertation, University of Birmingham).

Fee, G.
1976   'Hermeneutics and Historical Precedent—A Major Problem in Pentecostal Hermeneutics', in Spittler (ed.) 1976: 118-32.

1984   'Baptism in the Holy Spirit: The Issue of Separability and Sequence', in *Toward a Pentecostal Charismatic Theology* (Papers presented at the 14th Annual Meeting of the Society for Pentecostal Studies, 15-17 November, Gordon Conwell Seminary).

1991   *Gospel and Spirit: Issues in New Testament Hermeneutics* (Peabody, MA: Hendrickson).

1993   'Response to Roger Stronstad's "Biblical Precedent for Historical Precedent" ', *Paraclete* 27: 11-15.

Fowler, J.
1983   'Practical Theology and the Shaping of Christian Lives', in Browning (ed.) 1988: 148-66.

Freud, S.
1900   *The Interpretation of Dreams* (vols. IV and V in the Standard Edition; London: Hogarth Press, 1953).

1905   *Three Essays on the Theory of Sexuality* (vol. VII in the Standard Edition; London: Hogarth Press, 1953): 130-243.

1923   *The Ego and the Id* (vol. XIX in the Standard Edition; London: Hogarth Press, 1953): 3-66.

Frosch, J.
1990   'Viewpoint: Normal—Abnormal—Emotional Health—Emotional Illness', *Psychiatric Journal of University of Ottawa* 15 (1): 2-10.

Gadamer, H.-G.
1975   *Truth and Method* (trans. G. Barden and J. Cuming; New York: Crossroad).

Gause, R.H.
1976   'Issues in Pentecostalism', in Spittler (ed.) 1976: 106-16.

Geertz, C.
1973   *Interpretation of Cultures* (New York: Basic Books).

Gelpi, D.
1978   *Experiencing God* (New York: Paulist Press).

Gerkin, C.
1984   *The Living Human Document* (Nashville: Abingdon Press).

1986   *Widening the Horizon* (Philadelphia: Westminster Press).

1991   *Prophetic Pastoral Practice* (Nashville: Abingdon Press).

Gerlach, L., and V.H. Hine
1970   *People, Power, Change: Movements of Social Transformation* (Indianapolis: Bobbs-Merrill Educational Publishing).

Gilkey, L.
1990   *Gilkey on Tillich* (New York: Crossroad).

Girgis, H.
1990   'Regression', in R. Hunter (ed.), *Dictionary of Pastoral Care and Counseling* (Nashville: Abingdon Press): 1051-52.

Goodman, F.
1986   'Body Posture and the Religious Altered State of Consciousness', *Journal of Humanistic Psychology* 26: 81-118.

Grimes, R.
1986   *Beginnings in Ritual Studies* (Lanham, MD: University Press of America).

Haaken, J., and R. Adams
1983   'Pathology as "Personal Growth": A Participant Observation Study of Lifespring Training', *Psychiatry* 46: 270-80.

Habermas, J.
1971   *Knowledge and Human Interests* (trans. J. Shapiro; Boston: Beacon Press).

Hamilton, M. (ed.)
    1975   *The Charismatic Movement* (Grand Rapids: Eerdmans).
Hammond, G.
    1966   *The Power of Self-Transcendence* (St Louis, MO: Bethany Press).
Harrington, H., and R. Patten
    1994   'Pentecostal Hermeneutics and Postmodern Literary Theory', *Pneuma*
                16 (1): 109-14.
Harrison, R.
    1984   'The Concept of Priming Work in Professional Creativity', *Current
                Issues in Psychoanalytic Practice* 1 (1): 79-88.
Hartmann, H.
    1958   *Ego Psychology and the Problem of Adaptation* (New York:
                International Universities Press).
Heilman, S.
    1973   *Synagogue Life: A Study in Symbolic Interaction* (Chicago: University
                of Chicago Press).
Hiebert, P.
    1985   'Discerning the Work of God', in Robeck (ed.) 1985: 147-63.
Hillstrom, E.
    1985   'Decision Making', in D. Benner (ed.), *Baker's Encyclopedia of
                Psychology* (Grand Rapids: Baker Book House): 284-86.
Hollenweger, W.
    1972   *The Pentecostals* (trans. R. Wilson; Minneapolis: Augsburg).
Holt, R.
    1970   'Artistic Creativity and Rorschach Measures of Adaptive Regression',
                in B. Klopfer, M. Meyer and F. Brawer (eds.), *Developments in the
                Rorschach Technique* (New York: Harcourt Brace Jovanovich).
Hopewell, J.
    1987   *Congregation: Stories and Structures* (Philadelphia: Fortress Press).
Horton, S.
    1972   *Tongue Speaking and Prophecy* (Springfield, MO: Gospel Publishing
                House).
Hunter, H.
    1980   'Tongues-Speech: A Patristic Analysis', *JETS* 23: 125-37.
    1983   *Spirit Baptism: A Pentecostal Alternative* (Lanham, MD: University
                Press of America).
    1984   'What is Truth?', in *Toward a Pentecostal Charismatic Theology*.
Ironside, H.
    1912   *Holiness: The False and the True* (Neptune, NJ: Loizeaux Brothers).
Israel, R., D. Albrecht and R. McNally
    1993   'Pentecostal Hermeneutics: Texts, Rituals and Community', *Pneuma*
                15 (2): 137-62.
James, W.
    1902   *The Varieties of Religious Experience* (New York: Longmans, Green &
                Co.).
Janis, I., and L. Mann
    1977   *Decision Making: A Psychological Analysis of Conflict, Choice and
                Commitment* (New York: Macmillan).

Johns, J., and C. Johns
1992   'Yielding to the Spirit: A Pentecostal Approach to Group Bible Study', *JPT* 1: 109-34.

Johnston, R.
1984   'Pentecostalism and Theological Hermeneutics: Evangelical Options', *Pneuma* 6 (1): 51-66.

Jones, C.
1983   *A Guide to the Study of Pentecostalism* (2 vols.; Metuchen, NJ: Scarecrow Press and American Theological Library Association).

Jones, J.
1991   *Contemporary Psychoanalysis and Religion* (New Haven: Yale University Press).

Kelsey, D.
1967   *The Fabric of Paul Tillich's Theology* (New Haven: Yale University Press).

Kernberg, O.
1976   *Object Relations Theory and Clinical Psychoanalysis* (New York: Jason Aronson).
1977   'Boundaries and Structure in Love Relations', *Journal of American Psychoanalytic Association* 25: 81-114.

Kildahl, J.
1972   *The Psychology of Speaking in Tongues* (San Francisco: Harper & Row).

Knox, R.A.
1950   *Enthusiasm: A Chapter in the History of Religion* (Oxford: University of Oxford Press).

Kris, E.
1952   *Psychoanalytic Explorations in Art* (New York: International Universities Press).

Kroll-Smith, J.S.
1980   'The Testimony as Performance: The Relationship of an Expressive Event to the Belief System of a Holiness Sect', *JSSR* 19: 16-25.

Kuhn, T.
1962   *The Structure of Scientific Revolutions* (Chicago: University of Chicago Press).

Kydd, R.
1984   *Charismatic Gifts in the Early Church* (Peabody, MA: Hendrickson).
1988   'A Prolegomena to Pentecostal Theologizing', in *Pentecostalism in the Context of the Holiness Revival* (Papers presented at the 18th Annual Meeting of the Socoiety for Pentecostal Studies, 10-12 November, Asbury Theological Seminary).

Lamb, M.
1982   *Solidarity with Victims: Towards a Theology of Social Transformation* (New York: Crossroad).

Land, S.
1993   *Pentecostal Spirituality: A Passion for the Kingdom* (JPTSup, 1; Sheffield: JSOT Press).

Lapsley, J., and J. Simpson
1964a   'Speaking in Tongues: Token of Group Acceptance and Divine Approval', *Pastoral Psychology* 15 (May): 48-55.
1964b   'Speaking in Tongues: Infantile Babble or Song of the Self? Part II', *Pastoral Psychology* 15 (September): 16-24.

Lawless, E.
1983   'Brothers and Sisters: Pentecostalism as a Folkgroup', *Western Folklore* 43: 85-104.
1988   *Handmaidens of the Lord: Pentecostal Women Preachers and Traditional Religion* (Philadelphia: University of Pennsylvania Press).

Lawrence, B.F.
1916   *The Apostolic Faith Restored* (Springfield, MO: Gospel Publishing House).

Lederle, H.I.
1988   *Treasures Old and New: Interpretation of 'Spirit Baptism' in the Charismatic Renewal Movement* (Peabody, MA: Hendrickson).

Lindbeck, G.
1984   *The Nature of Doctrine* (Philadelphia: Westminster Press).

Loewald, H.
1978   *Psychoanalysis and the History of the Individual* (New Haven: Yale University Press).
1988   *Sublimation* (New Haven: Yale University Press).

Macchia, F.
1992   'Sighs too Deep for Words: Toward a Theology of Glossolalia', *JPT* 1:47-73.

MacDonald, W.
1964   'Glossolalia in the New Testament', *Bulletin of the Evangelical Theological Society* 7: 59-68.
1976   'Pentecostal Theology: A Classical Viewpoint', in Spittler (ed.) 1976: 58-74.
1979   'Temple Theology', *Pneuma* 1: 39-48.

Maddi, S.
1980   *Personality Theories* (New York: Dorsey).

Maloney, N.
1982   'Debunking Some of the Myths about Glossolalia', *Journal for the American Scientific Affiliation* 34: 144-48.

Maloney, N., and A. Lovekin
1985   *Glossolalia: Behavioral Science Perspectives on Speaking in Tongues* (Oxford: Oxford University Press).

Martin, H.
1970   'Discernment of Spirits and Spiritual Direction' (trans. I. Richards, *Discernment of Spirits* [Collegeville, MN: Liturgical Press]).

Mayers, M.
1973   'The Behavior of Tongues', in W. Mills (ed.), *Speaking in Tongues: Let's Talk about it* (Waco, TX: Word Books).

McConnell, J.
1983   *Understanding Human Behavior: An Introduction to Psychology* (New York: Holt, Rinehart and Winston, 4th edn).

McDargh, J.
1983 *Psychoanalytic Object Relations Theory and the Study of Religion* (Lanham, MD: University Press of America).

McGuire, M.
1982 *Pentecostal Catholics: Power, Charisma, and Order in a Religious Movement* (Philadelphia: Temple University Press).

McLean, M.
1984 'Toward a Pentecostal Hermeneutic', *Pneuma* 6 (2): 35-56.

McNeel, S.P.
1985 'Attribution Theory', in *Baker's Encyclopedia of Psychology* (Grand Rapids: Baker Book House): 86-88.

Meissner, W.
1984 *Psychoanalysis and Religious Experience* (New Haven: Yale University Press).

Menzies, R.
1991 *The Development of Early Christian Pneumatology with Special Reference to Luke–Acts* (JSNTSup, 54; Sheffield: JSOT Press).
1994a 'Jumping off the Postmodern Bandwagon', *Pneuma* 16 (1): 115-20.
1994b 'Luke and the Spirit: A Reply to James Dunn', *JPT* 4: 115-38.

Menzies, W.
1979 'Synoptic Theology: An Essay on Pentecostal Hermeneutics', *Paraclete* 13 (1): 14-27.
1985 'The Methodology of Pentecostal Theology', in Elbert (ed.) 1985: 1-14.

Metz, J.B.
1980 *Faith in History and Society* (ET; New York: Seabury Press).

Mills, W. (ed.)
1973 *Speaking in Tongues: A Guide to Research in Glossolalia* (Grand Rapids: Eerdmans).

Moseley, R.
1991 *Becoming a Self before God* (Nashville: Abingdon Press).

Mudge, L., and J. Poling (eds.)
1987 *Formation and Reflection* (Philadelphia: Fortress Press).

Myrdal, G.
1969 *Objectivity in Social Research* (New York: Pantheon Books).

Newman, L.
 'Pentecostal Hermeneutics: Suggesting a Model, Exploring the Problems' (Paper presented at the 21st Annual Meeting of the Society for Pentecostal Studies, Lakeland, FL).

Nichols, D.
1984 'The Search for a Pentecostal Structure in Systematic Theology', *Pneuma* 6 (2): 57-76.

Niebuhr, H.R.
1929 *The Social Sources of Denominationalism* (New York: Holt).
1929 *Black Pentecostalism* (Amherst, MA: University of Massachusetts Press).

Paris, A.
1982 *Black Pentecostalism* (Amherst, MA: University of Massachusetts Press).

Poling, J., and D. Miller
    1985   *Foundations for a Practical Theology of Ministry* (Nashville: Abingdon Press).

Reagan, C., and D. Stewart
    1978   *The Philosophy of Paul Ricouer* (Boston: Beacon Press).

Rieff, P.
    1966   *The Triumph of the Therapeutic* (New York: Harper & Row).

Riggs, R.
    1949   *The Spirit Himself* (Springfield, MO: Gospel Publishing House).

Rizzuto, A.
    1979   *The Birth of the Living God* (Chicago: University of Chicago Press).

Robeck, C.
    1980   'Written Prophecies: A Question of Authority', *Pneuma* 2 (2): 26-45.
    1988   'Prophecy, Gift of', in Burgess, McGee and Alexander (eds) 1988: 728-40.

Robeck, D. (ed.)
    1985   *Charismatic Experiences in History* (Peabody, MA: Hendrickson).

Rosenthal, R.
    1976   *Experimenter Effects in Behavioral Research* (New York: Irvington).

Samarin, W.J.
    1968   'The Linguisticality of Glossolalia', *The Hartford Quarterly* 8: 49-75.
    1969   'Glossolalia as Learned Behavior', *Canadian Journal of Theology* 15: 60-64.
    1973   'Glossolalia as Regressive Speech', *Language and Speech* 16: 77-898.

Schrieter, R.
    1985   *Constructing Local Theologies* (Maryknoll, NY: Orbis Books).

Schwartz, G.
    1970   *Sect Ideologies and Social Status* (Chicago: University of Chicago Press).

Shelton, J.
    1991   *Mighty in Word and Deed: The Role of the Holy Spirit in Luke–Acts* (Peabody, MA: Hendrickson).
    1994   A Reply to James D.G. Dunn's 'Baptism in the Spirit: A Response to Pentecostal Scholarship on Luke–Acts', *JPT* 4: 139-43.

Sheppard, G.
    1994   'Biblical Interpretation after Gadamer', *Pneuma* 16 (1): 121-41.

Spilka, B., R. Hood and S. Gorsuch
    1986   *The Psychology of Religion: An Empirical Approach* (Englewood Cliffs, NJ: Prentice–Hall).

Spittler, R.
    1983   'Suggested Areas for Further Research in Pentecostal Studies', *Pneuma* 5: 39-56.
    1988   'Glossolalia', in Burgess, McGee and Alexander (eds.) 1988: 335-41.

Spittler, R. (ed.)
    1976   *Perspectives on the New Pentecostalism* (Grand Rapids: Baker Book House).

Stromberg, P.
1986   *Symbols of Community: The Cultural System of a Swedish Church* (Tucson: University of Arizona Press).

Stronstad, R.
1984   'Trends in Pentecostal Hermeneutics', *Paraclete* 22 (3): 1-12.
1993a   'Biblical Precedent for Historical Precedent', *Paraclete* 27: 1-10.
1993b   'Pentecostal Hermeneutics: A Review of Gordon D. Fee's *Gospel and Spirit: Issues in Pentecostal Hermeneutics*', *Pneuma* 15 (2): 215-22.

Synan, V.
1971   *The Holiness-Pentecostal Movement in the United States* (Grand Rapids: Eerdmans).
1987   'Pentecostalism: Varieites and Contributions', *Pneuma* 9: 31-49.

Thatcher, A.
1979   *The Ontology of Paul Tillich* (London: Oxford University Press).

Thomas, J.C.
1994   'Women, Pentecostals and the Bible: An Experiment in Pentecostal Hermeneutics', *JPT* 5: 41-56.

Thomas, J.H.
1963   *Paul Tillich: An Appraisal* (Philadelphia: Westminster Press).

Tillich, P.
1951, 1957,   *Systematic Theology* (3 vols.; Chicago: University of Chicago Press).
1963
1952   *The Courage to Be* (New Haven: Yale University Press).

Tozer, A.W.
1963   *Knowledge of the Holy* (New York: Harper Brothers).

Tracy, D.
1975   *Blessed Rage for Order* (Minneapolis, MN: Seabury).
1981   *The Analogical Imagination* (New York: Crossroad).
1983   'The Foundations of Practical Theology', in Browning (ed.) 1983: 61-82.

Turner, V.
1969   *The Ritual Process* (Ithaca, NY: Cornell University Press).

Ulanov, A., and B. Ulanov
1982   *Primary Speech: A Psychology of Prayer* (Atlanta: John Knox).

Unhjem, A.
1981   'Paul Tillich', in *Encyclopedia Britannica* (Macropedia, 15th edn).

Wagner, C.P.
1988   'Church Growth', in Burgess, McGee and Alexander (eds.) 1988: 180-95.

Wells, D.
1978   *The Search for Salvation* (Downers Grove, IL: Inter-Varsity Press).

Wheelock, D.
1983   'Spirit-Baptism in American Pentecostal Thought' (PhD dissertation, Emory University).

Whitehead, J., and E. Whitehead
1980   *Method in Ministry* (New York: Harper & Row).

Willems, E.
    1967   'Validation of Authority in Pentecostal Sects of Chile and Brazil',
                JSSR 6: 253-58.
Williams, G., and E. Waldvogel
    1975   'A History of Speaking in Tongues and Related Gifts', in Hamilton
                (ed.) 1975.
Williams, J.R.
    1971   *The Era of the Spirit, Including Views on the Holy Spirit Held by Four*
                Eminent Theologians: Karl Barth, Emil Brunner, Paul Tillich and
                Rudolf Bultmann (Plainfield, NJ: Logos International).
    1985   'The Greater Gifts', in Robeck (ed.) 1985: 44-65.
 1988, 1990,   *Renewal Theology: Systematic Theology from a Charismatic*
    1992   *Perspective* (3 vols.; Grand Rapids: Zondervan).
Williams, M.
    1974   *Community in a Black Pentecostal Church: An Anthropological Study*
                (Prospect Heights, IL: Waveland Press).
Wilson, J., and H. Clow
    1981   'Themes of Power and Control in a Pentecostal Assembly'; *JSSR* 20:
                241-50.
Winnicott, D.W.
    1971   *Playing and Reality* (New York: Basic Books).

INDEX OF AUTHORS

DATE DUE

			Printed in USA

HIGHSMITH #45230